P9-DFD-694

Woman and Man

Biblical Encounters Series

Woman and Man

**Erhard S. Gerstenberger
and
Wolfgang Schrage**

Biblical Encounters Series

Translated by Douglas W. Stott

ABINGDON
Nashville

FRAU UND MANN

© 1980 Verlag W. Kohlhammer GmbH

WOMAN AND MAN

Translation copyright © 1981 by Abingdon

LIBRARY OF CONGRESS CATALOGING IN PUBLICATION DATA

GERSTENBERGER, ERHARD.
  Woman and man.
  (Biblical encounters series)
  Translation of: Frau und Mann.
  Bibliography: p.
  1. Man (theology)—Biblical teaching. 2. Sex (Theology)—Biblical
teaching. I. Schrage, Wolfgang. II. Title. III. Series.
BS661.G4713   261.8'343   81-10898   AACR2

ISBN 0-687-45920-6

MANUFACTURED BY THE PARTHENON PRESS AT
NASHVILLE, TENNESSEE, UNITED STATES OF AMERICA

CONTENTS

CONTENTS

CONTENTS

CONTENTS

Translator's Preface

The avoidance of sexist language has become a legitimate concern for us all, particularly for those engaged in the business of the printed word. Unfortunately, the elimination of such language often results in an awkward or even aesthetically offensive literary style. A translation from the German is subject to the additional frustration of German's multiple genders. God is a "he" for grammatical, not ideological reasons. In many cases only a fine line separates the legitimate elimination of sexist language from an illegitimate alteration of the author's—conscious or unconscious—intention.

Woman and Man, as one might imagine, had more than its share of such potential traps. I have tried to eliminate sexist language whenever possible while remaining true both to the authors' intentions and to stylistic considerations. Appropriately, the book itself, with woman and man as its theme, is intended to help us in precisely this—our attempt to understand the sexes anew in a balanced fashion.

Particular thanks go to Barbara Wojhoski for her keen eye, critical ear, and balanced advice in tight spots during the preparation of the manuscript.

DOUGLAS W. STOTT

Atlanta, Georgia
March 1981

A.
WOMAN AND MAN
IN THE
OLD TESTAMENT

I. The Unreconciled Duality

1. The Human Being: Woman and Man

We often speak about the "human being" as if it were an asexual, unified being: The human is born, lives for a time, and dies. The United Nations delineates and debates human rights, and the total number of human beings has now passed the four-billion mark. Catastrophes take the lives of hundreds or even thousands of humans; and countless books and treatises investigate the essence of the human being as if sexual differences were completely meaningless. Consciously or unconsciously they might well be taking their cue from the first biblical creation narrative: "God created man in his own image, in the image of God he created him" (Gen. 1:27). Only after making this programmatic statement does the priestly scribe of the sixth century then appear to pause before Christ—as if suddenly struck—and to add: "Male and female he created them."

What lies behind this unifying generic term, "the human being"? No doubt the universal experience that the male and female versions of this peculiar creature demonstrate an overwhelming number of common traits. No doubt also the assumption that the important differences between man and woman can be overlooked in certain situations. Here, however, we are already confronted with the dilemma. Who is to say whether and, if so, when this kind of hypothesis is really justified? When they speak of "the human being," do statisticians, planners, philosophers, commentators, and theologians in every case determine to what extent male and female self-understanding can be reduced to a common denominator? There is simply no way around the fact that the human being does not exist as a sexually neutral being; as such, it is only a statistical, abstract quantity on paper.

A serious suspicion arises in the face of this contradiction between the sexually specific reality on the one hand, and a manner of speech on the other which obfuscates those differences. It could well be that those who so gladly and so resonantly speak about "the human being" (or "man" in general) in reality mean only themselves, their own sex, or their own group. Human history offers more than enough examples of this kind of absolutization of the group ego. The American Declaration of Independence of 1776 insists on inalienable, God-given human rights, but in practice excludes both women and slaves from the enjoyment of these rights. Wherever the relationship between the sexes is discussed theoretically—as in Aristotle, Augustine, Thomas Aquinas, Luther, or Freud—one can easily come away with the impression that the man is the real human being, while the woman is only a creature derived from and subject to him (cf Gen. 2:18-23).

The human being is thus either male or female, and this difference often outweighs common human traits. This is why the tension between the sexes is noticeable at all times and in all cultures, even in securely ordered social systems. One can say that this tension represents an essential motivating force for life in general. Human history is unthinkable without sexual love and without the ubiquitous competition between the sexes. Just which roles women and men receive individually is irrelevant. From another perspective we can describe this state of affairs in the following way: The biologically determined and socially ordered polarity of the sexes has never been overcome or resolved in a higher unity. The yearning for unification has no doubt always been present, but it remains perpetually unsatisfied—if not on an individual, then certainly on a cultural level.

This already poses some initial questions for our topic. We experience today—for various reasons—this sexual duality as being particularly problematic. How did women and men during biblical times perceive their mutual relationships? How did they evaluate themselves? Are there any connecting lines from our own perspective back to the distribution of roles and sexual morality in the Old and New Testament? What kind of orientation aids can we, in today's difficulties, expect from the Bible?

2. The Human Being: Body and Spirit

Every human being, whether woman or man, directly experiences a personal corporeality as well as that other phenomenon which is so difficult to define: the spirituality accompanying every ego-consciousness. Thus, however one may assess the influence of cultural and social factors, a person's sex manifests itself both in the physical and spiritual dimension. Children discover their own external sexual characteristics quite early, and while growing up a person soon learns to focus—within the roles designated by society—upon the emotional reactions of the opposite sex. We find it essential here to emphasize the unity of body and spirit in man and woman. The biblical scriptures consistently take this integral view of the human being as their point of departure, and our contemporary psychological sciences emphatically support it as well. It is not enough to understand the relationship between the sexes only or primarily as physical contact, as is the case in many sexual studies. The obligatory bed scenes in otherwise quite serious and good films are often only a concession to public taste and as such a sign of collective, compulsive neurosis. Even less possible is the projection of an allegedly higher spirituality onto one sex—i.e., the male—while then considering the other sex merely as his material basis. Body and soul are inextricably fused in both woman and man in a characteristic way.

The question, energetically debated all the way into the present, is how the particular physical disposition of man and woman forms and determines their respective mental and spiritual existence. The ancients already saw that the woman during menstruation, for example, or the man during the cycle of his sperm production manifests certain characteristic effects. Our biological knowledge is immensely expanded today, for example, by the recognition of sexually specific hormonal changes. Still, we nonetheless are not sure just how bodily functions affect a person's thinking, wanting, and perceiving. Until only a few decades ago we still held obstinately to the view that the man, in accordance with his constitution, gradually develops all the traits one customarily designates as masculine on the basis of a long cultural tradition: activity, understanding, the will to battle, the gift of invention. The woman, on the other hand, because of her eternal destiny for motherhood, was chosen to cultivate the genuinely feminine qualities of self-sacrifice, sensitivity—artistic and otherwise—and so on. Contemporary anthropological research (cf M. Mead) has closed the door on these kinds of myths that only perpetuate the prevalent power structures. The fixation of feminine and masculine character traits is clearly a result of the socially fixed distribution of roles. One can be certain this fixation does not issue, with any sort of natural necessity, from bodily structure, since societal forms do exist in which the woman—according to our concepts—develops "masculine," while the man develops "feminine" traits.

We should not, of course, overlook how deeply this prejudice of the biologically determined spiritual disposition—a prejudice perpetuated for millennia—is rooted in us all. Vast segments of humanity as well as the various cultural circles of Western civilization are to some degree permeated by the ideal of the man called to rule and of the woman designated for subservience. It is quite interesting—and suspicious—that until now no fundamental change has come about, not even in the socialist countries whose theories of society quite clearly support the equality of rights between the sexes. There, too, we still find typical female vocations and an equally typical predominance of man in the political, administrative, and economic decision-making bodies.

We must therefore guard against an overestimation of the purely biological state of affairs. Better still: It is impossible to draw direct conclusions concerning predetermined, eternally unchangeable, "natural" character traits or behavioral patterns.

These are rather in every case culturally mediated. That is why one should not make an issue of (statistically determined!) smaller musculature when it is a question of admitting women into the vocation of locksmithing or engineering. Similarly, the absence of a uterus is no reason to exclude men from becoming trained to be midwives. This does not, of course, mean that we today can simply forget sexually specific experiences. Equality of rights should not be confused with leveling. Our femaleness or maleness ought indeed to be recognized within the present cultural context. It is, for example, ridiculous when the abortion debate is carried on and decided predominantly by men, without the equal participation of women. Excluding men from those decisions would be equally ludicrous, since both sexes together are responsible for life.

3. The Social Roles

What we have just discussed no doubt makes it clear: Just as so many other things in human life, one's existence as woman or man is not determined as much by natural as by cultural influences. The sexually determined behavioral models and mutual expectations have been preformed for millennia by the society in which one lives. We can find pre-stages of human behavior—including and even particularly in view of sexual roles—even in the animal realm. What occurs there as regards "the courting of brides," "matrimonial partnership," "the caring for the brood," and "familial solidarity"—above all with many vertebrates—often bears a striking similarity to the corresponding human behavioral models. It is no accident that we speak of the "proud roosters," the maturing young men who want to attract the attention of females; of the lovers who "coo like turtledoves"; of the mother who "defends her chicks like a hen"; of "bully" men and "feline" women. And yet these kinds of behavioral patterns, reaching far back into the tribal history of life, lie hidden in the deepest levels of our consciousness. Human development, continuing now for approximately a million years and probably decisively molded during the last ice age, has submerged all earlier constellations. We will have to look at more recent time periods in order to understand the social roles of the sexes and to develop better, more just forms of living together. Above all, we must consider the history of Western culture since the end of the third millennium, a period so well known from countless literary documents and from the results of so many excavations that we can easily identify the accompanying social structures—and with them the roles of the sexes. The Old Testament belongs in this context of ancient Oriental, Western cultural history; and as the sacred book of Judaism and Christianity it has up to this day helped determine the conceptions of what is typically male and what typically female. As such it warrants our attention. At this point, however, we still have to make some sociological clarifications.

The life of woman and man is in large measure determined by the conditions of existence of the primary group, which we can also call the family or tribe. How one lives, what experiences one has, depends for example on the work he must do in support of the group. That life is directed according to the manner of possession and educational tasks that are posed by one's progeny. Not least do the moral and religious conceptions that are common property of the group help determine one's personal existence. In a word, the group structure—with all its variations and consequences—is the primary factor responsible for the forming of sexual roles.

In a vague period of prehistory the primary group was the only form of human organization. Every tribe or clan lived by its own efforts from hunting and fishing, from wild fruits and sporadic agriculture. This picture was changed by the settlement and merger of several families into tribal confederations. Because of the need for regular field cultivation, for the exchange of goods, for marrying into other groups, and finally also as a result of the beginning city culture and establishment of larger realms, larger, secondary organizational forms arose. These secondary forms affected the life of the family in various ways. An example is the specialization of work, which has continued to this day. A band of hunters and collectors theoretically needs no distribution of labor, though at this stage the man may already have acquired the external work, and the woman the internal work in house or cave. The early agricultural family also remains relatively mobile, since man and woman can mutually replace each other as a work force. Both work in a limited and collectively governed area. All this changes with the specialization of vocations into crafts. Now the man (?) must focus completely on work production, while the woman remains in the domestic realm—which she seemingly has co-controlled since time immemorial. Modern factory work then provides the final separation of living place and work place; it takes economic independence away from the family and to a dangerous degree alienates the spouses from each other. We see a similar divisive tendency in the historical development of other family functions. The domestic rearing of children, for example, passes from the man—better, from collective responsibility—to the woman and state, and the private practice of religion becomes something for women. The man, on the other hand, acquires all legal and societal functions and obligations for himself. He becomes the only property owner and the head of the family, and must function as the real spokesman of that family.

In this entire development the fact that the woman has to go through pregnancy and birth—something keeping her temporarily out of "eternal service"—has no doubt played a role. More important, however, are the ideological conclusions the man has drawn from this state of affairs: The woman is less suited (by nature!) to represent the family externally. Be that as it may, the overall picture, in spite of occasional tendencies to the contrary, has during the course of history only become worse for women. The man has come away relatively better because he was officially the master in and of the house. In many ways, however, he has become the victim of this differentiation of roles. In the modern urban society in particular he sees himself subjected to pressures that make him into a caricature of himself.

What does all this mean for the relationship between the sexes? This above all: Because of the shrinking of the family and its loss of function, man and woman have to a large extent forfeited the chance for collective work and shared responsibility. Indeed, the possibilities for contact are limited, even at best, to the common time for meals, sleeping, and recreation. In addition, experience shows that this kind of divided life cannot be healed during free weekends either. For the children this life rhythm so hostile to the family starts at latest when schooling begins. This estranged orientation has cut its way too deeply into family members; each pursues his own interests.

4. Love and Power, Fairness and Faith

Within the biological and cultural framework just described there now occurs the quite personal encounter between the sexes. Several factors and reference points need to be considered here. In our own time we have learned to place love in the first position. Indeed, in vast areas of public opinion love appears to be the only, even exclusive content of sexual relationships. And even this concept is often enough narrowed even further to the act of sex. This idea of the absolute predominance of love can be traced back into the previous century, and its origins go hand and hand with the loss of function of the family. That is to say, the more the life partnership of man and woman lost its daily meaning, the more did personal attraction push itself into the foreground. It was supposed to provide the buffeted family ship with motivation and direction. We must recognize quite clearly that love did not always have this function, and we will do well not to equate that which the Old Testament says about it with our own concepts.

A critical evaluation of our own position is thus the prerequisite for the proper understanding of the Old Testament and the fruitful encounter with its statements.

Whenever the predominant contemporary ideology sees only sexual love between the sexes, it simply overlooks the fact that every sexual relationship simultaneously calls forth other human bonds and conflicts. We need only look at the question concerning superior and inferior positions, concerning the privileged position and attitude of faith of the partners.

Love—i.e., full, empathetic orientation toward the other—has its counterpart not only in hate, the destructive possession of the partner, but also in the simple power striving of the individual. Whenever two people live closely together, it is unavoidable that two different directions of will meet each other. Each would like to employ the other here and there for selfish purposes. We find the often unconscious struggle for leadership in the smaller group in all societal systems. This struggle is not always decided by the obtaining societal norms, but depends rather to a large extent on the constitution of the partners. Our contemporary democratic ideals would seem to correspond to a friendly, companionable, control-free form of life, particularly within the dual relationship between woman and man. This by no means excludes the possibility that one of the two will occasionally have to take the initiative and leadership role. In contrast to many basic views of the Old Testament and the Jewish-Christian tradition, it would be quite beneficial if these internal leadership problems of the small group were not burdened beforehand by a general fixation of sexual roles.

The question of privilege for man and woman both inside and outside marriage does affect our circle of problems to the extent that many of the norms set up by society are taken up by the individual and transformed into one's own concern, i.e., they are internalized. In a patriarchal society the man easily considers himself to be the only one with the right of decision, and the woman understands herself as the submissive one. Both will—against the soft voice of their conscience—seek to direct their mutual relationship according to this model. In a reverse fashion, we find many attempts today to replace these traditional norms with ones enabling both parties to develop their personalities freely. Here, too, one orients oneself according to basic rules devised by the (progressive) society. In a word, any understanding of norms taken from outside comes into conflict with the reality determining individual life. The daily experiences of a couple, those extremely personal joys and sadnesses of life with each other, cannot be figured according to any system of norms. From this we learn: Every ordering or privilege within an intimate life partnership between the sexes must be spacious enough not to strangle that very relationship itself.

Finally, we must mention the basic attitudes in questions of faith, since it of necessity influences the relationship between the sexes. The often hardheaded defenders of single-confessional partnerships doubtless have a good argument. Fundamental differences of world view can lead to arguments and alienation between a man and woman. The days, however, of uniform religious education are long past, and we are living in a deeply pluralistic society—at least as regards one's personal faith. Thus the dialogue concerning fundamental world views should not be excluded from the relationship between two people. One should examine mutual tolerance and as far as possible accept the difference in the partner's decisions concerning faith as a corrective and enrichment for one's own.

We are not making an extravagant assertion when we claim that all human predispositions, consciousness structures, patterns of behavior, and so on, flow into the relationship with the sexual partner. There is absolutely nothing that in principle might be a matter of indifference to me. Nocturnal snoring; daily work pace; the way one walks, speaks, laughs, dresses, behaves; preference for certain foods, landscapes, books, music; susceptibility to certain illnesses; disinclination toward this or that person or situation; fears, irritability, emotions; values and way of thinking—these and a thousand other things from the arsenal of one's personal character traits determine the tone of daily encounter with each other. This dual relationship between woman and man is—as we see it today—a comprehensive partnership between two quite different, yet equally valuable beings.

5. The Old Testament: God's Eternal Order?

We have tried to illuminate the contemporary problems and sexual roles and relationships as they appear in certain issues. In doing so, we naturally caught glimpses of the Old Testament now and then. It functioned in several ways: as a guide for relationships still holding today and as a witness for a long past culture. How are we to focus on this book that is equally sacred to Jews and Christians?

The Old Testament has no doubt remained a force in various ways up to the present; one need only think of the Ten Commandments and their continued power. As regards the role of the sexes, both theology and the church often demonstrate a blind trust in the Bible's unchangeable order of creation. According to that view, woman and man received once and for all the positions allotted them by nature, the man as lord and ruler and woman as the person subservient to him, his helping counterpart (Gen. 2:18, 3:16). The question is whether this typically male view of things correctly understands the Old Testament creation accounts and the overall witness of the Old Testament. If we assume this, then we immediately encounter an even more serious question. Our age claims to have acquired a deep understanding of the sexes, and it readily speaks about God's various concrete, temporally bound works in history. How, then, can one so glibly speak about an eternal order of creation? Why does one not take seriously the admitted mutability of *all* ideas of faith and ethical norms? How can theology go unpunished by the insights of other human sciences that view the human being primarily not as a creature of nature, but of culture, a creature continually recreating its own environment—and thus also itself. No, the Old Testament does not offer us the original model of an eternal form of partnership predetermined by God. It shows rather the temporally conditioned and completely fallible attempts of the people of those times to direct their world according to the will of God. In its thousand-year history, the people of Israel also quite clearly found different answers to the challenges of its time, including questions of the relationship between the sexes. The Old Testament has lasting significance for us for precisely that reason, since it has preserved the mutability of Israel's statements of faith. It shows us how people at that time, searching for the ultimate meaning of life, took up differing positions in the various life situations. It encourages us to do the same in our own time, to find in our individual situations the forms of partnership between man and woman that are commensurate with our time.

Viewed in this way, we are permitted to acknowledge and question without hesitation the alien character of the Old Testament as well. A superficial look will already show us that virtually all the Old Testament scriptures were written for men by men, and that they reflect primarily male interests and experiences. Religion in Israel—and in Judaism to this day—was almost exclusively an affair of men. The God of Israel was—and to a large extent still is for both Jews and Christians—a predominantly masculine figure. The doctrine of God's sexual neutrality and his occasional feminine characteristics (mercy!) by no means removes the fact of his patriarchal power. Thus it is not surprising that the image of women in the Old Testament is occasionally concealed by the veil of male ignorance and timidity. We take note of all this, recognize the temporally determined nature of the Old Testament witness, and try to learn something from the solutions found at that time. We can do this, however, only by continually looking at our own contemporary situation. Every direct transplant of Old Testament judgments would of necessity precipitate the most vehement defensive reactions from our society.

This is true because when interpreting biblical texts, it is in the final analysis a matter of drawing the right conclusions from the temporally determined form of the ancient witness for our own, completely different situation. Our world's societal structure and intellectual climate are immediately accessible to us. They provide the framework in which God acts today. We seek out an encounter with the biblical witness so that we, in our contemporary situation, can assume a similar posture and take similar, searching steps toward the one God and the ultimate meaning of life, just as they did.

Yet another consideration can be added. Since the days when Jesus of Nazareth preached and Christian congregations arose—almost two thousand years ago—the world has changed in significant ways. The congregation of believers is no longer an ethnic or national entity. Man and woman, through century-long struggles, have at least theoretically attained the position of equality that the early Christians already sought (cf Gal. 3:28). Neither as Christians can we return to the societal models of the Old Testament. In other words, we read the Old Testament from an enormous cultural distance that includes the entire development of the Christian faith. This does not, of course, mean that when interpreting the Old Testament we put on Christian glasses. We rather take seriously the existential conditions of today, conditions to a large part nurtured in the spiritual ground of Christianity. As far as possible, we study the Old Testament statements without prejudice and without intellectual haughtiness. How did one view woman and man in Israel in their relationship to each other? And what can we Christians in the twentieth century learn from that for our own situation?

If we have until now emphasized the distance and alien character of the Old Testament, then we must add: What a plethora of pulsating life and contemporary views we find in that ancient, sacred book! What honesty and openness in the portrayal of human conditions! What energy to endure this life, to rejoice in it, and to strive and hope beyond oneself! One reason for these writers' and narrators' often breathtaking proximity to reality and strength of faith is the fact that human beings, despite altered societal systems and ideologies, have for millennia remained the same obstinate and resigned, lovable and evil creatures they have perhaps always been. Another reason is the mysterious turning on the part of the Israelites to the one God, the God who above all became their partner and wandered, wrestled, sang, and suffered with humans.

II. The Circle of Life

In an initial round of conversation with the Old Testament witness, we will do well to describe—at least in rough outline—the typical life cycle of woman and man. Should we agree with those who say: Not a thing has changed since antiquity! Humans struggle for their existence and die! (cf Ps. 90:10, Eccl. 5:14)? Every life admittedly can be described as a curve showing growth, blossoming, and decay. In the case of humans, however, this image manifests important cultural and sexually specific peculiarities. Let us consider the main stages of life through which modern humans pass: childhood, schooling and vocational training, marriage and vocation, retirement. Theoretically these stages obtain for both man and woman. In reality, however, marriage interrupts the woman's vocational training; and pregnancy and birth, infant care and the task of rearing significantly hamper vocational activity itself. Furthermore, retirement has until today been a privilege of men. If we compare this kind of life scheme with what we find in the Old Testament, the differences become immediately visible. Israel never knew of schooling and vocation in the modern sense. The family and world of work constituted an organic unity. One spent his entire life within the family activity into which one was born or which one—so to speak as a branch of the patriarchal business—founded oneself. That held true for the man. Upon marriage, the woman moved into the clan of her "marriage lord" and thus experienced a deeper break in her development. Structurally and ideally, however, these family groups were virtually identical. One lived basically from agriculture, even in the small cities of the period. Skilled crafts and administrative functions were for the most part secondary activities and not official specializations. Today the family plays a pitifully subordinate part in the life path of woman and man. The integrating and meaningful impulses for the individual come above all from the vocational world. Furthermore, the industrial manipulation of dead materials has replaced any contact with the living world of nature. As regards our topic here we can assert that the modern economic world and technology must promote the equalization of sexual roles if women are not to be left to vegetate in a pre-industrial ghetto. In Israel precisely that visible familial economic system permitted a strong differentiation of reponsibilities and experiential realms.

1. Childhood and Youth

We know today that during early childhood, long before the onset of sexual maturity, a person has already begun to focus upon the roles society has assigned. As a rule, of course, this happens quite unconsciously. The young boy orients himself according to what he sees his father or other men do, while the young girl becomes accustomed to feminine or motherly activities and behavioral patterns. Society then guides the maturing person into the acceptable paths by means of parents, relatives, and other respected persons. We need only look at ourselves and how we figure out what to buy as presents for boys or girls. We need only listen when unreflected turns of speech occur such as: "A little boy doesn't do that kind of thing," or "Isn't she just a little darling?" We then become aware that this sexual differentiation begins extremely early and that quite unnoticeably those patterns are set that will be important for later behavior.

If this is the case for our own world, a world tending more and more to equalize sexual roles, how much more must this sexual conditioning during childhood have been at work during the Old Testament period. Unfortunately, the Old Testament gives us no direct information concerning these unconscious processes. Neither do we have a single text in the Old Testament in which a child as such is the central figure. We hear about the birth and rescue of Moses (Exod. 2:1-10), for example, only because one wanted to explain the national founder's name, origin, and significance. This is also the case in other stories that deal with children (cf 2 Sam. 12:13ff; 1 Kings 3:16ff; 2 Kings 11:2ff). The child (one should rather say, the son!) is of primary significance only in relation to the adult world. Nonetheless, we do gain from the available allusions an approximate picture of the influences to which Israelite girls and boys were exposed.

a. The Parents' Expectations

A newborn child's environment is decisively important. Old Testament evidence concerning the parents' expectations is clear: During the entire millennium of Israelite history, one wished for nothing more fervently than the birth of a son. The arrival of a daughter was a second-rate event if not an outright disappointment. A married couple who named its daughter Gomer, i.e. "Enough" (Hos. 1:3), likely wanted to hear nothing more of feminine progeny. And the name Dinah (Gen. 30:21) means something to the effect "bone of contention." To be sure, the positive female names passed down to us by the Old Testament sound quite conciliatory: Abigail, "father rejoices" (1 Sam. 25:3). In general, however, we can say that the Israelite society was patrilinearly directed, meaning that in all questions of lineage and inheritance only kinship with the father counted: the mother's side was of no consequence. It is not surprising then that one yearned with all one's power for a son and heir. This same mentality has maintained itself to this day in the

Islamic Orient, among orthodox Jews, and in many regions of the Christian West.

Let us have a look at a few examples of the Old Testament material. The Old Testament includes a great many ancestor or lineage tables; they appear first in Genesis 4:1-2, 17-22 and Genesis 5:1-32 and reappear in all the scriptures up to the final book of the Hebrew canon, Chronicles, which was written sometime around 200 B.C. (cf 1 Chron. 1–9). Sometimes these lists remark that an ancestor had "sons and daughters" (cf Gen. 5:4; 11:11; etc), but as a rule only the sons are mentioned by name. These generation registers were likely primarily used for legal purposes, and in such matters, as has been seen, the existence of women and girls was inconsequential. Only in exceptional cases do we hear of the birth of a daughter. Genesis 29:31–30:24, for example, tells of the birth of Jacob's first eleven sons. The story degenerates into a virtual competition between Rachel and Leah to see who can give the patriarch more sons (cf 30:8!). This list of the sons of Jacob does, as we see, also mention Dinah, Leah's daughter (30:21). It can clearly be seen, however, that this verse is extraneous within the framework of this birth competition, since the high point for Leah has already occurred in verse 20. She, the less beloved woman, can finally say after the birth of six of her own sons: "Now my husband will honor me." The following mention of the daughter Dinah is thus the subsequent addition of a later scribe who wanted to anticipate adequately the story of Genesis 34.

Outside these ancestor lists, references to the birth of daughters are equally rare. One reports that judge Ibzan, in addition to his thirty sons, also had thirty daughters whom he "gave in marriage outside his clan" (Judg. 12:9). The numbers of sons and daughters have been transmitted for some queens, and one notices that the daughters, too, gave the father a certain respectability and secured his position. Only a son, however, could continue the family (cf 2 Chron. 11:21; 13:21; etc). In David's case, too, only the sons are mentioned by name (2 Sam. 3:2-5; 5:13-16), although the full progeny formulation appears in 2 Samuel 5:13. Sons are the true sign of blessing and power;

daughters can only be welcome additions (Job 1:2; 43:13ff).

This becomes more than clear in all the passages that speak expressly about the hope for a son, often for the first son. For Abraham everything—absolutely everything—depends on the birth of a male heir (cf Gen. 15:2f). Sterile women, such as Hannah, who later became the mother of Samuel, yearned desperately for children, preferably for sons (cf 1 Sam 1:2ff, particularly v 8; Gen. 25:21ff; 30:1; Isa. 54:1; 66:7). In his most bitter outbreak of despair, Job describes the expectation that preceded his own birth (Job 3:2, 11); and Psalm 127:3-5 gives a more extensive explanation for the preference for male progeny:

> Lo, sons are a heritage from the Lord,
>   the fruit of the womb a reward,
> Like arrows in the hand of a warrior
>   are the sons of one's youth.
> Happy is the man who has
>   his quiver full of them!
> He shall not be put to shame
>   when he speaks with his enemies in the gate.

Beyond the future guarantee of the family's existence and possessions, sons are here the guarantors of the political and no doubt also economic power of a clan. This psalm also mentions the neutral expression "fruit of the womb" as well as the unequivocal designation "sons." In this context, however, it becomes clear that only male progeny can be meant. Only adult males could fulfill the legal functions of the community. Except for rare exceptions, women had no access to those proceedings in the gate (cf Deut. 25:7ff with Ruth 4:1ff). The linguistic emphasis on the son in the Old Testament goes hand in hand with a receding of the general designation for "child." The expression "son" may have sometimes had this general meaning, but in our Bible translations—because of our theoretical equal evaluation of boys and girls!—it is much too frequently rendered with "child" (cf Gen. 30:1!). This conceals the masculine character of Israelite society.

We can ascertain that the newborn child in the Old Testament period came into a world that was strongly and bluntly conditioned by the hope for male progeny and thus also by masculine values. In the Old Testament we find ourselves in a patriarchal society of the first order. This does not, however, mean that the woman had no place in this male world. Quite the contrary! She was given a quite specific role, an area of responsibility in which she could function with relative independence. But the entire public arena was geared to male views and needs. More exactly, it was directed toward the family head and beyond him to the maintenance of the larger family.

b. *The Maturing Girl*

According to our standards, the first life stage was particularly brief for the Israelite girl, since between the ages of ten and fifteen she was given in marriage. Climatically determined early sexual maturity and rigid societal structures promoted this kind of rapid development. In addition, one should not forget that the average life expectancy was not, as it is today, between sixty and seventy, but rather between thirty and forty; and that does not even take the high child mortality rate into account.

The young girl remained completely under the care of the mother during the period of growth and preparation. Infants were generally nursed for the first three years. Whereas the small son would then increasingly follow the father, the daughter stayed near the mother. Indeed, it seems as if the unmarried daughters basically also shared the sleeping room or female section of the tent or house with the mother (cf Song of Sol. 8:2). Just as in many other pre-industrial cultures, the young girl remained with her mother and followed the natural impulse for imitation. The mother then passed down—in a playful manner, as it were—all the necessary information and skills. True, in the well-known Old Testament song of praise to the efficient housewife (Prov. 31:10-31) this domestic educational function is not particularly mentioned. We can assume without hesitation, however, that the mother introduced her daughter to all those skills which made up the ideal image of the wife. This list is long and no doubt incomplete. In first position we find—in a rather summary fashion—the entire daily housework, summarized as "giving food." This encompasses above all the total kitchen service (v 15; cf Ps. 111:5, where the same turn of phrase is used in reference to God). The unknowledgeable husband can occasionally find out just how much skill this requires by taking on the preparation of a midday or evening meal himself. The text then extensively discusses the work of spinning, weaving, and tailoring (vv 13, 19, 22f, 24). These, too, presuppose a thorough apprenticeship. Peculiarly, verse 16 says that the wife is also responsible for the business of purchasing property. This activity would have to be based on a firm knowledge of legal implications, on experience in economic life, and above all on the woman's corresponding legal possibilities. The Old Testament says nothing about all this. Only Israel's surroundings relate something to us of that much female authority. Be that as it may, the Israelite girl was probably also initiated by her mother into the legal and societal rules of order. The echo of women's protests in the Old Testament (cf Num. 12; 27:1-11) leads us to believe that this instruction did not always occur in the sense of a blind subordination to men. The woman's social and charitable work is less surprising (v 20), since it issues almost effortlessly from domestic work in general.

To these few allusions in the "song of praise" we ought certainly to add the domestic instruction in questions of agriculture, vineyard cultivation, and animal husbandry, since the young girl no doubt also accompanied her mother during harvest and other work in the field (cf Judg. 21:20f). We also hear expressly that young girls tended the small animal herds (Gen. 29:9).

This strong association with the housewife's responsibilities from youth onward results in the Old Testament usually thinking of mother and daughter together (Mic. 7:6); according to the motto "a chip off the old block" one would then consider the mother responsible for an ill-bred daughter. Ezekiel 16:44 cites a common proverb: "Like mother, like daughter."

Admittedly one should not think of this domestic instruction as a preplanned course. Observations in pre-industrial communities show that this instruction and learning proceeds without any preconceived plan, but rather in the normal, daily routine without class plans, grades, or diploma. A great deal of time remains both during and after work for play and recreation. The young girl in Israel also had girlfriends in the usual sense. Dinah, for example, visits "the women of the land" (Gen. 34:1), apparently simply as a pasttime. Jephthah's daughter withdraws to the mountains with companions her own age in order to "bewail her virginity" (Judg. 11:37f); according to the narrator, she must have been between ten and fourteen years old at this time. We see that playmate groups of the same sex arose in Israel because of the strict separation of domestic and public responsibilities and because of the stringent sexual taboos for young girls; one need only consider the gang of "small boys" in 2 Kings 2:23f. When Zechariah 8:5 speaks of "boys and girls playing in the streets," this need not mean a mixing of the sexes; and the parallel passages Jeremiah 6:11 and 9:20 are probably thinking more of the small children between two and four years old who are simply playing outside in front of the house. Finally, let us briefly mention the peculiar, superstitious aversion to mixing "two different kinds" of things together (Lev. 19:19; Deut. 22:9-11) and to putting on the clothing of the opposite sex (Deut. 22:5).

We can now ask what significance this intensive association with the mother had for the Israelite girl. Only in a preliminary fashion was it a matter of instruction in domestic skills and practices. As regards the personality structure of the young girl, a strong, feminine self-understanding developed in the socially fixed areas. The daughter presumably identified to a large extent with the roles she associated with her mother. Neither must we underestimate the specific intellectual and emotional life that must have been predominant in the female activity of the Israelite home. Unfortunately, we have no Old Testament literary pieces from the hand of a woman, although figures such as Miriam, Deborah, Athaliah, and Huldah indirectly suggest the existence of an oral feminine tradition. From Israel's ancient Oriental surroundings we also know of literary documents that are sure to have been written by women, for example, letters concerned at least in part with political and economic matters (cf Romans).

c. The Maturing Young Man

Although we can only recognize the crude outlines of the way a young girl grew into the Israelite society, the picture of the young boy in his initial stage of life emerges much more clearly. He, too, remained with the mother during the nursing stage, usually two or three years. Hannah brings her son Samuel as a promised child to Shiloh after weaning, probably after the end of the third year; he then becomes a priestly apprentice with Eli (1 Sam. 1:21-28). Literally at the mother's breast during these initial years—according to our understanding today—the young boy is deeply influenced by the continual contact with the mother and corresponding absence of the father. The small child no doubt had other persons with whom to relate in the house—his small brothers and sisters, the grandmother and grandfather—but the mother had first claim and the full responsibility for the infant. She nourished him, cared for him in health and sickness, carried him around with her most of the time, taught him to walk, speak, and play, and joked with him. It is not at all surprising that sons developed a strong emotional attachment to the mother (cf Prov. 31:28; Jer. 15:10; 20:14-18). Grief for a mother was proverbially difficult (Ps. 35:14). The language of prayer—primarily in lament and supplication—refers again and again to one's own birth and to one's departure from the protective presence of the mother (cf Ps. 22:10; 71:6; 139:13). One enigmatic title of honor in the early period was "mother in Israel" (Judg. 5:7); and in the historical books one finds several examples of the significant influence a mother still exercised over the adult son. Rebekah persuades her favorite son, Jacob, to deceive his brother Esau (Gen. 27:6ff). Bathsheba twice becomes involved in questions of royal succession (1 Kings 1:11ff; 2:13ff), the first time for the sake of her son Solomon. We hear nothing of Oedipal conflicts except that one is forbidden sexual relations with one's mother (Lev. 18:7) or with another of the father's wives (cf Gen. 35:22; Lev. 18:8; 1 Kings 2:13ff). These laws suggest the conclusion that the problem of excessively close connection with the mother was not unknown.

However one may evaluate the dangers of this intimate mother-son relationship in the initial years of life, it appears that society in ancient times gave the child a better chance of growing up without emotional disturbances. The consistency and accessibility of this person to whom the child relates is no longer guaranteed today, not to speak of the extended period of nursing. The modern mother stands under the double pressure of domestic and vocational activity. She can no longer fully dedicate herself to her child, and child-care services do not offer a full substitute for the missing emotional attention. Today's father—who actually ought to be a much stronger relational person for the child in a democratic society—finds himself overtaxed by his vocation and thus virtually disappears from the domestic realm.

But back to the young Israelite boy. Weaning was an initial goal on his way to becoming a man, and was festively celebrated (Gen. 21:8; 1 Sam. 1:25). From now on, the father assumed the primary responsibility for education, though the mother still gave advice and instruction (Prov. 1:8; 31:1; Exod. 20:12; cf however Prov. 4:1ff: here the father is expressly the one giving instruction). A young boy had to learn all the skills of a farmer and particularly all the rights and obligations, traditions and values of his clan and people. Even the child must have seen clearly enough what kind of responsibility it would assume if it ever followed its father's footsteps and took over the leadership role in the family. As long as there was no professional army, the father also had to prepare his son for military service (Judg. 8:20).

The Old Testament has preserved numerous traces of how a father and son spent time together. The son asked questions, the father answered and explained: customs and traditions in Israel, the divine works of salvation in the past, the commandments, peculiarities of Palestine's geography, and so on. "If your son asks you . . ." is a permanent turn of phrase (cf Exod. 13:14; Deut. 6:20; Josh. 4:6, 21); and at least those stories from Israel's early period which want to explain something and end with the phrase, "And so it is to this day" (cf Josh. 4:9; 5:9; 6:25; 7:26; 8:29f; 9:27; and elsewhere), can be traced back to this kind of question-answer game. They simultaneously show how much of the Old Testament's narrative tradition was passed down within the family circle. The conversation between Abraham and Isaac is exemplary of the way a father and son associated with each other. Abraham has prepared for the trip without giving the son any reason at all, and these mysterious preparations must have seemed peculiar (Gen. 22:3). Isaac, however, goes along without any questioning, and only during the trip itself does he ask for an explanation:

> So they went both of them together. And Isaac said to his father Abraham, "My father!" And he said, "Here am I, my son." He said, "Behold, the fire and the wood; but where is the lamb for a burnt offering?" Abraham said, "God will provide himself the lamb for a burnt offering, my son." So they went both of them together. (Gen. 22:6b-8)

It is not just the tragic element alone in this scene that calls forth the measured, solemn style. No, the domestic instruction was so vitally important for the young boy, and the father's explanation so weighty, that this solemnity was indeed the suitable tone. The Israelite farmer avoided excessive verbiage. That experiential treasure of insights and rules, as well as confessions, prayers, stories, ancestral genealogies, or whatever else one had to "teach diligently to one's children" (Deut. 6:7), originally consisted of clear, short formulations. And whenever the father opened his mouth to speak, the son knew too well that it was a matter of life and death (cf Prov. 2; 3), since the young man could not possibly orient himself in his world without the father's and forefathers' teachings. A maladjusted, stubborn, rebellious son was also a source of shame for the family (cf Deut. 21:18-21; Prov. 17:25; 19:26; 28:24; and elsewhere). On the other hand, proper education—which could only be acquired from the father—resulted in the correct life content and the capacity to enjoy that life fully (cf Prov. 4:1ff). Well-reared sons were also the best recommendation for the family and the pride of their parents (cf Prov. 23:15ff).

At one time or another, we thus see the son step into his father's shoes. David is still a small boy, but he has already assumed full responsibility for the grazing flock (1 Sam. 16:11ff; 17:37). Joseph acts as a courier or messenger between his father's house and his brothers out with the herd (Gen. 37:14ff). The Shunammite's son runs out to the field when harvest is under way (2 Kings 4:18ff). Jether, Gideon's son, has a traumatic experience during the battle with the Midianites (Judg. 8:20). Jehoash was seven years old when he was crowned king (2 Kings 11:12; 12:1), and Azariah came to the throne when he was sixteen (2 Kings 14:21). Jeremiah resists his prophetic calling because he was "only a youth" (Jer. 1:6). Both Hosea and Isaiah draw their own children into prophetic service (Hos. 1:6-9; Isa. 7:3; 8:3f); and during times of war sons would suffer the same fate as their fathers (cf Deut. 20:13; Judg. 9:5; 2 Sam. 12:13ff).

The attention given the male progeny was naturally concentrated on the eldest son, since he would one day take over the leadership role within the larger family. Above all, he was the channel through which the patriarchal lineage was perpetuated, and was the person primarily responsible for the maintenance of family land holdings. Under his leadership, his brothers and their families could continue to live in the family house (Ps. 133:1); but to him alone belonged the double portion of the patriarchal inheritance (Deut. 21:15-17) as well as the position of superiority within the clan, a position manifesting itself in the reception of a special blessing for the firstborn (Gen.

27). This blessing, irrevocably bestowed only once, was the concentrated power, as it were, of the entire family, the unique charisma of this particular group of people, a charisma that passed from the dying father to the eldest son. The recipient represented the totality of his clan henceforth. The consecration instructions (cf Exod. 13:2, 12f; 22:28f; Num. 3:12f; Deut. 15:19f) concerning firstborn children confirm how high the Israelites valued the eldest son. In Pre-Israelite Canaan, the eldest son was sacrificed to God—exactly like the first-born animals or firstfruits of the harvest (cf 2 Kings 3:27; this custom was for a time also widespread in Israel; Ezek. 20:26; Mic. 6:7; 2 Kings 16:3).

The conclusion of childhood and apprentice years was probably festively celebrated in the Old Testament, although we have no direct reports of this. In Judaism today a young boy is still considered to have come of age after the end of the twelfth year. The celebration falls in the time of puberty and corresponds approximately to confirmation among Christians. Almost all cultures have structured this entrance into manhood in some ritual fashion. In pre-exilic Israel the circumcision was an important part of such initiatory rites (cf Gen. 34; Exod. 4:25; Josh. 5:2f) and was considered primarily a (religious-magical?) preparation and prerequisite for marriage. Circumcision was later changed to the eighth day after birth. The text dealing with this, Genesis 17:10-14, comes unquestionably from the post-exilic period when the surgical removal of the foreskin had already become a sign of the covenant and a symbol of the Jewish community (cf v 14!).

How should we today evaluate the intimate camaraderie between the young Israelite boy and his father between (approximately) the fourth and twelfth years of life? We can perhaps immediately see the disadvantages. In the first place, the growing boy apparently had absolutely no other alternatives as far as developing his personality was concerned. He had to grow into the vocation, educational level, and ways of thinking of his father. This fact is so self-evident that the Old Testament does not emphasize it anywhere. Whenever a son "went astray" from his father's ways, there had to be a certain reason for it; it was also viewed with mistrust (cf Gen. 4:19-22; Judg. 11:1-3; Gen. 37:23-28). We would not tolerate this kind of conformity. Furthermore, following his father's lead, the young Israelite boy identified with the power and authority of the head of the family; however, he also had to learn to subordinate his own interests continually to the higher welfare of the family. That, too, is self-evident for the Old Testament writers, though for us this kind of mentality means a severe limitation of personal freedom. In the third place, this total subordination to the father's educational power—until one came of age and often even far beyond—was no doubt sometimes a heavy burden for the son. Every Israelite probably accepted the fact that an Israelite father was not at all reluctant to make use of his disciplinary rights (Prov. 13:24). What happened, however, when his measure of punishment went too far and he did something like discipline his son to death (cf Prov. 19:18)? Legally, the son was also subject to the father's arbitrariness and brutality. Neither a judge nor a child protection agency could intervene in his favor. All those "wild, crazy, untamed" men the Old Testament sometimes mentions were, after all, also fathers. How did they treat their sons (cf Gen. 4:23f; 16:12; 1 Sam. 25:3)? Only rarely did a people succeed in saving a son from the execution of the patriarchal death sentence (1 Sam. 14:43-45).

Now, however, we must recognize that this severe limitation of the possibilities for personal development had a positive side as well, namely—again from our perspective—an enviable stability of social and intellectual-spiritual structures. The way of the fathers was known through the physical father, and it was absolutely binding (cf Jer. 6:16; Mic. 6:8). This is particularly the case for the masculine self-understanding and for the man's relationship to the opposite sex. Passages such as Proverbs 2:16ff, 5:1ff, and 7:5ff clearly show the intensity with which the Israelite father went about sexual education. Today's industrial society, on the other hand, lacks a binding ethos, a stable family or other primary group, and above all lacks the caring and exemplary figure of the father. It is no accident that the designation "fatherless society" has become a catch-phrase. A young man grows for the most part unaccompanied and misunderstood into a hostile, continually changing environment. Statistics and reports about young criminals, drug addicts, and youths who totally shut themselves out (youth sects, radical alternative cultures) are horrifying. In developing countries in which the effects of (rushed) industrialization appear even more glaringly, large portions of the young people are hopelessly uprooted. Family structures, particularly in the concentrated urban areas with their slums and favelas, have almost totally dissolved under the inhuman burdens and sacrifices.

2. Love, Courtship, Wedding

The second stage in the Israelite's life encompasses for all practical purposes the time from puberty until death. If the Israelite woman outlives her husband, then one can evaluate widowhood as a special kind of concluding stage. In contrast to the pronounced fourfold nature of modern life with its overemphasis on extra-familial vocational activity, the Israelite passes through two and at most three main stages: childhood and youth, marriage and independent work, and (perhaps) widowhood. The setting remains unchanged during one's entire life. Wherever a person is born in antiquity, so also does he live, work, and die there. The larger family unit and one's own arable land are the fixed points of orientation; no one leaves his place of birth of his own free will. The wanderings undertaken by Abraham, Joseph, Ruth, and others are occasioned by external causes and may reflect memories of the nomadic past. Nonetheless, the Bedouin restlessness has in the Old Testament long given way to agricultural settled life. One believed that a person could find happiness only "under his vine and under his fig tree" (Mic. 4:4).

We are devoting a special section to this transition into the second stage of life because this step into real life was so important in the Old Testament. The important thing here is that the instruction the parents have given their son and daughter prove good. The sexual roles and relationships have only been learned theoretically, but the text and example begin with the wedding. Has the daughter or son received the proper preparation and education?

Even today, sexual maturity marks an essential hiatus in the life of the young person. However, the complexity of life, the long educational process, and the heightened expectations have caused puberty and the step into adult responsibility to occur far apart from each other. Even after having come of age at eighteen, the normal European is at this time not yet able to establish a family. Things were different in the Orient of antiquity and thus also in Israel. Sexual maturity came quite early, at ten or twelve years. The Mishna figures that a boy is capable of reproduction from the ninth year onward (Yebam. 10:7-9). At the same, time, the children were considered economically and socially independent within the framework of the strong familial institution. We may assume that at this time the children had also attained a certain intellectual and emotional maturity. It is decisively important, however, that the family did not turn loose of these members that had just come of age, but rather accompanied and directed them further. Thus as a rule the parents, just as in most pre-industrial societies, had the deciding word in the matter of partner choice.

a. Becoming a Bride

To a large extent the Old Testament simply lacks any self-expressions of girls "of marrying age." Only in the Song of Solomon can we take a longer look into the interior world of lovers. The text of this unique book comes presumably from the post-exilic period. It is not so important to know whether it originally dealt with secular love songs or with cultic songs celebrating divine weddings, since the texts clearly go back to human experience and perception. What is surprising is that the girl in these antiphonies expresses her yearning for the beloved with great openness. The girl is seeking her friend in the dark city streets (Song of Sol. 3:2); but weren't young girls forbidden to go out at night and as punishment whipped home (5:7)? She would like to bring the beloved to her parents' house (5:4f; 8:2) or "give him her love" (7:12) out in the vineyards. The singer revels in the thought of his masculine beauty (2:9; 5:10ff) and imagines his tenderness (2:6; 5:2ff; 7:11ff; 8:3); in a word, she is "sick with love" (2:5; 5:8). How is all this possible if strict premarital abstinence is expected of the girl (cf Deut. 23:13ff)?

We must first look for the answer in the life situation in which these songs were sung. One should probably think about the wedding festivities. Song of Solomon 8:8-10 also presupposes, in a kind of flashback, the courtship of the young bride. But even if one considers other possibilities—such as the harvest work in gardens and vineyards during which the young girls possibly sang love songs, or even mourning ceremonies for a deceased spouse to whom one sang the phrase "for love is strong as death" (8:6)—it is clear that sexual yearning could be freely expressed in such passages. The ancient Israelite society was certainly patriarchal, and women were given a subordinate position in public. However, this is by no means the same as prudery or false shame. At the proper time and under even halfway legitimate circumstances, one gave oneself to love. There were no doubt many sexual taboos and significant limitations for a woman, but the girl not yet engaged was able to love her friend if she was certain that he would marry her (cf Deut. 22:28f; 2 Sam. 13:13, 16). The parents' consent was in such cases probably quite easily acquired, since the parents had to fear the shame of having a deflowered, unmarried daughter in their family. In this sense the emphatic "she had never known a man" (Judg. 11:39; 21:12) meant the same as the statement "she is still not engaged."

In spite of all we might deduce from the Song of Solomon, the free encounter of the sexes did not play a decisive role in Israel. In any case, Old Testament laws and stories presuppose the relative separation of the male and female spheres of life, the sexual purity of the bride, and precisely that parental initiative concerning the choice of spouse. Nothing was left for the young girl to do but wait anxiously for her groom. Only within this overall situation might she then diplomatically adeptly tell her parents of her own wishes (1 Sam. 18:20). The subordination under the will of the older generation from childhood on probably excluded conflicts between daughter and parents to a large extent. Furthermore, the girl saw in flesh and blood the fundamental truth that a woman without a husband—and thus a woman without sons—was worth nothing. What other possibilities for existence could a girl in Israel, under these circumstances, have dreamed up for herself? She could languish away as an old maid in her parents' house, become a prostitute, or perhaps go underground as a medium of the dead (cf 1 Sam. 28:7ff) or some other kind of sorceress (cf Exod. 22:17; Deut. 18:10f; Ezek. 13:17ff). No, in that case it would be better to wait for the husband chosen by her parents. Personal love for the spouse often did indeed arise even when the bride was not able to influence the parents' decision (cf Gen. 24:67). We can justifiably assume that the girlhood dream of a shining groom was fulfilled just as frequently in Old Testament times as in our own. In addition to the Song of Solomon, the allegorizations of the bridgroom images in the prophetic-eschatological language witness to this fact (cf Ezek. 16; Isa. 62). Zion or Israel then played the female role, and church hymns such as "Daughter Zion, Be Glad" or texts from Bach's *Christmas Oratorio* (cf Nr. 3, 4, 19, etc) have taken up and carried forth this sexual symbolism.

Although almost all the Old Testament courtship stories are told from the male perspective, we also occasionally see in them reflections of the reality of the young wife who more or less consciously saw her life's most important decision being made. We see, for example, the prototypical story of the selection of Rebekah as Isaac's wife (Gen. 24). Father Abraham would most like—according to good Hebraic custom—to select a girl from his own relatives for his son. He thus sends his confidant to his old home in Mesopotamia. The decisive first scene of bride selection takes place at the well that also has a place for watering camels. Abraham's messenger wants to have a look at the local girls. He prays for divine guidance (vv 12-14), and already Rebekah comes, who like no other corresponds to Abraham's idea of a good daughter-in-law. Assuming Bethuel is not—as in verses 15 and 24—Rebekah's father, but rather—as in verses 50, 53, and 55—a younger brother, then she is Isaac's first cousin, daughter of Nahor, Abraham's brother. Probably because of legal inheritance reasons, the marriage to a first cousin—the daughter of a father's brother—was considered optimal. The course of the narrative reveals that Yahweh had already solved the problem and made the best decision for Abraham at the well scene. The messenger's prayer of supplication (vv 12-14) and the thanksgiving (vv 26ff) indicate that marriages were first and foremost "made in heaven." The human side of spouse selection, however, also makes an appearance; and in this context the young girl's behavior is noteworthy.

At the well, Rebekah is first tested. Is she caring and does she traffic without fear with man and beast? Will she be able to execute her function as household organizer and maintainer? Even more, the Old Testament often compares women with wells (cf Prov. 5:15-18). It is her biological and familial task to quench the man's thirst for sexual satisfaction and progeny. Every Israelite who heard this story in Genesis 24 will have understood the allusions and been glad: Rebekah is a woman in the fullest sense of the word! She takes up female work energetically and confidently. She quenches the stranger's thirst and does more than asked; she also waters the camels and offers the hospitality of her father's house. Besides that, she is beautiful (vv 16-20, 25).

In the second main scene (vv 29-54) Rebekah remains the object of action. Thus it was in Israel: A young girl's wishes were subsumed under family interests, and probably often submerged. The father and brother (or brothers) gave her over to the person courting (v 51). Not until the concluding scene, when the guest is about to leave early, is Rebekah questioned as to her own opinion (v 58). The selected bride is not quite without choice. Only after her agreement does the caravan set off.

The Israelite girl had to be prepared to leave her own family and join her husband's clan. The decision—or the conscious acceptance of a stranger's decision—required strength of character. This break with one's own past was only required of the woman, not of the man. The Israelite woman's personality structure was no doubt also determined by this particular circumstance. Thus we occasionally observe a certain aggressiveness on the part of women toward their fathers or the betrothed. Rachel and Leah, two sisters who belong to one husband and who can be as mean as spiders, make a common front against their father, Laban (Gen. 31:14ff). Both of Samson's wives successively show their self-willed natures and in each case betray him to the Philistines during the wedding festivities (Judg. 14; 16). For the sake of her husband's family, Ruth leaves her Moabite home (Ruth 1).

The Israelite bride places herself completely at the service of her husband's family. Her own relatives receive the bridal price or marriage present in exchange for her (Gen. 34:12; 1 Sam. 18:25), but then have no more claim to their daughter. The bride in Israel possibly also received (as is known from Assyrian-Babylonian marriage contracts) a dowry in the marriage (cf Judg. 1:12-15); this could serve as a cushion in the case of widowhood or expulsion. Later sources deal extensively with this affair, for example the Mishna tract Ketuboth. In case of extreme danger she fled—as is still customary today—back into her parents' house (Judg. 19:2). Nonetheless, the orientation to the husband's family was in every case a significant and lasting alteration of her life. During a royal wedding the bride was advised:

Hear, O daughter, consider, and incline your ear;
    forget your people and your father's house;
    and the king will desire your beauty.
Since he is your lord, bow to him. (Ps. 45:10ff)

Every bit of this advice held true for every Israelite farm girl as well; compare the exemplary significance of the story in Esther 1.

b. Becoming a Husband

After reaching sexual maturity, the young Israelite boy waited, just as did the girl, for the day of his wedding; the one difference was that the pressures and limitations on him were not as severe or were of a different nature. Admittedly, the man who does not establish a family or adequately care for his own is worthless. The book of Proverbs repeatedly scourges the lazy or drunken fellow (cf Prov. 20:13; 23:29-35; 24:30-34; 26:14-16; and elsewhere). Yet one can more easily imagine, given the situation, that a man might choose a vocation other than that of head of a house and farmer. A wandering priest, for example, enjoyed great respectability (Judg. 17:7-13). Did he really have to marry? Or the leader of a band or army, as David in his early years, or Jephthah: Was he not basically allowed to be a bachelor? There were possibly also traveling merchants or sailors (cf 1 Kings 9:26-28) who chose not to marry for the sake of greater mobility. We know nothing of this. It simply seems that the Israelite man, because of his preferential position, might sooner have the possibility of breaking out of the traditional life-style. If we are not deceived, then David's son Absalom was a confirmed bachelor. Why else would he have erected a pillar for himself during his own lifetime—in the absence of sons (2 Sam. 18:18).

The unmarried man's greater mobility becomes even more apparent in the question of premarital sexual relations. A young man can fall in love with a girl and seduce her—as long as she is not engaged—and go relatively unpunished (Deut. 22:28f; 2 Sam. 13:3ff). If it comes to light, then he must either marry her or pay a bridal price as punishment (Exod. 12:15f). Only the intimate relationship with a married or engaged woman is a dangerous affair, one that can cost him his life (Deut. 22:22ff). The Wisdom literature and instructions of the Law tirelessly warn against contact with the "other woman," meaning someone else's woman (cf Gen. 39:7ff; Prov. 5:1ff; Exod. 20:14, 17). "He who commits adultery has no sense; he who does it destroys himself" (Prov. 6:32; cf the drastic description of the seductive art of a loose woman: Prov. 7:6-23). Apparently Israel's young men were real hotheads who had neither the patience nor the means to conceal a premeditated act of adultery by means of murder and then marrying the widow—as did David (2 Sam. 11). Breaking into another's marriage meant a risk of life. On the other hand, society tolerated sexual relations with prostitutes (Gen. 38:13ff; Judg. 11:1; 16:1; 1 Kings 3:16).

The impulse to establish his own family, however, governed the young man more than animal desires. Love pointed beyond the two lovers. To be sure, the portions of the Song of Solomon to be sung by the man also praise the partner's physical charms (eg Song of Sol. 1:8-11, 15; 2:10-15; 4:1-15; and elsewhere). Judges 14:1-4 and 16:1, 4 speak about Samson's sexual urge, and in a preliminary fashion this is also the case in several other passages that speak of love and being in love. Nonetheless, according to the Old Testament understanding as a whole, there stood behind this yearning for sexual union the desire to transcend oneself as well as—from the perspective of the man—to complete oneself (Gen. 2:23f; cf below IV 1). Essentially, love has a social dimension, and is the expansion of the ego to the partner and family. For both man and woman, being blessed means having numerous descendants (cf Gen. 12:2; 24:60). As the future head of the family, the young man knows of this prospect when he marries; it is also, however, a matter of concern for the perpetuation of the clan (cf Gen. 15:2). The wife shares the same concern, but does so in the function of her husband (cf Gen. 30:1; 1 Sam. 1:7f). From the perspective of these general expectations, it is then quite understandable that marriage was warmly recommended to the young adult. "He who finds a wife finds a good thing, and obtains favor from the Lord" (Prov. 18:22). And in a reverse fashion, whoever lives in fear of the Lord can be promised the following:

Your wife will be like a fruitful vine within your house;
your children will be like olive shoots around your table.

(Ps. 128:3)

Psalms 127 and 128 could even be understood as best wishes for the groom on his wedding day.

Thus as regards the expectations of the young Israelite, marriage connects the realization of his own, personal yearnings with the interests of the family community as well as with the promises of Yahweh's blessed activity. No wonder the wedding represented a high point in the full sense of the word in a man's life. According to Judges 14 and Genesis 29:28, the festivities lasted seven days and even at that time were likely celebrated with Oriental revelry—with song, dance, games, and rich festive meals. Above all, we find the groom's friends of the same age invited as guests (Judg. 14:10). As is still customary in the Orient today, the bride was given to the groom in a cermonious procession (cf Ps. 45:15f). The decisive act was then the bringing together of the bridal couple late in the evening in the bridal tent or chamber (Gen. 29:23-25; cf Ps. 19:6). This room was decorated in the finest fashion and filled with fragrant perfumes (cf Prov. 7:16f). The bride was led in veiled, and the couple then "enjoyed love," the bridal night.

In this context, one custom was important in Old Testament times which has been preserved until today by some Arabian tribes. The bride's parents and relatives waited in front of the bridal chamber until the first sexual act had been performed and the bride deflowered. They received the bedsheets and blood traces with a cry of jubilation and passed them around among the guests. The bride had gone into the marriage as a virgin! The sheets were stored and served later as proof of the bride's purity in case of doubt (Deut. 22:13-21; the Luther translation reads to the effect: "tokens of virginity"). Thus the bridal night had double legal significance. The first act of sexual intercourse sealed the marriage contract drawn between the parents; at the same time, it provided proof for the girl's blameless reputation. We can see that the interest of the man dominated the structure and interpretation of the wedding ceremony.

3. Daily Life in Marriage

It is no secret that youthful love and bridal excitement must soon give way to daily life with its demands and amusements, its routine of high and low points. Life together and in a family is not the way one imagines it to be during the initial period of love. It seems to me that this fact held true for the Old Testament married couple as well, though to a lesser extent than today. This wave of disappointment, that today comes over young marrieds after about six to twelve months, was probably weaker then because of the openness, order, and clarity of living conditions within the smaller group, the sobriety with which the father and mother prepared their children for their roles, and the preeminence of collective interests over individual needs. Perhaps we can even conclude with some certainty that in Old Testament times there were in general fewer unhappy and unsuccessful marriages than today, since marriage relationships today are based not on overriding goals, but rather almost exclusively on personal, often selfish love or individual drive for happiness. Another burdening factor is that the fragmentation and complexity of our life-style make it impossible to evaluate before the marriage the partner's personality and potential for development. This kind of evaluation, so extremely necessary for both personal and shared happiness, is not even possible for oneself. To a much larger extent, then, the future must remain hidden to young couples today, and highly tensed expectation replaces the orientation to reality. We will now investigate some aspects of married life using examples of Old Testament couples.

a. Abraham and Sarah: The Dual Relationship

The chapters Genesis 12–23 occasionally speak about the patriarchal couple, though God deals for the most part only with Abraham, and the ancestor's wives are only the organs through which the divine salvation plan is carried out. As such, however, they are highly valued by the narrator. Sarah, the "princess," accompanies Abraham on all his wanderings as a confident housewife. She displays extremely human, concrete characteristics and is not an abstraction. Only subsequent generations idealized her portrait (cf 1 Pet. 3:6; Heb. 11:11).

In the daily life of this aging, childless couple, the strict division of labor is immediately noticeable. Just as Proverbs 31:10-30 describes, Sarah takes care of the kitchen and prepares the festive meal while Abraham talks with the guests in the shade of the tent entrance, where a light breeze makes life more pleasant (Gen. 18:6-15). The bedouin wife's place is decisively "in the tent" (v 9), at the hearth and among the cooking pots. She is proud to bring a good meal to the table. The guests' question concerning where she is is thus superfluous, unless they wanted to speak with her (v 9; cf v 15). This same kind of division of the tent into female and male parts and the corresponding specialization of daily work is still dominant today among Arabian bedouin. Indeed, with a few variations this division of space and tasks still exists in our own highly developed industrial society. The wife's place is still in the kitchen, while the husband's is often in the living room in front of the television, or perhaps in the garden, the study, or in the hobby room.

Abraham's guests eventually turn the conversation to Sarah. She is yet to bear a son (v 10). The tent walls are thin, the air is not disturbed by any traffic noise, and perhaps the housewife is even eavesdropping a bit; in a word: "So Sarah laughed to herself, saying, 'After I have grown old, and my husband is old, shall I have pleasure?'" (v 12). In the first place, this scene shows that as a rule the wife took part in outside events from the kitchen and through her husband (more about this in the next section). In the second place, it suggests that married life normally meant sexual satisfaction for both partners. Third, already during Sarah's time sex during old age was no longer suitable or no longer possible. The fourth point is the main problem of the narrative section as a whole: the absence of an heir (vv 11-15).

Thus sexual relations were important to the Israelite couple beyond the honeymoon. The Old Testament makes numerous references to caresses and sleeping together as regards married couples. Isaac "teases" or "fondles" his wife such that one could see it from the street through the open window (Gen. 26:8). Wisdom literature tries to promote the practice of love in marriage in order to avoid the chaos of promiscuity (cf Prov. 5:15ff). The old Book of the Covenant even prescribes that the man who has taken a second wife (because he has become tired of the first) is not allowed to withhold the first wife's rightful portion of sexual relations (Exod. 21:10; cf Gen. 30:14-15: The man belongs alternately to the one and then to the other wife). One ought accordingly to presume that sexual behavior in Israel was balanced and without problems. The frequently documented visits to prostitutes and adultery on the part of the men (cf Gen. 38; 2 Sam. 11) as well as extramarital relations on the part of the women (Gen. 39:7-18; Prov. 7:6-23) are all the more astonishing.

For our own purposes, it would be more important to investigate the intellectual and emotional partnership between spouses during Old Testament times. How did the division of labor in the family affect the human cohesiveness between the couple? Our sources at this point are rather meager. The man's interests stand in the foreground, emotional ties are rarely brought to expression; we should not allow ourselves to impose our own standards for personal ties without further ado. Nonetheless, even this information is limited. Collective action of wife and husband is mentioned only rarely, and when the Old Testament narrators do report something of this, they often choose negative examples. Jezebel and Ahab plan Naboth's murder (1 Kings 21); Eve and Adam both succumb to the temptation of wanting to be "like God" (Gen. 3). In both stories the woman plays the role of the temptress. Hosea demonstrates Yahweh's judgment and grace in his own marriage to a harlot (Hos. 1–3). Positive examples are the collective pilgrimage to Shiloh that Elkanah makes in the company of his two wives Hannah and Peninnah (1 Sam. 1) or the common concern Jeroboam I and his wife share for their ill son (1 Kings 14). It will be worthwhile to look closely in this sense at all the conversations first between spouses, and then more generally between men and women. Abraham and Sarah speak not a single word with each other in Genesis 18; the patriarch gives her only a short word of instruction (v 6). This same situation is more grave in two texts in which Sarah becomes the victim of male behavior. Abraham asks her to pose as his sister so that he may avoid endangering himself (Gen. 12:11-13; 20:2); and we hear neither protest nor queries nor any other expression of opinion from the woman who is thus subjected to the arbitrariness of strange men. It is crystal clear to the narrators that Abraham's wish is a command for the woman. A kind of exchange of opinions between the spouses arises actually only because of the other wife, Hagar, and her son Ishmael (Gen. 16:1-6; 21:9-12). Both times Abraham "obeys" his wife and expels the disagreeable rivals. Otherwise Sarah plays an active role only in Genesis 21:1-7 (Isaac's birth, naming). In Genesis 17:15-19 Abraham receives for her the promise of rich descendants. On the other hand, the patriarch's wife does not appear at all in the extremely important sections Genesis 15:1-21; 17:1-14; 22:1-19. All this appears to admit the conclusion that the wife had the right to express her own opinion in certain questions concerning her own status or realm of activity. In matters concerning the husband as head of the family, however, she could at most express her opinion "unofficially," even if her own life were at stake.

It is not possible for us to analyze all the Old Testament conversations between partners. Let us refer a few examples. Elkanah loves his sterile wife Hannah (1 Sam. 1:5) and consoles her tenderly and warmly: "Am I not more to you than ten sons?" (v 8). In Judges 13 Manoah's wife twice reports the appearance of an angel of God (vv 6f and 10). She receives no answer at all from her husband, who instead himself turns to Yahweh in prayer and then deals directly with the divine messenger, even in the name of his wife (cf vv 15-21). Only at the very end is there a dialogue between the spouses in which the wife proves to be theologically much more sensitive and realistic (vv 22f). Second Samuel 6:16, 20-23 shows us a graphic marriage quarrel between David and Michal.

Additional interesting conversations between spouses can be found, for example, in 1 Kings 1:11-31; 2 Kings 4:21-24; Job 2:9f; Esther 5:1-8; 8:3-8. A comparison of these texts with dialogues between unmarried men and women reveals that in the portions yet to be discussed, women present themselves more freely and represent their own concerns with greater precision, and that the dialogues contain more arguments than do those between spouses (cf 1 Sam. 25:24-35; 28:8-14, 21-25; 2 Sam. 13:8-20; 14:1-20; 1 Kings 3:16-28; 10:1-13; 17:10-24; 2 Kings 6:26-29; 8:1-6; 9:30f; Ruth 3:7-15; Esther 4:12-17; and elsewhere). These do not yet, of course, say anything about the exchange of opinions between individual Israelite married couples as it might have occurred in reality as opposed to literary stylizations. These literary documents do, however, give us an idea how the Old Testament narrators and writers imagined this kind of human and intellectual cooperation, as it were, before the eyes of the public.

The problem of male progeny and sterility in the woman was a serious problem for Israelite marriages; people did not take the sterility of the man into consideration probably because of a lack of knowledge about the pertinent biological factors. We have already mentioned this problem earlier. The Abraham stories, however, give the opportunity to reflect on both external and internal threats to the marriage partnership that may seem a bit alien to us. We can undertake this reflection, however, only to the extent that it illuminates the structure and resistance power of the marriage institution in the Old Testament.

Polygamy no doubt brought with it an inner threat to the marriage institution. Several wives in one household—that could not always run smoothly (cf Gen. 16:4ff; 21:9ff; 1 Sam. 1:6f)! This kind of cohabitation of two or more women with one man is quite rare in the Western tradition. Today this situation corresponds perhaps most closely to the fixed triangle relation known to all the participants, a relation in which one spouse maintains a relationship to a spatially separated lover or mistress. The feelings of jealousy and hate generated by this constellation are virtually identical with those the Old Testament describes. Among external threats in Old Testament times we can mention, above all, war, bad harvests (eg, because of extensive drought), and sickness or epidemics. In the majority of these emergencies, the Israelite families no doubt developed strong feelings of solidarity (cf Gen. 46; Lam. 4; 1 Kings 17:12; and elsewhere). In certain extreme situations, however, a list of priorities went into effect that we find unacceptable. From our perspective it appears that in such cases the weakest family member would be sacrificed first. It was possible, for example, that during a drawn-out seige of a city, mothers could be brought to consume their own children (2 Kings 6:24-29). Above all, however, we need to mention the legitimate sacrifice of the wife for the sake of her husband (cf Gen. 12:10-20; 20:1-18; 26:1-11; Judg. 19:22-30). The stories proceed from the understanding that a Hebrew married couple in a strange environment is in a certain sense legal prey. What can a man do upon entering an area with his wife in which he enjoys no legal protection? If danger is imminent, he sacrifices his wife. Is that an act of the purest cynicism? Wouldn't he on the contrary have to jump into the fray for his wife? We recall the British SOS rule: women and children first! Old Testament ethic—compare Genesis 19:8 and Exodus 21:7 as examples of the offering of children—does not proceed in such situations from medieval courtly ideals, but rather from the sober consideration: Which family member is most expendable in a serious situation in which the survival of the family itself is at stake? Who can be replaced most quickly? The answer: Daughters and women can be replaced most easily, whereas the clan stands or falls with the family father or the sons.

b. The Shunammite and Her Husband: External Relationships

We have already occasionally referred to the married couple's relationships to its environment. The basic model seemed to be Sarah's behavior: Through her husband and from the kitchen she took part in what happened (Gen. 18:9-14); not until verse 15 does she appear directly confronted with Abraham's visitors. This model appears again in several narratives and legal texts in which the husband is the spokesman—one sometimes wants to say, trustee—for his wife. Compare Numbers 5:11-28, 30; Judges 13:6-21 with Genesis 20 and elsewhere. Only the adult male is the fully privileged representative of the family in the locale or tribe's decision-making bodies. He represents his family members to other groups and powers, including to God. A sign of his dignity and public responsibility is, for example, his membership in the council assembly in the gate, an extremely old democratic institution in the various communities (cf Ruth 4:1ff; Jer. 26:16; Job 29:7ff; Prov. 31:23), or in the council of the elders of the tribe or possibly tribal confederation (cf Exod. 24:9ff; Num. 11:16ff; 1 Kings 12:6ff; Ezek. 8:1; 20:1; and elsewhere). The husband's function in war, as well as his economic tasks in the family business as owner of the land and herds, resulted equally in numerous contacts with the external world. Our task now is to see whether this image of the husband as the only one with external contacts holds true for the Israelite family in its full scope. We have already encountered texts that lead us to doubt this hypothesis, for example, Proverbs 31:16!

Our best example is a narrative that lets us see the woman's relative but unexpected independence in her dealings with the external. In 2 Kings 4 we read the following story: The prophet

Elisha, a penniless, wandering man of God, regularly visits a rich family in Shunem (v 8; in the parallel story about Elijah the hostess is a widow from Zarephath, 1 Kings 17:9). Or more precisely: The housewife considers it valuable to have him as a guest, and it is she who suggests to her aging husband (v 14) to fix a nice, quiet room for the guest (vv 9f). It is astonishing that, according to the narrator, this simple bit of advice to the spouse suffices to decide the plan and put it into effect. There is not the smallest bit of suspicion that the rich lady might in a clever fashion be wanting to give herself access to a lover; this idea does not even arise within the context of the announcement of the birth of a son (vv 16f). When the son, already long grown, suddenly dies (v 20), the Shunammite woman gives us an even more impressive example of her internal and external independence. She instructs her husband to prepare a slave and an ass, since she must quickly seek out the prophet Elisha (v 22). Just imagine: The only son lies dead in the house, and the wife wants to go off on a trip! Isn't a word of explanation to the spouse in order here? The Shunammite's husband is portrayed as extremely easygoing if not feebleminded. He does not jump up in a rage and chase his wife out of the house so that she secures mourners and prepares the dead son's burial; no, he asks quite harmlessly: "Why will you go to him today? It is neither new moon nor sabbath" (v 23). This sounds as if he had already grown accustomed to his wife's taking excursions on holy days and now can only ask a bit curiously: Does she have to go now, too? The peak of non-solidarity, however (and this would also be true if the husband did not yet know of the child's death), is the Shunammite's answer: "It will be well!" or "Good-bye" (v 23: the Hebrew word is *shalom*). Nothing more; then she speaks once more only with the slave (v 24) and rides away.

The Shunammite of our story has apparently turned the tables and has trained her husband to be a docile subordinate. She is the master in the house; it is no accident that in verse 8 she is called a "great," "strong," or "rich" woman (cf 2 Kings 8:1-6). Neither is her behavior rather striking only against the background of a patriarchal society. What husband today would stand by silently if his wife prepared a nice attic room for a traveling evangelist and left the house in a serious crisis situation without giving a reason? Today one might still offer the explanation that religion and the church are female matters. This excuse did not, however, apply in Old Testament times!

This story of the dominating Shunammite is not the only one of its kind in the Old Testament. We encounter a great many texts that grant to women an extensive freedom in contacts with the external world, texts that thus do not limit her to the kitchen and female chambers. First Samuel 25, the story of the energetic Abigail and her arrogant, unstable husband, belongs here. Verse 25 goes so far as to offer a feminine critique of this master of creation: "For as his name is, so is he; Nabal [i.e., fool] is his name, and folly is with him." We have already spoken of Manoah's wife. Before she brings in her husband, she, too, speaks with Yahweh's messenger on her own behalf (Judg. 13:2-7). In the case of the well-known judge Deborah, one must ask whether her husband Lappidoth has not become known to posterity because he was married to a famous wife (Judg. 4:4). The same is true of Shallum, the husband of the prophetess Huldah (2 Kings 22:14). Drawing the circle a bit wider, one encounters Israel's midwives—who negotiate with Pharaoh and will not be intimidated (Exod. 1:18f)—and the rest of the impressive figures in the Old Testament: Miriam, Jael, Jezebel, Athaliah, Esther, Judith, Ruth. They would certainly have smiled at our assertion that "only the man could represent the family in Israel before the public forum."

The previously cited Old Testament documentation of the woman's need for a guardian and spokesman is by no means abrogated by this discovery of her relative freedom. But how are we to interpret these contradictory finds? Four factors are of importance here. They would, it seems, have to be distinguished historically and regionally, since no one would want to assume that one and the same behavioral pattern dominated all through Israel's thousand-year history and in all its various tribal traditions. We will suspend these differences for a moment, however, and try to ascertain the basic situations:

1. The maintenance of her own specific realm of activity doubtlessly brought the Israelite wife into direct contact with her surroundings. (Unfortunately we know nothing about domestic money matters, shopping necessities and habits, and so forth.)

2. The husband was the family representative in all public and legal matters; in addition, he theoretically held the disciplinary power in the family and—as the "owner" of the land, the house, the livestock, and of all those belonging to the family—made all the decisions concerning both his animate and inanimate property.

3. Because of common responsibilities, eg, for the rearing of the children, the Israelite married couple shared some liability within the community (cf Deut. 21:18-21).

4. Every societal system tolerates, indeed even demands in some cases, the reversal of the obtaining rules of cohabitation. This toleration of a reversal of the patriarchal principle was apparently relatively great in ancient Israel, whereas in Judaism the woman's limitations became increasingly tighter (cf the legal considerations concerning the wife's duty of obedience in Esther 1:16-20).

c. *Moses and Zipporah: The Problem of Mixed Marriages*

The previously neglected historical dimension of marriages in Israel should now briefly be presented at least as it concerns a special problem. How, in the various epochs of Old Testament history, was a marriage structured between an Israelite man and a foreign woman? The reverse of this—the marriage of a foreign man into an Israelite community—also occurred (cf Num. 10:29-32; Judg. 4:11), though it was never of great significance. These various treatments of mixed marriages in the Old Testament should remind us that changes are possible even in extremely stable, static social organizational forms.

The religious-historical background in rough outline is the following. Marriages with women from other tribes was not a problem in the early Israelite period; at any rate, it was not a question affecting the Yahweh faith. Members of other nations came to Israel by means of female prisoners of war or other kinds of female slaves (Deut. 20:14; 21:10-14; cf Judg. 5:30; 2 Kings 5:2). They adapted to the "guest" country's social order and were fully integrated. In spite of what many later literary pieces would have us believe (cf Exod. 34:11-16; Deut. 7:1-3), the early Israelite tribal confederation was in no way ethnically separated or excessively oriented toward religious purity. External confederations, clans, or tribes occasionally joined (cf Josh. 14:6ff). The only apprehensions directed against intermarriage with the Canaanites in Israel's early period were a result of inheritance considerations (cf Exod. 24:2-4): The Canaanites held to a different set of property rights, and the inhabitants could have raised claims because of daughters who had married into Israel. This is also the reason one preferred marriages within the man's clan (Exod. 24:4). In the period of kings, too, marriage with foreign women was still quite customary, at least at the royal court itself and probably also in diplomatic and military circles. The marriage politics of Solomon (1 Kings 11:1-6) and of the northern Israelite king Ahab (1 Kings 16:31; 21:5ff; 2 Kings 9:30-37) are famous. Not until the exilic and post-exilic period did Israel increasingly close itself off from its neighbors and particularly from any occupation forces. This ethnic and religious encapsulation was a reaction against the loss of civil and religious independence. Israel protected its identity in a clear-cut frontal position against everything foreign. This ultimately led to the prohibition of mixed marriages (Ezra 9–10; Neh. 13:23ff) or of any relationship with the "unfaithful." Within the framework of a doctrine of sin that already blamed the woman outright and sexual desire as well for the fall of man (cf Gen. 3:1-6), the foreign woman was increasingly suspected of being responsible for Israel's defection from Yahweh and its turn to foreign gods (1 Kings 11:2, 7ff; Deut. 7:11ff; and elsewhere).

One must read the various stories about Moses and his Midianite wife Zipporah against this historical background. The Midianites were one of Israel's southern neighbors. At first there were friendly relations between the two groups (cf Exod. 18), and one has reason to believe that Israel first became acquainted with the Yahweh religion through the Midianites (cf Exod. 3). An extremely deep hatred developed later (cf Judg. 6f; Num. 31).

Exodus 2:16-22 tells us quite openly how Moses came to meet his Midianite wife—again, by the way, in a typical well scene. Exodus 18:2ff also views his marriage to her as quite normal. Two texts, however, in contrasting ways, incorporate some extraordinary aspects into the story. According to Exodus 4:24-26—an extremely ancient and difficult text to understand—Zipporah circumcises "her son" (originally perhaps "her husband"?) and touches the bloody foreskin to "his feet" (whose? the son's? the husband's? it probably touches the man's genitals!) and speaks the dark words: "You are a bridegroom of blood." This story can presumably be traced back to ancient Israelite or Midianite legends according to which the circumcision was a defensive ritual—during the bridal night?—against the attack of bloodthirsty and lascivious demons, demons who kill the young groom in order to overcome the bride (cf Gen. 38:6-10; Tob. 3:7f). In-laws are occasionally called "circumciser" (male or female) (Exod. 18:1ff; Deut. 27:23). Is this the faint reflection of an old matriarchal custom that instructs the bride (or her mother) to perform the circumcision?

The other story points in precisely the opposite direction. In Numbers 12:1 Moses receives severe criticism from his sister Miriam and his brother Aaron because of a "Cushite" woman he has married. This would be either an Ethiopian woman or, according to Habakkuk 3:7, a woman from the region in which the Midianites also lived. We must no doubt understand this outbreak of xenophobia within the context of Numbers 25:6-15. There an Israelite and his Midianite companion—their names are Zimri and Cozbi—are slain by the Aaronite Phinehas. The narrator considered this association with the foreign woman to be a serious sin prompting God's punishment. Yahweh accepts the death of the two sinners as a propitiatory sacrifice and ends the plague (v 8). The text echoes the spirit of the time of Ezra and Nehemiah. The process of isolation from all that is foreign is in full swing. Not even Moses escapes criticism because of his marriage (Num. 12:1), and he is justified to a certain extent only as God's prophet and spokesman (Num. 12:2-16).

The problem of mixed marriages in Israel can, in my opinion, teach us the following: The theological elite among this oppressed Jewish people in the exilic and post-exilic period forges a doctrine of God's strict exclusivity and of Israel's corresponding election, a doctrine leading to a separation from all that is foreign. This formation of theory occurs at the level of the people as a whole, while the consequences manifest themselves at the level of the primary organizational form, the family. Free mobility as regards marriage—a centuries-old custom—is violently changed from above. This not only discriminates against women from other tribes and sacrifices them, as it were, to the interests of the exclusive Jewish community, it also redefines the roles of woman and man within the Jewish cult community. The man becomes the half-innocent victim of the woman's temptation. He becomes the protector of the pure doctrine and of the pure worship service, becomes a student of the Torah and the absolute head of all family spheres of activity. The woman, on the other hand, falls completely to the level of a servant maid: she is apparently more vulnerable to evil; she is incapable of coming into contact with God on her own; she lives under the curse of Eve and must thus obediently subordinate herself to man in all things (cf Abot 1:5; 2:7; below B I 4 a).

4. Divorce and Death

Every goal one attains allows the traversed path to become comprehensible once more. In this sense, the end of a life partnership illuminates the meaning and structure of the shared years. We will see that the end point of an Israelite marriage can only with some qualification be compared with what we today designate as retirement, widowhood, and remarriage.

In Old Testament times, too, a marriage was basically intended for one's entire life. Pragmatically, however—and people were pragmatic during Old Testament times—one did not know of any declaration of obligation corresponding to our "till death do us part." The legal formulation was presumably, "You are my wife, I am your husband" (cf Hos. 2:4; this was significantly expanded in view of the relationship Yahweh-Israel: Hos. 2:21f). The intention is nonetheless clear: One wanted a stable family, so one married permanently. Associations for a certain period of time were too severely subjected to the pressure of time. The problem of incompatability between spouses in Israel was alleviated somewhat for the husband by his being able to marry one or more additional wives. The existence of polygamy proves once again how much the institution of marriage was geared toward the man, and to what a large extent it was a patriarchal arrangement.

The man's interests also demanded the possibility of divorce, in case of emergency. Deuteronomy 24:1-4 and Jeremiah 3:1 witness to the man's right to release his wife without legal proceedings and without giving a reason. What does it mean: "because he has found some indecency in her" (Deut. 24:1)? The law gives the impression that male arbitrariness was sanctioned. A mere "bill of divorce" gives the divorced woman a certain degree of protection and the possibility of remarrying. We can no longer ascertain just how the reality of divorce looked or just how high divorce statistics were. King Ahasuerus of the Esther story expels his disobedient wife Vashti (Esth. 1:19). Women of a harem, released by a king, were held prisoner because of political considerations (2 Sam. 20:3), since a pretender to the throne might make claims based on possession of a royal wife (2 Sam. 16:20-22). Abraham permits Hagar to be sent out into the desert (Gen. 16; 21:8-21). Hosea releases his wife and then takes her back (Hos. 3:1). In one instance, a husband's betrothed wife is taken away again because of political considerations (2 Sam. 3:14-16), in another a wife runs away from her husband (Judg. 19:2). Those are all the passages relating to a premature separation of spouses, and only with some difficulty can one reconcile them with the law in Deuteronomy 24:1-4. According to them and our own perceptions we can say that the Old Testament divorce law does not basically seem intended for the dissolution of a partnership between two people, but rather for the release of an unsuitable party. The family or tribe remains intact; in the place of its old, pruned branch a new one can easily be grafted.

If death dissolves a marriage, then the Old Testament more clearly shows the emotional bonds shared by the partners. The violent separation ordered in 2 Samuel 3:14ff and Ezra 10 manifests the same aspect of death for those concerned (cf also Job 19:17). First, the death of the wife. The story of Abraham again offers the best example. The patriarch personally conducts the mourning ritual for Sarah, mourning her and having her interred in a royal fashion (Gen. 23). He later remarries (Gen. 25:1), but is then himself buried next to his first wife (Gen. 25:10). Otherwise the Old Testament rarely reports the death of a woman (cf Gen. 35:8, 19; 1 Sam. 4:19ff; 2 Kings 9:30ff; 11:13ff); dying during childbirth, however, probably occurred often enough. The prophet Ezekiel, on God's command, is not permitted to grieve for his wife in public (Ezek. 24:15ff). His behavior is so unusual—since the woman is, after all, "the delight of man's eyes" (v 15)—that his neighbors quite indignantly question him and thus give him occasion to deliver God's message (vv 19ff). A priest, on the other hand, is not permitted to defile himself for his dead wife, since she is not related to him by blood (Lev. 21:2f).

The death of a man, whether at home or on the field of battle, was apparently largely an affair of men. In the hour of death it was above all important to gather one's sons around, to bless them (cf Gen. 49), and thus to pass on the family estate. This was no place for sentimental departure scenes between spouses. It was, however, the wife's obligation to mourn her husband ritually (cf 2 Sam. 11:26; Jer. 9:19ff; Joel 1:8). The consequences of the death of the head of a family were much more incisive. The survival of the family was virtually called into question in two cases. If the surviving children were not yet of age, then the widow fell into economic and legal difficulties (cf 1 Kings 17:10ff; 2 Kings 4:1). If there were no children at all, then a brother of the dead man, or some other male relative, had to take the widow as his wife according to strict stipulations and to bear with her an heir for the dead man (Deut. 25:5ff; Ruth 3ff). We see again how strongly life in Israel was determined by the idea of preserving the family beyond the death of the individual.

III. Sexual Roles

We now prepare for a new round of conversation with the Old Testament. It will treat the double themes of "sexual roles" and "relations between the sexes" and will take our present reality more strongly into consideration than before.

In retrospect we can easily see that we have already touched, in chapter 2, on the problem of sexual roles and relations between the sexes. We tried to reconstruct according to stages of life the behavioral patterns, problems, and values for young boys and girls, men and women during Old Testament times. What is behind the terms "sexual roles" and "relations between the sexes"? Put bluntly: the contemporary, fashionable sociological manner of observation. This is not at all meant in a derogatory fashion, but is rather only a question of honestly recognizing the temporally conditioned nature of one's own thought and research. For the rest, however, we are dealing with fundamental facts as regards this presentation of female and male roles and relationships. To this day, both women and men have had to adapt to certain behavioral patterns preformed in their own society. The Israelites also knew this. Contemporary sociology and anthropology have merely systematically and critically researched the role distribution and mutual relationships between the sexes, and have described the mechanisms through which every person is forced or reared by his environment into the adequate role. In addition, these disciplines have drawn comparisons between the various cultures. Seen in this way, the social-scientific viewpoint can sharpen our own view of both antiquity and modern reality. This does not obviate or replace the basic theological concern prompting us to speak with the Old Testament witness. On the contrary, the contemporary humanities provide a strong motivation for it. The more clear and the more complicated the picture of the human being becomes, the more pressing are the questions concerning both the meaning of life and God.

In the third and fourth chapter we thus want to examine more closely the roles and relationships concerning woman and man in the Old Testament, and we will compare these with the behavioral patterns we follow today. This comparison is necessary not only because it corresponds to the intention of this series of books, but also—incredible as it may sound—because at decisive points the relationship between the sexes today was preformed during Old Testament times. In spite of revolutionary insights concerning the equality of woman and man, the New Testament community basically did not change the traditional models at all (cf below particularly B III 2 *b*). In any case, subsequent Christian tradition returned overwhelmingly to the Old Testament conceptions. Indeed, one must say even more. Today we can say with certainty that the roles and relationships of the sexes developed over a period of millennia in the ancient Orient. They were then fixed in a certain way in Israel under the particular influence of the Yahweh faith and Israelite culture. Because the Old Testament became the sacred book of Jews, Christians, and to a certain extent Muslims, these fixed elements have had an unusually permanent effect. For many people to this day, what the Old Testament says about woman and man, particularly in the creation story, has the character of irrevocable divine truth. People fail to recognize the temporally conditioned character of all the human statements in the creation narratives, for example, because one believes oneself to be encountering the eternal order of nature itself there. Not until after the Second World War did a much wider group of people begin to ask questions concerning the origin and meaning of sexual roles. On the subject of "roles" and "relationships," we are somewhat arbitrarily separating these two aspects, although they actually belong together. Anyone playing a certain social role necessarily comes into contact (a relationship) with other people through this role. Nonetheless, one can separate the two perspectives and present the role-player before the actual appearance, as it were, and only then in action.

A fundamental preliminary remark still needs to be made here. We cannot pretend to achieve a complete, definitive investigation in this encounter with the Old Testament reality. If we wanted to carry this juxtaposition through in its entirety, we would have to analyze and compare every single societal relationship. That, however, extends far beyond the scope of this study. All we can do here is present a few important points and then leave it to the reader to investigate further. We can, however, point out a few cultural and civilization-related differences.

a) The Israelites lived for the most part in a farming culture, in exceptional instances in a weakly differentiated urban culture. We exist in a highly technological urban context, and even the remnants of contemporary farm life have long been inundated by industrial considerations and habits. (A farm boy quite possibly does not know how to milk a cow, he does not know how a wheat kernel germinates, and he spends as many hours in front of the television as does his peer in the city.) In other words, Israelite society was pre-industrial, ours is totally industrial.

b) A significant difference in Israel's spiritual posture

corresponds to these differences in manner of production and life then and today. We can classify Israel's world view as mythical-religious, ours as empirical-scientific. This does not exclude the possibility that any culture can contain within itself traces of the opposite point of view.

c) For Israel, the totality of the world consisted of the ancient Orient and its nations; both now and then the Mediterranean realm is included. The majority of Asia, Europe, Africa, and of course the rest of the world lay outside Israel's experiential horizon. Today every reflection concerning the human being must actually take the entire planet into consideration with its unimaginably large population.

d) Finally, we should not forget that Old Testament faith and Old Testament customs were transformed and further developed in Christianity. The relationship between the sexes did, it is true, remain the same in its basic contours, but it also underwent important changes in its details (cf below W. Schrage).

1. Division of Labor

We already ascertained, particularly in section II 3 *a*, that woman and man in the Old Testament went about their daily tasks in clearly separated spheres of activity that nonetheless were related to each other. This division of labor issued quite naturally from the necessities of agricultural work and the rearing of children. There existed no other interests or forces that could have disturbed this dual work rhythm on an Israelite farm. The Old Testament accepts this order of things without a great deal of reflection. It is sober enough not to trace these differences in sexual roles back to differences in body structure, intellectual constitution, or emotional disposition in a way rendering females useless as far as male tasks are concerned. No, this division of labor issued just as it is, and therefore it is good and intended by God. Primal history, which reflects most deeply on the relationship between the sexes, is just as laconic here as are the narrative and Wisdom texts we have already heard. The man is responsible for agricultural work (Gen. 3:17-19): the woman is to bear children (Gen. 3:16) and—we can add—rear these children and take care of housework (cf Prov. 31:10ff). Man is the tiller of the soil (Gen. 2:8, 15), and woman is to be his "helper" (Gen. 2:18). The word means "support" or "aid" and probably refers to the woman's complementary work. It was always this way for the Israelite and would always remain this way. He considered the world of farming to be the only possible one, and for this reason he told the story of creation such that his world, and not that of his nomadic ancestors, had its start in that story. The world of the nomads was long forgotten, and the unstable world of small livestock herdsmen was at most only a bad dream for the Israelite farmer (cf Deut. 26:5; Judg. 6:3-6).

That which no Israelite author could have imagined, has occurred: The human being's manner of life has changed significantly. We, who have experienced the industrial (or already the post-industrial?) age, have the same obligation as the ancient Israelites: to order responsibly our lives under God's claim and guidance. This includes the roles of the sexes, roles that—as we know today—are formed by one's culture and manner of life. Concerning one's daily work we must ask: Must we today maintain the traditional, agricultural division into external and internal tasks; must we limit the woman to domestic activity and the man to the earning of income? To ask this question at all means to answer it in the negative. This kind of division of labor is impossible today; following it strictly would cause the collapse of the entire economic system.

What has changed since the Old Testament was written? Put briefly and incompletely, this: The majority of people no longer lives from the land, but rather from wages. Basic schooling and vocational training are still basically the same for young boys and girls. The number of pregnancies for the individual woman has drastically decreased. (One sees how strongly old prejudices still affect us by the fact that many firms do not like to employ young women; they are afraid of absence and extra costs in the case of pregnancies.) The mechanization of work equalizes men and women in virtually all vocations (there are female crane operators, policewomen, female engineers, and so on). Above all, industry, government, schools, and society at large need an army of female workers because the male potential simply does not suffice. Because of this general state of affairs, untold numbers of women since the turn of the century have paved and often fought for their own way into the previously male-exclusive vocational world. The division of work spheres may still exist in some Arab emirates or in Pakistani farming villages, but not in the Western industrial world. Should one then not conclude that this separation presupposed in the Old Testament between the spheres of responsibility of woman and man can no longer hold true today? Should one not recognize that wage-earning has to a large extent generated a sexually mixed work situation? By no means! The old conceptions of the woman as house mother and the man as external worker continue to exist. A few years ago I met a young physician who forbade his wife—an educated physician herself—to practice. "Your place is now with housework," he told the as yet childless woman. This kind of behavior is by no means an isolated case, even though it sounds totally anachronistic.

As a control measure, let us look back a moment at the Old Testament. A peculiar fact emerges. With the exception of the vocation of priest, the Old Testament imposes no real vocational limitations on women. There is one prohibition, namely against women wearing male clothes and vice versa (Deut. 22:5). Here one may discover the fear still widespread today of a leveling of sexual differences. The division of work spheres in the Old Testament, however, is a pragmatic and not a theoretical affair. As far as I can see, the Old Testament contains none of the malicious remarks about the one or other sex—usually the female—of the kind we hear so frequently in Jewish-Christian history. When the Old Testament speaks disparagingly or disapprovingly about a woman, it does not do so because of her weakness or stupidity. Eve is a conscious temptress (Gen. 3:1ff), and Athaliah is the prototype of a cruel despot (2 Kings 11:1–3:20). The prophets point an accusing finger at the ostentation of ladies in the upper strata of society (Amos 4:1; Isa. 3:16). These are not, however, general judgments against women. And one more thing: The first tentative steps toward freely chosen vocational activity for women are taken at the royal court in Israel. The king employs female perfumers, cooks, and bakers (1 Sam. 8:13) as well as female singers (2 Sam. 19:35; 2 Chron. 35:25).

To the same extent that the male vocational world opens up to women, so also does the previous female sphere of work become accessible to men. Expressed positively: Because of vocational equality the man is permitted to return to the household with all its tasks, for his own enrichment, to lessen the burden of the vocationally active woman, and to the joy of the children. If basic human rights are worth anything at all, then society should not be allowed to burden doubly the woman with both an external vocation and household tasks. The man must assume a proportional amount of housework. Put in another way: Not only should the woman have the opportunity to develop her life fully in both spheres of household and vocation, but the man, too, is allowed to emancipate himself for the sake of this kind of comprehensive life experience. It is clear that this demand would transform the entire world of work. Vocationally active women and men would have to work only half a day in order to do justice to household obligations during the other half. In addition, the foundation for this kind of partnership would be laid in schools in which both young boys and young girls learn home economics as well as child care with equal seriousness.

Now, however, we must also mention the objections against this modern way of dividing labor. The demise of fixed role models also erases the traditional female and male activity characteristics, and with them—to a certain extent—the character traits of the person involved as well. Certain vocations demand of its employee primarily hardness, perseverance, or quickness; others require patience, sensitivity, imagination, and so on. Yet all these allegedly female or male characteristics are present in every human being in larger or smaller measure. Free choice of vocation guarantees that every person can develop inclinations and talents without regard to sex. The man is allowed to express his feelings, feelings that were repressed in the old system of tough male vocations. The woman is allowed to employ her natural gifts for rational thought and leadership. Every married couple acquires the freedom to distribute between themselves, according to their own evaluation, the roles to be played. He can become a house-husband, she a politician; he a friend of children, she the representative of their common interests—or it can all be reversed. The arc of sexual tension between the sexes is not suspended by the kind of role distribution that does not follow the clichés fixed by society. One wonders in general, and finds no satisfactory answer explaining why human beings developed culturally sanctioned female and male behavioral models with their corresponding separation of work spheres. Would it not have been better from the very beginning to avoid role clichés and to adopt rather as a model the kind of free mobility (Deborah!) we sometimes encounter in the Old Testament?

At one point—let this now also be subjected to debate—nature does indeed offer resistance to the expansion and admixture of the old, sexually determined spheres of activity. Only the woman is involved in pregnancy, birth, and nursing. However, compared with the situation in antiquity (or with that in developing countries), these genuinely female activities have diminished to an almost incredible degree in today's industrial societies. At most, a woman experiences two or three births during her seventy or more years of life, and is involved with nursing an infant at most two or three years total. This bearing and nursing function can thus not possibly be the factor causing the woman to be limited her entire life to the existence of a housewife. On the other hand, one can easily see that society must grant the vocationally active woman special rules for the short span following a birth. To play this problem out fully, what would our reaction be if that news bulletin was correct according to which one successfully implanted a fertilized egg in a male body? I must admit, I have trouble imagining a pregnant man. But supposing science made it possible, what would we have to say about it? In view of the desire for comprehensive human experience, equality between the sexes at this final point as well would certainly have to be welcomed. And yet one becomes terribly uneasy at the thought. Imagine a pregnant man who has grown breasts as a result of hormone treatment, whose previously hairy skin now feels soft as silk, and who now speaks in a soprano voice. Does this extreme image—which might mark the end point of the present development—render untenable the whole idea of a new distribution of work spheres and of the dissolution of the ancient spheres of responsibility for woman and man? I don't think so. This futuristic projection shows only that the human being is responsible for its actions and is not permitted to follow to the end every path open to it.

One problem still remains. As already suggested, the Old Testament excludes women from the vocation of priest. At this one point we find tangible evidence of purely sexual reasoning. The physical constitution, actually: menstruation and birth render the woman cultically impure (cf Lev. 12; 15:19ff). Note well, there is no express prohibition against a woman being a priest. But the practice we recognize in the Old Testament speaks an unmistakable language (cf eg Exod. 28f; Lev. 8f; 21; Deut. 18:1-8; 2 Sam. 6:17; and elsewhere). Only men are permitted to bring offerings to God. Apparently this mysterious bleeding, toward which one has a magical disinclination, excludes the woman from direct contact with God. Or the female sex was considered particularly vulnerable to demonic temptations (cf Gen. 6:1-4). Be that as it may, the woman was de facto unsuited for priesthood. This Old Testament taboo retains an unusually strong power even today. The Catholic church, with every possible reason and in repeated announcements, has held tightly to the verdict against women. Women are permitted to be ministers or pastors in the Protestant churches, but must struggle a great deal against deeply rooted prejudices, as in Sweden or in the Anglican Church. Can we—indeed, are we allowed to—follow the Old Testament model in this matter? In my opinion, the answer is an unequivocal no. Considering the apparent alteration of the demonic model of the world and the relativization of sacrifices by the prophets—both events documented—the Old Testament actually already should have overcome this magical taboo-practice against the female sex. According to Jesus' preaching, the conceptions of cultic purity and impurity that led to the exclusion of women from the priesthood, are totally untenable. Accordingly, the Christian community cannot fall back on this argument, and other tenable arguments do not exist.

To summarize: Considering our contemporary presuppositions, the spheres of vocation and responsibility of woman and man respectively can be ordered according to sexually specific concepts and role models neither inside nor outside the marriage partnership. In addition—and this must be emphasized in view of the Old Testament—marriage is no longer the uncontested ideal situation for man and woman. There are countless bacheloresses and bachelors who live fully within their vocations and who perform valuable services for society at large. How could one want to declare certain vocations to be female or male domains? How could one want to reduce the unmarried woman to a housewife's existence? It's absolutely impossible! And according to the Old and New Testament spirit of judging with the fairness and love God gives and asks of humans, the burdens and opportunities both of vocational life and of home economics should be divided equally among the partners in view of contemporary societal presuppositions. Division of labor, yes! But not according to preformed sexual roles!

2. Superiority and Subordination

The Old Testament, patriarchal societal system theoretically demands the subordination of the woman and supports the power of authority of the family head over the entire family. We saw this in chapter 2, and at the same time we took cognizance of the abundance of exceptions to this rule. We can now deepen our observations with further texts and progress forward to an evaluation.

We saw that in the Old Testament the husband in many respects occupied the role of an owner of wife and children, house and livestock. "You shall not covet your neighbor's house; you shall not covet your neighbor's wife, or his manservant, or his maidservant, or his ox, or his ass, or anything that is your neighbor's" (Exod. 20:17). This commandment encompasses all movable and immovable property of one's neighbor; this includes—and this was self-evident for the Israelite—both wife and slaves. The same fact is expressed by the designation "husband" (Hebrew *ba'al* or *'adon*: Gen. 18:12; Exod. 21:22; 2 Sam. 11:26; Prov. 12:4; and elsewhere). A common term for "to marry" is "to take possession" (Deut. 21:13; 24:1; Isa. 62:5) or simply "to take" a wife (Exod. 2:1; Judg. 14:2). Some exegetes consider the stealing of wives practiced by the Benjamites (Judg. 21) to be an echo of the old, common custom of forcefully kidnapping the wife from a neighboring tribe. It may well have happened often enough that Israelites acquired wives during military campaigns (cf Deut. 21:10-14), but the rule appears to have been the contractually ordered marriage. Within its own context, Judges 21 also is described as an exception (vv 1, 7f). In a word, Israel's legal language and legal customs are full of references to certain property claims for the husband as regards his wife. We have already mentioned the payment of a bridal price before the wedding (cf Gen. 34:12; Exod. 22:16; Deut. 22:29; 1 Sam. 18:25-27; in this last passage David has some initial apprehension about becoming Saul's son-in-law because he cannot pay the bridal price, v 23). Society at that time even more frequently puts man into the role of spokesman for his wife. This male privilege appears quite blatantly in Numbers 30:2-17. A woman's vow before Yahweh is only valid if the man immediately over her, be it father or husband, takes express cognizance of the promise and thus puts it into effect. The "jealousy ritual" (Num. 5:11-31) also places the suspected woman into the unenviable position of someone without either her own voice in the matter or any right of protest or appeal. One can speculate that these last texts come almost certainly from the post-exilic period. Was this increasing spokesmanship for women a result of the fact that the male world had lost its political independence and now passed the pressure exerted by the victorious powers further down the social ladder? One can refer to the Old Testament reality in which the husband often "obeyed" his wife; however, this legal inequality of the sexes in the Old Testament cannot be argued out of existence.

According to our contemporary view of things, this kind of legal discrimination against the woman and preferential treatment for the man is totally unacceptable. We have behind us, after all, a long history of Christian culture with its message of the dignity of all people, a message we have never totally forgotten. Above all, we are experiencing today a difficult, belated, and repeatedly canceled movement toward universal human rights which are valid without regard to race, religion, or sex. To a large extent, equal rights for women and men are already on the books. In the emotional sphere, however—our own subconscious—the millennia-old ideas of hierarchy have hardly diminished in significance. Even the most enlightened male will occasionally catch himself thinking that the woman ought to obey him, to share his opinion, and to be at his beck and call. The old desire for ownership and power have not died simply because the man's privileged position has been eliminated from constitutions and law books. As a man one must also recognize clearly that the same desires still exist in a different form in women. The myth of a woman's natural subordinating character and of her passivity has always been a lie men tell themselves for their own reassurance. E. Vilar, in her to a large extent one-sided book *The Well-Dressed Man*, has at any rate described in a lively and accurate fashion the hidden female urge to dominate.

Another example of the perpetuation of hierarchical

structures in marriage is the following: A pastor seeks new female volunteers and aids; yet he often hears the excuse, "I would really like to take on a position in the church community, but my husband won't allow it." History has programmed a woman just enough in the direction of external subordination that she can speak such a sentence without losing her self-esteem. In a similar situation, a man can only give complicated explanations about his vocational obligations and burdens; he will not refer to his wife's will. A psychoanalytical observation shows just how deeply this hierarchical, patriarchal ordering of the sexes still clings to our consciousness. Young couples who break out of this system of domination and want to live together in a real partnership often fail precisely because of these subconscious desires for possession and domination (H. E. Richter).

What can be done in such a schismatic situation? To repeat once more: We do not believe that female behavior must always include humility, passivity, and surrender with some sort of natural necessity; nor that male behavior must necessarily always be characterized by strong power of decision, the will to dominate, and a feeling of superiority. We cannot, however, deny the millennia-old inheritance of models of superiority and subordination within the relationships between the sexes. It is extremely difficult to work one's way out of this inheritance. Perhaps some fundamental reflection on the Old Testament can help us further.

We must first see that, indeed, the Old Testament did say something theoretical about the question of a hierarchy of the sexes and did define a rule. The creation story tells us that God sought a "helper fit for him" for the first man (Gen. 2:18, 20). This new being, that is not like the animals because it is made from man's rib, is subordinate to his authority for precisely that reason. According to the narrator's popular etymology, this being is called "woman," the one derived from man (v 23). Despite verse 24, she is obviously intended for a complementary and serving function. The following story of the fall then says much more sharply: "Yet your desire shall be for your

husband, and he shall rule over you" (Gen. 3:16). A comparison
with other Old Testament statements makes it clear that the
domination of one human being over another is an extremely
two-edged and dangerous affair. One brother is not allowed to
place himself over his other brothers; this controverts the spirit
of brotherhood (Gen. 37:8). The power of a master over a female
slave with whom he has had sexual relations is limited (Exod.
21:8). Whenever slaves become masters, things do not go well
at all for the new subordinates (Prov. 19:10; Lam. 5:8). Rich
people dominate the poor and probably exploit them (Prov.
22:10). Whenever enemies take over power, there is then fear
and trembling (Ps. 106:40f). Even a king's power—which in
and for itself is beneficial and good (cf 2 Sam. 7:8ff; Ps. 21;
72)—stands in the ambiguous light of the misuse of office (cf 1
Sam. 8:11ff; 2 Kings 21). And according to the schematic
passage Genesis 3:16, precisely this husband is to rule over his
wife? What was the Old Testament author thinking when he
wrote this incredible sentence that flies in the face of all
conceptions of marital love? He apparently wanted to
characterize the perversity of marital relationships. Marriage,
too, stands for him under the curse the first two humans
brought upon themselves. In the patriarchal system of his time,
this superior male position could easily degenerate into
violence that would bring the curse over humanity into
realization. Subsequent generations unfortunately took this
statement of curse over the woman more and more to be a
description of the normal state of affairs and increasingly less as
a warning against possible degeneration. That is how Jewish
and Christian ideas concerning the subordination of women
and the corresponding societal forms used Genesis 3:16 as their
point of departure. The New Testament recognition of the
liberating, new order of the kingdom of God—a kingdom also
removing the curse over the sexes—already had faded into the
background in some of the later New Testament writings (cf
below B II and III).

At this point we ought to look a bit deeper and show how
Israel's historical experience under foreign rule and exile

heightened its sensitivity for all forms of the misuse of power and use of force. During the period of darkest oppression and humility there arose that unique yearning for redemption, the wish for peace, justice, nonviolence, and happiness (cf Isa. 11:1-9). The oppressed and outlawed are then rehabilitated (cf Isa. 42:7; 56:4ff; 61:1ff; 66:2). Two passages apparently discuss women after mentioning all other marginal people; the structures of oppression under which they suffer are to be suspended when God's salvation becomes reality (cf Jer. 31:8, 22: "A woman protects a man" is a rather obscure passage. However, it apparently alludes to the reversal of the patriarchal state of things. Joel 3:1f: The spirit of God overcomes sexual differences and structures of oppression).

Let us now return to our contemporary reality. Just as little as a certain skin color, eye formation, skull type, or hair texture predestine a person to a second-class being, neither should sexual differences provide a basis upon which to establish an ideology of subordination of the allegedly weaker sex. The equality of woman and man is a genuine Christian concern from the perspective of the biblical witness and on the basis of modern developments during the past centuries. For the relationship between the sexes in the family circle this means that the patriarchal superior position of the male in the Old Testament is a temporally conditioned affair; it cannot be transferred to our society. On the contrary, woman and man stand next to each other as equal partners. The bases of this partnership are mutual respect, mutual trust, and continual dialogue. Life in the family is carried on with shared responsibility. The problem of leadership is not eliminated by this kind of partnership; one solves it, however, in a human fashion. If leadership becomes necessary within this democratic framework, then the person with the best qualifications in a given situation ought to take the initiative or active role. Experience shows that gifts and inclinations are always unevenly distributed in a married couple. Weaknesses in one partner often correspond to strengths in the other and vice versa. If decisions must be made, then according to our understanding things should be clarified in dialogue. The partner with the best prerequisites can take over the execution and thus also the leadership role in the matter at hand. Many married couples indeed proceed in this manner. There can then be no question of the domination of the one over the other. Why, then, do we still need this ideology of male superiority?

We will not address the question whether it is easier to eliminate the structures of oppression subordinating women that we find in public life. We hear enough complaints to the effect that women must exert themselves twice as much as men in order to be recognized in a leadership position. Let us hope that the excellent example of female heads of state, ministers, physicians, nurses, and countless other women in positions of responsibility will slowly but surely convince the "man and woman in the street" of female leadership qualities.

3. Being a Mother and Father

Among young married couples in the Western industrial nations, the roles of mother and father have become particularly problematic. It begins in good Old Testament fashion with the woman having to take on all sorts of burdens during pregnancy with which a man never has to deal. Nausea, circulatory disturbances, weight gain, and varicose veins are only some of the normal effects. Those pregnancies which made being a woman the greatest happiness have become rare. In any case, they exist more in the textbooks written by men and theologians. The reasons behind this contemporary suffering because of pregnancy and birth are not so much physical and medicinal as they are spiritual or emotional. The general nervous pressure on a (vocationally active) housewife is doubtless also a factor. Equally important is the widespread social hierarchy in which the house, job, and car all rank far above the child. The pregnant woman often elicits sympathy or misunderstanding from her surroundings. During a baptism conversation in the spring of 1979, the mother—a former confirmation pupil—told me: "My sister thinks I'm crazy because we want a second child. She would rather add ten dogs than a child." That is a logical position in a society that has buried human values under the pressures of production and consumption. A child means lower income, additional costs, and many other sacrifices for both parents. Beginning with the birth, the young mother must interrupt her vocational career and then remain tied to the house for two or three years. Under contemporary living conditions this is a real sacrifice for the woman. She gives up the external vocational contacts that make up a part of her life and then walks through parks and playgrounds with her baby carriage. During house visits I have repeatedly met young women whose "house was threatening to fall in" on them because they couldn't stand the isolation in the house. The husband, on the other hand, stands more or less helplessly before the small child and often flees into his job. As much as a child is anticipated and greeted in any given individual case, the living circumstances and societal attitudes in central Europe are nonetheless normally quite hostile toward that same child.

In view of the modern skepticism toward progeny, one needs to recall the joy prompted by the birth of a son in the Old Testament and the full social recognition the child enjoyed in Israel. Some examples are the words of praise the midwives direct to the grandmother Naomi (Ruth 4:14f) and Hannah's wonderful song of praise after Samuel's birth (1 Sam. 2:2-10; cf above II 1 a). One encounters a similar attitude toward children in developing countries and in southern Europe. In these regions, material living conditions have not yet forced the child from its place among the earthly things of value (cf Ps. 127:3). The full attention given progeny in the Old Testament—based, as we saw, on the high estimation of the family—can thus only be described as optimal.

On the other hand, we cannot agree with the Old Testament custom according to which the mother is the only person serving as a reference point for the child in the early years (cf II 1 b and c). Under our own presuppositions we would have to encourage a division of that child care between both parents. Not only does it not hurt anything, it is on the contrary a necessity that the father actively participate in caring for the small child. He should already be accompanying his wife during pregnancy and trying to lessen some of her burdens. If at all possible, he should be present during birth and should not—as was customary among the Israelites and still is among pre-industrial peoples—stay as far away as possible because giving birth is only a female matter (cf Gen. 35:17; Exod. 1:15f; 1 Sam. 4:19f; Ruth 4:14; only the midwives are always there! Extremely old fears of the demonic are probably behind all this). It would be ideal if the infant could see from the very first days of life—during bathing, diapering, feeding, and playing—that it is deaing in this world not only with female, but also with male people.

It is a good sign that many young married couples during the past decades have learned to assume the roles of parents together. Men with baby carriages are no longer so unusual a sight. Complete success for this kind of shared care for the small child, however, is still a thing of the future. Several factors hinder the full implementation of many of these ideal conceptions: societal structures with their work pressures; lack of education particularly on the side of the man; and the general mentality of the public, according to which a man still degrades himself if he has too much to do with housework. Unfortunately, the story of the widower who gives up his job in order to become a "house husband" and care for his four young children—this story still belongs in Germany to those touching pieces blown up so big in the gossip tabloids; they move one to tears but never bring about any change in society.

From about the third year of life on, the second phase described above in section II 1 *b* and *c*, the Israelite married couple begins sharing the responsibility for rearing the child. This does, admittedly, occur in separate spheres of life and work; nonetheless, a high degree of mutuality does become visible. Both father and mother appear in many texts as the familial points of reference, as the educational authorities from whom the growing child receives orientation. We will turn away for a moment from the parental rights concerning children; they range in the Old Testament from the right to discipline the son or daughter, to the right to sell them (cf Prov. 29:17; Exod. 21:7). We are interested here in the parental solidarity in rearing the children. "Honor your father and your mother," says the commandment for children growing up; or in the reverse order: "Every one of you shall revere his mother and his father" (Exod. 20:12; Lev. 19:3; the term "to revere" or "to fear" contains more than our "to have fear"). We find numerous warnings to those who transgress against this commandment (cf Exod. 21:15, 17; Deut. 27:16; Prov. 19:26; 20:20; 23:22; 28:24; 30:11). In all the passages, father and mother are mentioned together. A small child's first words are "my father, my mother" (Isa. 8:4). Indeed, the child is there for the joy of both parents (Prov. 23:25); the lot of those left by father and mother is extremely hard (Ps. 27:10; cf orphans as a peripheral social group: Ps. 10:14, 18; 82:3; Job 6:27, often mentioned with the widow and called a fatherless child). Even the move away from the parental house (Gen. 2:24) means a painful break. Other examples could be mentioned as well. Admittedly, the Old Testament very frequently speaks of the father's house instead of the parental house, or of the father instead of both parents; we may, however, on the basis of these passages, assume that in educational questions the Israelite parents essentially acted together, even though the father embodied the highest family authority and instructed the son in male matters. Thus emphatically both father and mother accept their son Samson's marriage wishes (Judg. 14:1-4).

As regards content, Old Testament parental obligations involve not only the mediation of knowledge and standards, but particularly involve the necessary love and care for the child (son). The highest commandment for the father is to pity "his children" (Ps. 103:13). The word derives from the Hebraic designation for "womb" or "body" and means the affectionate care given a child. The example of David shows just how much fatherly emotions can undo all considerations of reason (2 Sam. 18). Absalom, the son and candidate for the throne before whom David had to flee Jerusalem (2 Sam. 15–17), is killed by troops loyal to the king. David receives news of the victory and is "deeply moved"; he withdraws to a chamber over the gate and weeps as he goes, "O my son Absalom, my son, my son Absalom! Would I had died instead of you, O Absalom, my son, my son!" (2 Sam. 18:33c). The same cry of lament is repeated in 2 Samuel 19:4; the king's despair turns the victory into defeat (vv 2ff). Joab, the commanding general, then speaks sharply to the unhappy father's conscience in the name of political reason (vv 5-7).

A mother's love is so strong that she disregards her own feelings and decides in favor of the child; thus it is in the story of the two women who argue over a child (1 Kings 3:16ff). It says of the true mother: "Her heart yearned for her son" (Luther: "Her motherly heart flamed in love for her son," v 26). In the case of sickness or death, the parents are beside themselves in grief (cf Gen. 37:34f; Judg. 11:35; 2 Sam. 12:15ff; 1 Kings 14:1ff; 17:17f; Job 1:20). Indeed, one notices with what emotional energy the Old Testament narrators tell of the fear and grief of parents for their children. Usually they are hesitant in the portrayal of strong feelings. The solidarity with children, however, the hopes one puts in them, makes these outbreaks of feeling understandable. No wonder that this parental love—just as in the entire ancient Orient—has influenced theological language. Yahweh is responsible for his people like a mother (one must in any case conclude this from Num. 11:12) or a father (Exod. 4:22f; Isa. 64:7). He "comforts as a mother" (Isa. 66:13) and rejoices at his son "as a father" (Prov. 3:12).

Let us conclude. The roles of father and mother are extremely important in the Old Testament; the parent-child relationship appears to count at least as much as that between parents as a fundamental constellation of human life and society. Let us disregard the temporally conditioned references to arbitrary behavior toward children (how do things actually stand with child abuse in democratic societies?); there remains then in the Old Testament documents a lively picture of parental solidarity and concern for one's progeny that can serve as a model for us.

4. Political Roles

We were surprised to find a few outstanding female figures in the Old Testament patriarchal society that gave to women very few external possibilities for development (cf II 3 *b*). We ask once again: How are these exceptions to the rule possible? What conclusions can we draw from this for our present situation?

First, the rule again: The man is not only the head of the family, but also quite naturally fills all the other offices of superiority. Men take care of all legal matters (Exod. 18); comprise the tribal or confederation council of the elders (Exod. 24:9-11; Num. 11:24ff; Ezek. 20:1); are alone admitted to temple service and the office of the priest (Num. 18; 1 Chron. 24–26); occupy the realm's administrative posts (2 Sam. 8:15-18; 20:23-26); and of course they make up the entire army (2 Sam. 23:8-38).

The exceptions are those women in public offices already mentioned: Miriam, Deborah, Huldah, and so on. We will look at the most classic example, the judge Deborah. Unless we are being deceived, the narrator of Judges 4 even wants to make a hidden caustic remark to the proud and strong male world. The Israelites, he begins, are again suffering under Canaanite domination and cry to God for help (vv 1-3). This time, however, Yahweh specifically chooses a woman as savior, Deborah, the wife of a certain Lappidoth (v 4). She had for a long time been an extensively recognized judge in the area of the tribe Ephraim (vv 4f). This woman summons the chief (or some other important person) of the tribe of Naphtali and gives to him the divine task (disguised as a rhetorical question in the original text): Go and defeat Sisera, the Canaanite general, with his terrible armed power of nine hundred chariots (vv 6f).

Barak, the person summoned, gives the interesting, reflective answer: I will do that only if you, Deborah, will go along (v 8). We listen and are astonished: a man says *this* to a woman as an answer to a divine task! Deborah declares herself willing to go along on the campaign; at the same time, however, she chides the lack of faith of our hero Barak and releases him from the final execution of the saving deed: A woman is to defeat the foreign general instead of a man (v 9). And so it happens; Jael kills Sisera after he seeks refuge in her tent (vv 17f).

It is no accident that the report of the decisive battle against the Canaanites so emphatically places two women in the foreground. This can hardly mean that Yahweh wants to work through the weaker, powerless female sex. After all, Barak and his ten thousand warriors also fight energetically (vv 14-16). I believe that the narrator wants to criticze the patriarchal order of things with the figure of the folk-heroine Deborah and the Sisera-victor Jael. Women possess just as many leadership qualities as men and are quite capable of filling public offices! Deborah unites in herself no less than three important functions otherwise reserved only for men: the judicial, prophetic, and the military. She took the reins at a critical turning point in Israel's history. Men ought to take note of that!

We have already found a similar critical attitude in Numbers 12. Miriam not only challenges the political leadership qualities of her brother Moses, but his prophetic office as well. Has Yahweh "not spoken through us also?" is her provocative question (v 2). We do not find this kind of criticism with the other political female figures. They are presented both positively (Judith, Esther) and negatively (Jezebel, Athaliah). From the post–Old Testament period we can mention Queen Salome Alexandra (75–67 B.C.). She exerted influence on politics long before her own period of rule and must count as an example of how female leaders were possible even during the periods of Judaism most decisively hostile to women.

The Old Testament thus did not basically deny that women had the capacity to fill leadership positions in public life. Proverbs 14:1, for example, contains no general denigration of women; it says in a straightforward fashion: If a woman acts intelligently, the family prospers; if she acts stupidly, it falls apart. Both woman and man can be stupid; 1 Samuel 25 gave us an incisive example of a man's stupidity. In addition, Proverbs is full of chiding remarks directed at foolish, lazy, weak men (cf Prov. 10:1, 4, 5, 8, 10, and so on).

We can with relative ease draw a conclusion going beyond the previous remarks on the subject. The practical separation of the male and female worlds in the Old Testament has no fixed theoretical basis yet in the canonical writings. The subordination of the woman in practice has not yet generated any doctrines concerning her alleged inferiority as happened in later Judaism and in Greek philosophy (cf below B I 4). In Israel one still lives unreflectively in a male world in which a gifted woman can quite possibly fill public offices. The privileged position of the male has not yet been ideologically solidified, though it finds theological expression in the second creation story (Gen. 2f).

IV. Relationships Between the Sexes

Fortunately, the Old Testament sexual roles assigning woman and man to separate life spheres could by their very nature never lead one to construe separate social organizational forms for them. The fundamental principle of "equal but separate," which plays such a large role in racial separation, cannot be applied very easily to the relationship between the sexes. The interests and common things, the mutual dependence of man and woman, are simply too strong; they allow no full organizational separation of male and female worlds. Despite the deep cleft between the sexes in the strict Islamic countries, for example, the relationships between man and woman cannot be denied. Regardless of how patriarchal the organization of the Old Testament world was—and it was so to a significantly lesser degree than the orthodox Muslim world—the society at large encompassed the separate spheres of life and work of woman and man and formed from them a higher unity. History has occasionally seen strict and unreconcilable separation of male and female spheres, including the renunciation of propagation, for example, in the Jewish Qumran sects, the strong Marcionite church of the initial Christian centuries, and the monastic orders (both monks and nuns) that arose in the Middle Ages. One wanted to exclude sexuality and relationships between the sexes completely in these groups because they were considered anti-divine and hostile to salvation. The Old Testament, however, and the mainstream of Judaism in general, has never been tempted to split the world into two hostile parts. It withstood the dualistic manner of thinking that came primarily from Persia.

1. Being Alone

The human being cannot live in a human fashion alone. "It is not good that the man should be alone" (Gen. 2:18). He stands in reference to a counterpart, a being like himself (Gen. 2:23). Contemporary philosophers, psychologists, and social scientists have expressed the same thing in this way: The ego needs a thou if it is to come to a recognition of itself at all. It needs human reference points. A child with whom no one speaks soon falls into an intellectual twilight condition. Total isolation from the environment can make a prisoner go mad. The human being is thus a deeply social being, and is for its own sake dependent on its fellow humans. Thus it must seek out the other, who speaks, works, and plays with it. Community in a variety of forms is a fundamental presupposition of life. The impulse toward the opposite sex is a particular kind of search for community.

Should one—indeed, is one allowed to—conclude from

this human striving for community and union that each individual being, within itself, is only a fragment of a larger whole? Is it legitimate to understand the desire one experiences in sex—the desire to lose oneself in the other person—as a recollection of a primal time when humans were supra-sexual, or bisexual, androgynous, unified beings? Oriental myths, Greek and Hellenistic philosophers, and later even Christian theologians dreamed in this way of a harmonious primal condition to which humans must return by overcoming the physical and sexual (cf B I 1). The Old Testament is more concise in its statements and more sober in its evaluation of reality.

It recognizes and values human community in all its peaceful and supportive nuances. It praises friendship (cf 1 Sam. 20; Prov. 17:17), and as we have already seen, it views the family as a source of refuge and meaning for the individual. It fears the dissolution of social bonds (cf Mic. 7:5f; Ps. 88; Job 19:13ff). It condemns the wanton destruction of the community by means of injustice, violence, hatred, lying, or envy (cf Hos. 4:1f; Amos 2:6ff; Isa. 5:8ff; Jer. 22:13ff; Prov. 15:27; 16:28; Eccl. 31:6). The Israelites find all good forms of human relationships worthy of praise; the best, however, appears to them to be love between man and woman, that kind of love that joins two independent people together without dissolving their individuality in ecstasy. That is the sense of the oft-cited passage Genesis 2:24: "Therefore a man leaves his father and his mother and cleaves to his wife, and they become *one* flesh." Sexual union doubtless stands in the foreground here, the sign of a wedding couple's unity and happiness. They physically become *one* body, joined and interwoven into one another. Coitus, however, is not a mechanical act. It is performed by people who have left their families behind them because they love each other. Thus more is happening here than just sexual satisfaction. The passage means to say that when two merge into one body, a new social being emerges, the core of a new family. This loving solidarity between spouses also becomes clearly recognizable in the story of Michal and David. Saul's daughter loves David (1 Sam. 18:20), and David receives her as his wife. Saul's idea is to destroy the suitor by means of the woman (1 Sam. 18:21, 28f). Michal, however, does not go along with it; she inwardly separates herself from her father and rescues David from his snares (1 Sam. 19:8-17). This puts her own life in danger, but the solidarity with the beloved is stronger than the duty of obedience to the father.

One would have to investigate all the Old Testament texts that speak of love and attachment between spouses and inquire as to what kind of partnership they mean (cf Gen. 29:18, 20; 34:3; Judg. 19:3; 1 Sam. 1:5, 8; 2 Sam. 3:16; 13:1f; Song of Sol. 8:6f; and elsewhere). One would find that sexual enjoyment—that the Old Testament otherwise highly praises (cf Prov. 5:15-19)—is imbedded in the feeling of belonging together and trust between two independent people. If the mutual respect breaks down, so does the partnership. The story of Amnon's rape of his sister Tamar illustrates this with utmost clarity (2 Sam. 13). The young, apparently immature man is consumed with passion for Tamar. Without thinking much about propriety or the girl's dignity, he plans an act of force with the help of a "crafty" friend. Tamar tries to bring him to his senses (vv 12f), but it doesn't help; his egoistic will must prevail. After the coerced intercourse, "Amnon hated her with very great hatred; so that the hatred with which he hated her was greater than the love with which he had loved her. And Amnon said to her, 'Arise, be gone'" (v 15). The story is masterfully told. It portrays the actors with their emotional impulses as do few other Old Testament narratives. Above all, however, it shows the basic Israelite view: An egocentric, narcissistic love cannot create community; it only sows hatred and destroys a person (vv 22, 28).

The first creation story also speaks about this unity of the sexes, although from a completely different perspective. The older form of its creation statement probably went as follows: "God created man (the 'Adam') in his own image, indeed, in the image of God he created him" (Gen. 1:27a). Adam: that means humanity in general, and includes woman under the overriding concept man. For Adam is not only a species designation (cf Gen. 5:2), but also the proper name of the first man (cf Gen. 5:3). From God's point of view, and particularly from the perspective of the human beings being created in God's image, humanity is a unified form. Sexual differences—that naturally are present—play no role here. Only a later author (from whose hand we have the remark in Gen. 5:1-2) emphasizes dual human sexuality: "Male and female he created them" (Gen. 1:27*b*). The polar contradistinction of all living creatures had enormous theological significance for him, particularly because of cultic considerations (cf Gen. 7:15f; Lev. 1:3, 10; 3:1; and elsewhere). According to Genesis 1, then, the unity of human beings has a universal dimension. There are ways of looking at things for which sexual differences are insignificant (especially if they do not violate the privileged position of the male!).

Let us return to the human urge to unite with a person of the opposite sex, to "be attached" to him or her. One clearly notices the attempt in the Old Testament to integrate the sexual impulse into the familial, patriarchal society and the dominant system of values. The numerous prohibitions against dangerous or perverse sexual traffic give us an idea of how difficult the taming of these primal impulses was in antiquity as well. Beyond these lists of prohibitions, one must imagine the actual transgressions. Nonetheless, it appears that during Old Testament times society determined and protected the unity of woman and man to a much larger degree than we can imagine. Leviticus 18:7-18 transmits to us, for example, a list of "forbidden degrees of relatives." The determinations are motivated overwhelmingly by the interests of the larger family unit. Chaotic relationships between men and women within this group would have catastrophic consequences. Thus actual sexual community, the group's perpetuating principle, is limited to married partners. Considerations because of incest played no role in the original form of the prohibition table; they were read into it only during the course of time. Things stand differently as regards the frequent prohibitions against homosexuality, intercourse with animals, and various other sexual "perversions." Their background is no doubt the societal organization, but they are nourished by religious and magical considerations that presumably extend far back into human history (cf Gen. 9:20-27; 19:5, 30-38; Exod. 22:18; Lev. 18:19, 22f; Deut. 23:18f; 27:21; Ezek. 22:10f; and elsewhere).

In my opinion, a comparison of Old Testament findings with our present reality yields the following. We experience sexual community basically in the same way as did the ancient Israelites. As they did, we too—one hopes—perceive the happiness of a person-to-person encounter that does not extinguish the individual, but rather raises that individual above itself. As they did, we too experience surrender and security, meaningful cohabitation, and physical union with its tenderness and its intoxicating satisfaction. The Song of Solomon, quite apart from its Oriental graphic imagery, is as fresh and relevant as ever before:

> You have ravished my heart, my sister, my bride,
>   you have ravished my heart with
>   a glance of your eyes,
>   with one jewel of your necklace.
> How sweet is your love, my sister, my bride!
>   how much better is your love than wine,
>   and the fragrance of your oils than any spice!
>   (Song of Sol. 4:9f)

We may be unaccustomed to hearing of the beloved's jewelry and perfume in a song of love, but the text is easily understandable. It sings of the bride's charms and of the joy of anticipating union with her, just as does the entire Song of Solomon in its male parts. The girl answers with truth just as timeless:

> O that his left hand were under my head,
>   and that his right hand embraced me!
> I adjure you, O daughters of Jerusalem,
>   that you stir not up nor awaken love
>   until it please.
>   (8:3-4)

What could be more beautiful than the union of lovers?

Just as the joys of living together, the frustrations and conflicts appearing in the Old Testament are also with us today. The difficulties besetting sexual encounter today, however, show how things have changed.

We have spoken repeatedly about the various accents falling both then and today on primary and secondary societal organizations. The development of the consumer-oriented industrial mass society has deeply disturbed the familial structure; it has robbed it of meaning and function and has rendered homeless the intimate togetherness, the cohabitation of woman and man. How are two people supposed to form a partnership between them when, because of an inundation of vocational and other external obligations, they hardly have the opportunity to speak with each other? Whence can this community come if each spouse understands so little of the other's tasks and concerns that mutual accompaniment becomes impossible? What must the effects be of the increasing recognition that the larger organization cannot, in the final analysis, lend meaning to the life of the individual? Contemporary analysts repeatedly emphasize the deadly antithesis between our society's micro- and macro-structures. Despite all the countermeasures of charitable and social-political organizations, intimate relationships and partnerships are almost defenselessly subjected to the pressures and contortions of mass society. The family is like a mussel without its shell. Thus under these circumstances, it is not the high divorce statistics that astonish us, but rather the marriages that against all expectation really do manage to create a life partnership. My own experiences from pastoral care and research of degrees of satisfaction among German married couples show that a great many people feel bound to their partner in an extremely sober way. During long years of living together, the partnership aspect itself more or less adapts well. One delineates spheres of interest and responsibility, respects the partner's idiosyncrasies, each helps the other—in short, most of the married couples around us live in a kind of peaceful coexistence. They are not particularly successful in actively and consciously making use of common interests or in creating a dynamic partnership from this interdependent proximity, a partnership bubbling over with joy and radiating warmth and humanity. Yes, that is it: Out of thousands of married couples we meet only an isolated few possessing that shared radiant power. The passive, static feeling of belonging together, on the other hand, is undeniable.

This threat to and encroachment on the intimate partnership is thus also a reality in intact marriages. Everyone appears to perceive this fact without, however, being able to analyze it consciously. The themes of love and marriage are central problems of modern life. They are discussed everywhere, both with a great deal of display as well as occasionally with insight and helpful results. The mass media, popular literature, and church activities all try to solve the recurring problems. Over all these efforts there hovers the fear of not doing justice to the mutuality of the sexes. Many people think sexual love is the only remaining way out of mass society's anonymity and dehumanization. The pressure to find this safe harbor then becomes all the more urgent, cost what it may. An army of anxious and insecure people thus fills the waiting rooms of physicians and counselors. Conversations with young people, students, and married people of all ages confirm this general state of insecurity on the part of both sexes. Modernity is hard-pressed to develop new, adequate role models for woman and man. Thus no one really knows "how things stand with oneself or with one's partner." The only relevant goal society gives to everyone is personal, vocational, and economic success. This guiding model is thrown up to everyone both from above and from without. Under no circumstances, however, does it lead to an intimate partnership with someone, since that other person simply cannot be subordinated to one's success drive. One's individual striving for happiness is hostile to real partnership. One cannot be surprised that when it dominates, the relationship between two people becomes emptied. This happens everywhere pure sexual contact is glorified. Whenever one loses hope for genuine human partnership and community, sex is praised as the panacea for the wounded individual. This egoistic satisfaction of one's needs by subjecting and exploiting the other person, however—a person who then becomes an object—is a sick and neurotic aberration according to everything we have been able to learn both from the Old Testament and from contemporary human sciences (cf 2 Sam. 13).

It would be more than interesting to study the reflex of our situation in the various realms of research, art, and literature. We will make only a few remarks here. Psychological and psychoanalytical science contributes a great deal to the understanding of love relationships. It shows that the human being, with its multilayered consciousness, is continually searching for a higher unity. (Anthropologists point here to the aspect of human incompleteness at birth, a condition making that human into a being desiring to transcend itself.) The ego needs a supra-ego in which to secure itself. It is even prepared to "sever off part of itself" and give this over to that higher ego. Lovers construct a common supra-ego. Expressed in a different way, things look like this: The human being tries to reach positively beyond itself with its inclinations and emotions, and creates emotional ties with the beloved. Its emotions are "occupied" by the partner, confiscated, and in this way satisfied and rendered useless for other ties.

This kind of scientific language sometimes sounds mechanistic, as if it came directly from the chemistry laboratory. Nonetheless, it provides help in understanding the phenomenon of sexual partnership. This is particularly the case for the historical dimension brought into the discussion by psychoanalytical research. The capacity to love is not an unchangeable, given factor. It arises as the end product particularly of one's childhood development. Love must be learned, and it can only be learned if it is lived out as a model. The child must receive love; otherwise it can never open itself up in a trusting and self-giving manner to its surroundings. Psychoanalysis has apparently unconsciously picked up biblical insights about "one must first be loved" that we find already in the Old Testament.

Social psychology illuminates the societal relationships in which the encounter of the sexes takes place. Medicine, pedagogy, sociology, anthropology, and many other sciences pay a great deal of attention to sexuality. One sees that there is no dearth of scientific interest; apparently, however, it stands in a reverse relationship to the success of sexual partnership.

The plastic arts, theater, film, and literature would all be unthinkable without the themes of "love" and "unity" between the sexes. Instead of enumerating a great many famous examples, let me rather cite two novels that correspond approximately to both the Old Testament and modern posture of expectation. Let it thus be documented that historical and cultural epochs do not simply pass on, but rather often exist both next to and in one another. In his 1936 book *Farmer's Psalm (Bauernpsalm)*, Felix Timmermans portrays the obstinate love of the hero Knoll for the soil of the field and for his two (successive) wives. This bond to the land and to the family is a unique passion refined by daily struggle. Timmermans describes the community of man and woman in his plastic, graphic language:

> On Sunday afternoon, when I walked with Fine through the fields in order to inspect the fruit, I was always ten steps ahead of her. We would speak hardly five words in an hour, yet we were close together, here, in the heart. Fine and I could sit together for hours without having to speak a single word. The quietness did not disturb us; it comforted us.

Things stand quite differently with Karin Struck in her novel *Loving (Lieben)*. She portrays the torturous search for the partner with whom the most intimate partnership is possible. The searching woman is a midwife and is called Lotte. She hovers constantly near death because her personal relationships break apart and disappoint her. The terrible conclusion drawn from these encounters is that "love means being alone."

One of her insightful observations is a contrasting piece to Timmermans' wordless love:

> How I fear the silence between lovers. I watch an older married couple in a restaurant waiting for their food. They are continually silent, even while eating. It is a coerced, not a good silence. It is a silence issuing from a dying life, from being cut off from a stream of life.

2. Partnership

The love relationship, or more precisely, the relationship between two people who love, does not consist simply in the effort to transcend oneself in order to establish a new common entity. It is also a matter of affirming and supporting the other person—the counterpart—in that person's own particularity. Genuine partnership respects the otherness and guards against wanting to subsume or level it. As we have already seen (see above, II and III), the Old Testament recognized this kind of equally weighted togetherness of woman and man—within the framework of the overall patriarchal system, of course. Just as the love yearning for union can occur within structures of privilege and subordination, so also is mutual respect possible in the marriage of antiquity. The clear division of male and female spheres of responsibility no doubt made this mutual respect easier.

Except in the book of Esther—and that is an extremely late document, presumably from the second century before Christ—we have no indication that the woman in Israel was to obey the man in all things. The texts we have queried show that the man indeed spoke for his family, and they also mention his power of authority in certain instances. A considerable number of stories and statements, however, show the woman to be a relatively independent spokesperson within her own sphere of work. The husband is to bow to her in many questions (cf above, II 3 *a* and *b*). We may thus speak of partnerships in Old Testament times. A strong feeling of justice prompted the husband and wife in Israel to help each other attain what each could rightfully claim. The good housewife "does her spouse good, and not harm, all the days of her life" (Prov. 31:12). She lets him sit undisturbed with the elders in the gate and carry on important conversations (Prov. 31:23) while she does housework. The man, on the other hand, watches over the honor of the woman given over to him, be it wife, daughter, or sister (cf Gen. 34:7ff; 2 Sam. 13:20-29; Song of Sol. 1:6). He tries to remain loyal to his wife, though law and custom are very considerate of him at this point (cf Job. 31:1; Prov. 5:18; Mal. 2:13ff). Of the figures known to us by name, Elkanah and Boaz behave in an exemplary fashion. Quite against social convention, Elkanah wants to console his favorite wife, Hannah, who is childless. Sterility was doubtless a reason for divorce. Elkanah wants to bring Hannah to accept her fate and to be happy with him in spite of it (1 Sam. 1:8). Unfortunately, social norms cannot be transcended so easily by the decisive will of an individual. Boaz grants the widow Ruth her rights (Ruth 3f). In doing so, he puts both his reputation and property on the line; we cannot say whether he does this in a completely selfless fashion.

Love naturally comes into play in the mutual aspects of the relationship between husband and wife. The firm inclination toward the partner is enough to make a person capable of supporting as far as possible the partner's uniqueness; capable since this kind of support of the other automatically means a limitation of oneself. This renunciation is suggested both in the case of Elkanah as well as of Boaz. It becomes clear as day in the example of Michal, that was already rightfully interpreted as an instance of solidarity. That example also contains signs of intervention for the male partner. She makes David's flight possible at her own risk (1 Sam. 19:11ff). After David is the unrivaled king and has a full harem (2 Sam. 5:13ff), this same Michal intervenes again on behalf of her husband's reputation in this concerned (?) fashion (2 Sam. 6:20); the narrator suggests, however, that she does it from ulterior motives and out of self-interest (cf 2 Sam. 6:16, 23). And how should we understand Abigail's intervention for her foolish husband Nabal in 1 Samuel 25? Could she protect him from the revenge of the army leader in any way except by denunciation? Another example is one standing in an ambiguous light. A Levite who later sacrifices his wife without a second thought, initially puts himself in an impossible situation for her sake. Four months after her flight he rides after her, going the "unmanly," low way, speaks in a kindly way with her and wins her back (Judg. 19:3).

We see that in the Old Testament a man seeks and values a good housewife (Prov. 18:22; 19:14), and the woman respects her husband as the protector and provider (cf Isa. 4:1). It is merely all too human that doubts can arise in specific instances concerning one's true motivation.

The doubts and ambiguities that can arise precisely in a relationship between partners gives us an idea of just how great the possibilities for conflict are. Any strict command system represses expressions of dissatisfaction. The relationship between partners, on the other hand, encourages criticism and self-criticism. The Old Testament knows well the precise tensions that grow out of this possibility of the exchange of opinion. It warns the "quarrelsome" or "insubordinate" woman, with whom it is impossible to live under one roof, the following:

> It is better to live in a desert land
>   than with a contentious and fretful woman.
>
> (Prov. 21:19)

> A foolish son is ruin to his father,
>   and a wife's quarreling is a
>   continual dripping of rain.
>
> (Prov. 19:13)

These and similar proverbs (cf also Prov. 11:16, 22; 27:15f) allude to a real phenomenon. The "housewife sickness" has apparently existed since even before the beginning of industrial work. This characteristic "contentious" housewife was probably a result of the chronic overburdening of the female spouse. And without fear of going too far astray, we can no doubt add that the aggressive, lazy, or arrogant husband (cf Prov. 14:14-19 and elsewhere) also had a poor relationship with his wife; the difference is that his is not treated as a literary theme. Is it also possible that the husband sometimes could not quite endure the burdens of work in the field, family and public responsibility? The ideal conceptions contained in Proverbs 31:10ff and the Song of Solomon may occasionally have led to frustrations and unforseen developments. Other factors could have been coerced marriage, economic misery, incompatability between spouses, traumatic childhood experiences, and so on. In any case, this unloading of pent-up aggressions is a part of any marriage partnership. It should not, however, become a permanent situation; otherwise the sitation becomes untenable.

The experiences and insights reflected in the Old Testament hold true in similar fashion for our own altered societal system and for the dual relationships found there. It remains the task of married couples not only to put up with each other's personality, inclinations, disinclinations, strengths, and weaknesses, but also to support them actively to the extent that the relationship between them and the family unity as a whole are not endangered. Nonetheless, we can see graphically that life partnerships today have become much more difficult than in Old Testament times. The immensity of the external vocational world, the difficulties inherent in caring for a modern household, the insecurity of roles, and the extremely narrow basis of the small family—these and other factors cause additional dilemmas. How can I adequately support my partner in her vocational frustrations? To what extent can I expect or accept self-limitation from my partner, or even sacrifice of his interests? Who performs the task of re-educating the man for shared domestic responsibility? How should married couples behave who discover in themselves ambiguous attitudes and varying feelings regarding the partnership ideal? Shared responsibility can be so burdensome that one of the partners would like to be led! The questions are endless, and they constantly recur both in the reported experiences of partnership marriages and in research projects concerned with the subject.

3. The Family: Germ Cell of Society?

We will conclude this chapter with two excurses that detour away from our main theme but that nevertheless are extremely important for the relationship between man and woman. Both sections deal once again with the question already mentioned concerning the radiating power of intimate partnership. Can one consider this relationship between two people as the motivating and formative power within society and the church? Is the family the building block for all of society's secondary organizational forms? Even though the Old Testament deals with the question of progeny from the very beginning, even as regards love and marriage, and even though all the authors are thoroughly steeped in the importance of the family—the Old Testament does not itself give us any clear answer to our question.

We have often suggested that the family unity had absolute priority over other organizational forms in Israel. Clan and tribe were expanded families, and even the later national community was always strictly ordered according to blood relation (Num. 1; Ezra 2). According to this finding, one could assume that the overall society was considered to be an organic unity from bottom to top. This appearance, however, is deceiving. Israel clearly encountered problems of the larger organization, of pressure directed from the top toward the bottom, particularly during the period of kings.

In the Song of Deborah, composed during the eleventh century before Christ and predating the monarchy, Israel is still a loosely ordered bundle of tribes, clans, and living communities (Judg. 5:13-17, 23). Among the individual groups, special interests are correspondingly quite strong and virtually preclude the possibility of solidarity against an enemy. In the period of kings this tribal identity still plays an enormous role (cf 2 Sam. 19:12f, 42ff); indeed, it soon results in a division of the larger Davidic kingdom (1 Kings 12). The flight and separation formulation found in 1 Kings 12 goes as follows:

What portion have we in David?
We have no inheritance in the son of Jesse.
To your tents, O Israel!
Look now to your own house, David.

(1 Kings 12:16)

This saying uses familial-legal ideas and concepts throughout. It gives the impression that political leadership in a multi-peopled state in the second generation after David was still the affair of a small family leader. In truth, however, a fundamental refusal of obedience to David's grandson Rehoboam lies behind this abdication on the part of the ten northern tribes. They simply no longer wanted to participate in this development toward a centralized state with its bureaucracy and inevitable tax burdens (1 Kings 12:4ff). This protest, according to our interpretation, is thus directing itself against the modern monarchy in the name of the old family and tribal organizations. All the Old Testament texts critical of the monarchy (collected and expanded during the exile for theological reasons) betray the same apprehensions (cf Judg. 9:8-15; Deut. 17:14-20; 1 Sam. 8:10-18). The passage in Samuel shows in great detail how brutally the desired king intervenes into the private sphere. He conscripts the sons into military service, recruits the daughters for his court, confiscates the clan's land, and raises a 10 percent tax (vv 11-17).

Secondary social organizations are never content merely with the function of protection they assume for the families. They also always exert pressure in their own interest, pressures to which the subordinate units must conform. We became acquainted with the dissolution of mixed marriages in the time of Ezra and Nehemiah as an example. These interventions from above are the warning sign that a secondary organization has made itself independent. From this perspective, we could describe the history of the Israelite families as a regressive movement. The free clans lost more and more of their independence to larger organizations. The increasing enslavement of the woman goes hand and hand with this, possibly the result of the political disenfranchisement of the man. Within the larger historical framework, however, the Old Testament family still remained a functional unit. Not until the appearance of industrial work in our own time was it totally destroyed and reduced to the sad, remnant-like state of parents with a child. This family remnant vegetates away in a big-city apartment; its members hardly have common tasks and have little contact with neighbors. Its intellectual nourishment consists of the poorer television programs.

Can the family today be the basic element of society? Is Catholic social doctrine correct in continually trying to reflect upon secondary organizations from the perspective of the family? Old Testament skepticism and today's reality speak against such attempts. The mass organizations determine and control the world. They force families and small groups into their sphere of control and appear to be totally inaccessible for reorganization after the model of the old, intact family structure. This has never become as clear for me as in the documentary film *Raoni* by Jean-Pierre Duttileux and Luiz Carlos Saldanha (1979). The strip shows the daily life of an Indian tribe in the Brazilian jungle, familial togetherness, hunting expeditions, work in the field, rituals, meals. The "civilization's" bulldozers break into the reservation and tear down the forest with giant chains in order to turn them into livestock pastures. The chief of the threatened village wins representatives of neighboring Indian settlements for a common request action. They finally get through to the head of the Indian protection agency, General Ismarth de Oliveira, who answers with vague promises. He is himself the helpless instrument of an expansive civilization unable to respect the microstructures of society. The concluding scenes take place in the teeming city Sao Paulo. The village chief, now in European clothes, wanders through the concrete desert and traffic accompanied by the anthropologist Orlando Villas Boas. He shakes his head and incredulously observes the human masses, the filth, and the closed faces. This, then, is the paradise of technological humans with its larger organizations. Clan life in direct contact with nature on the one hand, and existence in the industrialized world on the other, are two totally irreconcilable ways of life.

We cannot, however, flee back into a "natural" condition, a condition our predecessors left behind them a hundred years ago at the latest. Can we then at least realize the more modest dream of a humanization of these larger structures? Can the familial realm, and particularly the encounter between the sexes, still offer standards and values of personal respect, human compassion, and giving, that would be useful on a higher level in helping to make mass society more bearable? It is possible, and we ought not to give up hope; the difficulties, however, are obvious. One no doubt cannot run a factory according to the principles of a family household. How, in a huge company based on economy and efficiency, can one still save a place for the small joys and worries of the individual worker? A modern hospital must apparently function according to economic considerations. With that, however, it immediately loses the atmosphere of security and personal care. The administrative apparatus of cities and states, of the Federal Republic, and of the Common Market, are mammoth governing bodies in which personal contact is objectified and emotional life is suppressed. As a rule, then, authorities appear publicly with absolutely correct protocol or overbearing roughness.

The only possible way out will consist in taking the Old Testament skepticism seriously: We must reflect anew on our social structures without any false romanticism. We will not be able to do away with mass organizations. Perhaps, however, we can succeed in putting the brakes on their unbridled and autocratic growth. Perhaps we can find more possibilities for decentralizing the anonymous power centers than we previously assumed. Above all, Christians will work for the strengthening and reconstruction of the smaller group units that develop—in critical distance toward mass society—human forms of living together.

4. The Family: Rooting Soil for Faith?

The Old Testament never expressly designates the family as a refuge of the Yahweh faith. We have occasionally ascertained, I think, that the transmission of Yahweh's salvation activity in Israel nonetheless took place to a large extent in the family. The instruction a son received from his father offered the clearest reference to this fact (see above, II 1 c). If we go back to the pre-Mosaic period, the familial reference point of faith becomes apparent. The "God of the fathers" is a family and clan god, named after the head who first received the revelation (cf Gen. 31:53f; Exod. 3:6). This group reference then passed over to the god Yahweh, who revealed himself anew at Sinai. The covenant scene in Joshua 24 says emphatically: "As for me and my house, we will serve the Lord" (v 15). The narrative in Exodus 19, on the other hand, speaks about a well-organized holy people (v 6). That is Israel's post-exilic condition. The Psalms are full of addresses to the personal God oriented toward the clan (cf Ps. 22:2f; 23; 31:15; 71; and elsewhere). The original Israelite main festival was one going back to a nomadic custom: the celebration of the Passover. It was and still is celebrated among Jews overwhelmingly within the family circle and has for ages taken up the traditions of the Yahweh faith (cf Exod. 12). Characteristically, the son's question is posed precisely within the context of Passover: "What does this mean?" (Exod. 13:14), to which the father is to respond. Other annual festivals were added later, reflecting the rhythm of the agricultural year (Exod. 34:18, 22f, and elsewhere) but no longer occupying the same firm position within the clan. However, one also went to these celebrations as a family (cf 1 Sam. 1:3, 21). The great annual celebrations in Shiloh or at other sacred locales, however, were only part of Israelite religious observance at large. Until all cultic sacrifice was centralized in Jerusalem (Deut. 12), however, the family-oriented sacrifices and cultic celebrations in the home were probably more important yet (cf 1 Sam. 9:12; 16:2f-5; 20:29; and elsewhere). When sacrifice in the provinces was then forbidden, and the worship of Yahweh was to take place exclusively in Jerusalem—this date falls almost at the same time as the deportation to Babylon—the idea of a huge congregation slowly developed, one encompassing men, women, and children (cf 1 Kings 8:2 with Neh. 8:1-3; 12:43; Josh. 8:35). Synagogues then arose shortly after the exile and served the local congregations.

Regarding the role of the woman in the Israelite cult, let us only recall that menstruation made her cultically impure each month and thus significantly curtailed her active participation in the cult. Discharge of semen on the part of the male or other kinds of contamination occurred less frequently; nonetheless, the man had to abstain from sexual intercourse before worship (cf Exod. 19:15; Lev. 15:16; 1 Sam. 20:16; 21:5ff; Jer. 36:5). Despite the woman's disadvantage because of bodily functions, she did participate in the sacrificial meal during the early period (1 Sam. 1:4f) and was able to pray and make vows on her own (1 Sam. 1:10f). In the vow prescriptions of Numbers 30 and other passages we can see that the woman's religious rights became increasingly limited during the course of time, until during the Jewish period she could participate in the worship service only as a spectator from the synagogue gallery. In Jeremiah 44:15ff and Ezekiel 8:14 we hear about special female cults that were possibly also conducted as a protest against these discriminations.

Above all, however, we are interested in the Israelite family. In the beginning, the faith in the God of the fathers and in Yahweh was entrusted to it. Gradually, however, the tribal confederation (cf Josh. 24 and Exod. 19), the monarchy, and the theocratic community usurped the small group's religious powers; this development ran parallel to the civil-political one we earlier discussed. Yahweh increasingly became a god of the realm and of the people at large (cf 2 Sam. 7; Ezra 9; Neh. 10).

The Old Testament's ambiguous witness here poses the question at just which level God encounters us and where we are to place him first. A long Christian tradition has made God primarily into the protector of the superstructures. In the saints, the Catholic Church possesses mediators who are responsible for the social substrata. In the Protestant confessions God remained above all the Lord of the world, the protector of the state, of good morals, and of the economic order; or he became the partner of the individual soul apart from any social structures. In the first instance, God's word reaches the individual person through a larger organization (church, state); whereas in the second all social reference points are insignificant in the face of the necessity of extracting the soul from this world. Both conceptions fail to respect the individual person in its human relationships.

Let us forget these distinctions for a moment and pose the question more precisely. What is the position of the Christian church as regards the family? It is an indisputable fact that the church in Germany and other European countries is not composed of or above families. And how could it be? Strictly speaking, the family no longer really exists. The church is financed through the larger state organization and is variously coupled with it both legally and ideologically. The painful question is just where cause and effect can be found here. Has the church—by opting for the superstructures since approximately the time of Constantine the Great—contributed to the destruction of the family? This would indeed explain why it finds it so difficult to stand by the ill-treated, pursued individual in the smaller group, and to reflect upon and live the gospel in the middle of daily human life.

V. Sexuality and Religion

One basic theological problem both during the Old Testament period, and probably our own as well, is this: What does God have to do with sexuality? At first glance the question seems absurd. Doesn't God stand beyond any sexual specificity? It is not that simple.

Israel lived in an environment in which sexuality was highly significant. In Babylon, for example, the holy or sacred wedding was celebrated annually. The king or his representative was joined with a priestess in the temple tower, a symbolic act designed to represent and portray sacramentally the renewal of life forces. All kinds of sexual symbols and customs were known from the Canaanite religion in Israel's immediate proximity. According to the heavy attacks of the prophets Hosea and Jeremiah against the cultic mountains and the practices carried on there, cultic prostitution was apparently a frequent occurrence (cf Hos. 4:12-19; Jer. 2:20-25). This is probably a reference to the custom of having young girls deflowered in the sanctuary after they reached sexual maturity or before they were married. In this way one wanted to guarantee the divine fertility or blessing. In Egypt, too, we know of myths according to which the seasonal creation of the world is a sexual act. In its own environment, then, Israel experienced how sexuality was elevated to the divine and expanded into a universal force. The power of generation, represented in the steer-likeness of the God Baal; the power of birth, imagined as the fertile earth goddess; the power of love, uniting both male and female elements and represented by the Venus-goddess Ishtar, Anat, or a similar goddess—these and many other sexually specific divine figures populated the religious world of Israel's neighbors.

If we consider the living conditions in antiquity, the status of the sciences, the close association people at that time had with nature and the land, then we must admit that this personification of natural forces and of life cycles in the form of gods and goddesses must have been unusually suggestive. Neither did the alluring effect of these neighboring religions on Israel miss its mark. The settlement in Palestine soon posed the weighty question: Who gives us here the fruit of the field and the wine (cf Hos. 2:7-10)? That could only be the indigenous earth goddess who let the plants spring forth from her body. Who in the final analysis took care of a woman's fertility? That had to be a god with the force of generation, since there was no doubt that not every instance of intercourse with one's husband resulted in impregnation. Was it not completely sensible and in order to honor the divine power everywhere one found life and everywhere new life emerged? Wasn't sexual power the driving force of all existence? It was then only logical to ascribe sexuality to the gods themselves, and to ascribe a goddess to each god. Only in this way could the gods participate in the universal life process. They could motivate life both in a generative and bearing fashion and bless all human and animal sexuality by their presence. We thus see all of Israel's neighbor's sky and earth gods ordered into pairs, each god with his spouse and each goddess with her partner. (A difficult question is whether the—in part—more free position of women in the ancient Orient can be traced back to the fact that powerful goddesses existed. In general one can say that this had little influence on the social position of women. All ancient Oriental cultures of historical times lived more or less according to patriarchal systems.)

Our initial, overwhelming impression from the Old Testament suggests that—except for a few exceptions—Israel radically excluded sexuality from its concept of God. Yahweh was a single, probably male, but unmarried God. The significant exception to this rule is given us by the excavations of the Jewish military colony on the Nile island Elephantine. During the fifth century before Christ—at the same time Ezra and Nehemiah in Jerusalem were separating out all heathen elements under the name of the one Yahweh—Jews here worshiped not only Yahweh in the temple but also goddesses like the warmongering virgin and seductress, heavenly queen and vegetation goddess Anat. Jeremiah 44, by the way, sharply condemns the worship of the same goddess. Aside from this kind of deviation on the part of popular or heretical theologians, however, the Old Testament witnesses cling with iron strictness to Yahweh's male-tinted transsexuality. The central confesson of the Jews to this day is: "Hear, O Israel: The Lord our God is one Lord" (Deut. 6:4). Regarding the amorphous nature of this God and the impossibility of representing him graphically: "You shall not make for yourself a graven image, or any likeness" (Exod. 20:4-6; cf Deut. 4:12ff); this also excludes any human, sexual figure. The Old Testament does, admittedly, make shy or even naïve attempts to imagine God as a person, and then usually as a man (cf Gen. 3:8; Ezek. 1:26; Dan. 7:9), but these carry little weight. Yahweh remains an individual god, the only, sublime god.

Astonishingly, however, the sexuality one had so decisively struck from the concept of God appears somewhere else. In some prophets Yahweh is the man who has chosen the people Israel to be his bride (cf Hos. 2:4-10; Jer. 2:32f; 3:1-5; Ezek. 16; 23; Isa. 54; 62). The main statements of this theological view are, for example:

There were two women, the daughters of one
    mother. . . .
They became mine, and they bore sons and daughters.
                                                (Ezek. 23:2, 4)

For the Lord has called you like a wife forsaken
    and grieved in spirit,
like a wife of youth when she is cast off,
    says your God.
                                                (Isa. 54:6)

For the Lord delights in you,
    and your land shall be married.
For as a young man marries a virgin,
    so shall your sons marry you,
and as the bridegroom rejoices over the bride,
    so shall your God rejoice over you.
                                                (Isa. 62:4f)

This free association of sexual symbolism with Yahweh is quite noteworthy. Was the concern of Old Testament theologians about pulling the God of Israel down to the level of fertility gods perhaps not all that strong? Be that as it may, Israel did not exclude sexual language from its theology; indeed, it did ascribe sexual activity to Yahweh, if only symbolically, and made him responsible for fertility at large (cf Hos. 2:10; Ps. 65:10ff).

This Old Testament ease regarding sexual symbolism also generates questions for our own understanding of the Bible and our own church doctrine. After centuries of repressing all sexuality, it is time to discover, in dialogue with the Old Testament, that God the Creator wants the fertility of all of nature. We ought to be allowed to rejoice in this, and as sexual beings we are indeed permitted to participate in the continuing creation. The Bible says even more. God the savior liberates not only the sexually neutral individual person, but rather precisely the human being in its social relationships. He liberates the sexual impulse from its pressures and egoism, and thus also the sexual partners both from themselves and for each other. And God the Spirit fills resigned people and antiquated forms with new life; he creates so that the rejoicing happiness of those who love will not cease.

We have now ended a few rounds of conversation with the Old Testament, though certainly not exhaustively or with any finality. We hope, however, that the reader can now question and study further in a necessary to and fro between the realities of the older world and our own. Both realities illuminate each other mutually, and neither can be understood without the other. For the rest, the following contribution of Wolfgang Schrage from the perspective of the New Testament will look more closely at just this last question, that concerning the redemption and sanctification of sexuality. This will once again cast a light on the temporally bound witness of the Old Testament.

B.
WOMAN AND MAN
IN THE
NEW TESTAMENT

Introduction

As ever, this topic is extremely relevant and is still a favorite literary child. The intention of our New Testament treatment cannot be merely to expand this flood of publications—publications indeed promising enlightenment and guidance—by yet another. The exegete would already be a bit out of place to the extent that he or she does not share the prejudice that knowledge and information of itself leads to new experience, liberated sexuality, and relations with the opposite sex in the fashion of genuine partnership. Neither, however, will this exegete add a voice to the chorus of those who assure us—after the wave of emancipation and sex has ebbed with all its exaggerated fantasies and promises of happiness—that they knew better all along. Knew what? That nothing can ever really be changed in the stability of traditional roles and ideals. And perhaps they even still consider their conservative posture to be biblically correct.

It does make sense, however, to recall anew all those impulses and experiences in the New Testament that on the one hand did indeed become documented in language and text, yet on the other still remain only vaguely conscious; this is particularly true because of the long tradition of obfuscation by non-Christian elements. Nowhere else has the history of interpretation and effect so obscured the in part extremely subversive potential of the New Testament, so much so that people have widely accepted the idea that hostility toward the body and cramped sexuality were good Christian traits. Indeed, precisely the New Testament texts were held responsible for a cramped and neurotic taboo on the physical and on sexuality. Up to the present the New Testament still gets credit particularly for the model of patriarchal structures that promote a privileged position for the male and repression of the female.

This can no doubt be partially explained by the presence in

the New Testament of unequivocal initial steps toward this view of things; the alien character of biblical texts often appears most clearly when one reads certain pertinent passages. Despite some justification, one thus cannot really object that only earlier exegesis was sexist and, as everywhere else, wrote "history" in the sense of "his story." This is also why one cannot reverse direction and measure everything with the standards of feminist ideas, or replace the factual degradation of females in patriarchal cultures and in exegesis with the claim that one ought now to treat this subject from an exclusively feminine perspective. Whoever is convinced that male exegetes evaluate from a male perspective and with androcentric interests is invited to further common understanding by objections within the pertinent exegetical questions.

This is particularly necessary because the New Testament does not contain any unified answer to the question concerning the proper relationship between woman and man. It is no accident that the church can refer to the New Testament in support of both the subordination as well as the ordination of women; one finds both patriarchalism and feminism equally supported by the New Testament—and is for the most part justified in doing so. Without content criticism *(Sachkritik)* within the diverging interpretations, however, these kinds of contradictory conclusions are, to be sure, not possible. *Sachkritik* is at any rate unavoidable. If it is not simply to orient itself toward its own favorite ideas of fashionable trends, then one needs certain standards and reference points. The Jesus tradition and Pauline passages should particularly serve as such. The Synoptic Gospels and Pauline Letters will probably stand in the foreground of the presentation of biblical attitudes and will often even be played off as critical authorities against certain faulty New Testament developments; this is so because precisely they are where we must seek the thematic center of the New Testament. Their texts are where an inner connection exists between this center and the evaluation of the relationship between woman and man. This preferential treatment of Jesus and Paul is also a kind of compensation. For centuries, other texts—the Pastoral Letters, for example—have dominated the field in a fateful way. It is no accident that these texts have prompted people to accuse the church of preaching a morality that drives human beings into all sorts of complexes and guilt feelings, of limiting the woman to home and the kitchen, and of making her keep her mouth shut in church. We don't have to "rewrite" the New Testament to make it support women's rights.[1] At certain points, however, we must ask the New Testament to testify against itself; and under some circumstances we must even measure an author according to some of his other statements. A kind of "de-patriarchalization" will then take place of its own accord; not all New Testament material, but certainly some specific strands and tendencies do stand in need of this. The New Testament itself, however, offers the most effective beginnings of this kind of *Sachkritik*.

Of course, the evaluation of some of this content depends on certain theological and exegetical presuppositions that can only be partially explained here. We cannot, for example, discuss at any length whether the Pastoral Letters do indeed come from the hand of Paul, something that in any case I consider quite impossible. Nonetheless, some arguments important for our topic ought not to be overlooked. I hope we will find, for example, that a judgment concerning whether the *mulier taceat in ecclesia* (1 Cor. 14:34f) is Pauline or post-Pauline, is not really a question of male or female prejudice, but rather of the weighing of exegetical arguments (cf III 2 *b*). We can easily see how important exegetical differentiation is and how catastrophic, on the other hand, ignorance can be, by considering the common but completely abstruse simplification suggesting that Jesus' freedom was betrayed by Paul, whom many consider to be a "defamer of women and marriage"[2] or "the eternal enemy of women" (G. B. Shaw).[3] Of course, we cannot exegetically really help anyone who considers passages such as Galatians 3:28 to be an obligatory theological exercise designed to cash in on male privileges; or who interprets such passages in the sense of a false doctrine of two realms, according to which the secular-"natural" relationships (usually meaning those prescribing "subordination") are left unchanged and the passage's validity is limited to a relation *coram deo* (cf II 3 *b*). One cannot, of course, toy back and forth with "subordination" to the point that "equal rights" comes out; we should ask, however, in what context it stands in the New Testament and just what scope it really has, particularly as compared with corresponding Jewish and Hellenistic statements. This naturally depends in part on the evaluation of the environment in question, something we can describe here only in a rather perfunctory fashion. We should, of course, be fair in all this; one can easily comprehend that any evaluation of New Testament material will appear in a different light if compared with the high marriage ideals of the Stoics or, on the other hand, with the most crude statements of certain Jewish or Hellenistic forms of misogyny. In the final analysis, however, it is less important to see how early Christianity comes away from such comparison or whether it can offer us something original and specific; what is important is rather whether it can be persuasive as regards real substance. As we shall see, it cannot always do this.

This suggests that one ought not to repress and silence those traditions and behavioral models that indeed do need to be criticized. The criterion for selection is not, however, what happens to confirm a certain position or fit best into someone's pet concept. Any given option is not, of course, forbidden; indeed such things are unavoidable. It must, however, enter into a debate with whatever represents the opposite view. Texts from the Jesus tradition or the Pauline corpus are not, of course, excluded from such critique. Whenever the radical antitheses of the Sermon on the Mount sit uncomfortably with our contemporary permissive society, that is certainly no reason to overlook or criticize them. When, however, the exclusively male circle of the twelve is said to go back to Jesus himself, then we must ask whether this kind of post-Easter position—a time when women were also chosen as resurrection witnesses and missionaries (cf concerning the apostolate III

1 *c*)—can really say anything substantial concerning the question of admitting women to "office." Jesus, after all, did not yet pursue any universal mission to the gentiles himself, and yet the church let itself be sent out into the world by the resurrected One. The example of the Canaanite woman shows that one could contradict Jesus. She was not satisfied with his refusal, and to Jesus' no she countered "but . . ." This led him to change his position (Mark 7:24ff; Matt. 15:21ff).

There are dangers inherent in any thematically centered presentation that does not proceed through the texts in a linear fashion, but rather—as is customary with the Biblical Encounters—tries to summarize central problems of the biblical witness. One is naturally a systematization not always without problems. Nonetheless, this inherent danger is worth the risk for the sake of avoiding unnecessary repetition. One's efforts, however, are directed toward ordering as representative texts as possible—possibly even contradictory ones—under certain themes. In any case only basic positions and essential outlines can be shown without having to abstract too much from the historical, cultural, and social determining factors and implications. A text's value is not, to be sure, diminished by the fact that most of the texts are actually statements elicited by certain "occasions." We do, however, continually need to bear in mind that a great deal is missing from the New Testament only by accident, and that just as much is found there merely by accident; all systematic development and reflected doctrine remains in the background. These heterogeneous occasions and temporally fixed reference points from which the individual texts emerge do not as such either explain or justify anything. They are a substitution neither for the question of the texts' motives and reasons, nor—and this needs to be particularly emphasized—for their inevitable "encounter" or confrontation with the present. The latter will indeed be treated in the concluding section, but the exegetical yield in the preceding sections will nonetheless not simply be presented in a historical-positivistic fashion. We will rather be trying from the very beginning to relate the exegetical finds to our own present.

I. Woman and Man as Creatures of God

1. Corporeality and Sexuality

The entire New Testament concurs that God as the Creator of heaven and earth created the human being in its corporeality and sexuality as well. This was already critically emphasized in the confrontation with dualistic-ascetic currents both inside and outside the church in early Christianity (cf I 3 e). The New Testament traced neither one's physical constitution nor the sexual differentiation of humans back to the Fall. An androgynous primal human, whose separation might be considered the beginning of sin and death, plays just as small a role as does the idea that one condition for entry into the kingdom is that "you make the male and the female one and the same, so that the male not be male nor the female female" (Gos. Thom. 22). The New Testament, just as the Old, does not know of any human being as such, but rather only as a woman or man, as woman with the man and man with the woman; and one can hardly use Mark 12:25 to suggest that sexual differentiation represents a sign of estrangement.[4] A person's existence as woman or man, one's sexuality, is not something added secondarily to human existence—be it higher or lower—nor is it something we can ignore. It is rather indivisibly given in a person's very existence as a human being.[5] Just as a person does not *have* a body, but rather *is* a body, neither does a person *have* femininity or masculinity, but rather *is* a woman or man.[6] This is why the Old Testament creation story is cited *verbis expressis,* a story emphasizing sexual differentiation and whose acquaintance and validity one can presuppose even when no specific reference is made to it:

> But from the beginning of creation, "God made them male and female." (Mark 10:6)

> Have you not read that he who made them from the beginning made them male and female . . . ? (Matt. 19:4)

This alone forbids any negative evaluation of women, the kind that has been traditional from then up to the present. Woman and man *both* come from the hand of the Creator and are thus of equal stature and equal dignity.

A fundamental similarity thus augments any differentiation; unity augments polarity. This is why no distinction at all is usually made between man and woman; one speaks rather in a manner including them both. "Man" shall not live by bread alone (Matt. 4:4); the sabbath was made "for man" (Mark 2:27); there is nothing outside a "man" which by going into him can defile him (Mark 7:15), and so on. "All flesh is like grass" (1 Pet. 24; Isa. 40:6); "all flesh shall see the salvation of God" (Luke 3:6; Isa. 40:5); "for every one who asks receives" (Matt. 7:8) and "he who humbles himself will be exalted" (Luke 14:11). "All have sinned," but "all believers" are justified by faith apart from works of law (Rom. 3:23ff; cf 5:18); thus in a truly universal fashion *every* human being is exonerated. This is not supported by any ideal of some sexless or bisexual human existence or by some creature abstracted from sexuality, but rather by the recognition of a common element connecting woman and man, above all the fact of their creatured nature.

The inheritance of the Old Testament creation tradition also plays an extraordinarily important role in the understanding of partnership and marriage. God not only created human beings as woman or man, he also created them for partnership. The orientation of the sexes to each other is most clearly and impressively experienced in the sexual impulses between woman and man, in the physical "becoming one" of marriage.

Again, an Old Testament citation elucidates this: "For this reason a man shall leave his father and mother and be joined to his wife, and the two shall become one flesh" (Matt. 19:5; cf Mark 10:7; 1 Cor. 6:16; Eph. 5:31). This is precisely why it is impossible to consider human sexuality either divine or diabolic, or, for example, to misunderstand marriage either as a paradise or a hell on earth. In the New Testament view, sexuality is just as removed from its romantic glorification as a power of heaven, as from its demonic degradation to an animalistic power of nature. As a gift from the Creator it is not to be disregarded as purely secular, and certainly not disqualified as sinful—as if it did not also come from the Creator. Neither is it to be infused with sacramental significance or exaggerated cultically or religiously (cf the cultic prostitution of ancient Oriental fertility rites), as if one could draw a special bead on God's mystery in it. It is rather a positive arrangement by the Creator, a part of the creature's created nature and an integral part of its personality.

The significance of this view for us today is obvious. Sexuality is neither an absolute nor a panacea, but rather one component of the *totus homo*, an integrating and integral aspect of the physical-spiritual totality in which we all exist. The New Testament views the human being completely as a unity; the individual anthropological elements almost always stand for the totality. This is significant for the New Testament and excludes both an overestimation as well as an underestimation of individual aspects. One virtually never forgets one's corporeality or is ashamed of one's sexuality. There is thus neither prudery nor hypocrisy, neither rigidness nor humiliation in the relationships between the sexes. This sobriety is not the result of experiences of disappointment or frustration; and it is certainly not the result of some enlightenment campaign appealing only to knowledge, but then accordingly void of any capacity for genuine experience of humanizing—because knowledge is not enough here. It is rather the consequence of faith in the Creator, from whom only good and whole gifts come (James 1:17). "For everything created by God is good, and nothing is to be rejected if it is received with thanksgiving" (1 Tim. 4:4).

Whereas the so-called sexual emancipation of our own time often enough not only does not liberate at all, but rather makes one just as neurotic and cramped as did the puritanical-rigoristic morality, the New Testament safely passed between the Scylla of repression and the Charybdis of libertinage. At the same time, however, we cannot deny that the later church for centuries not only preached a monstrously anti-corporeal morality—thus creating for many people a permanently bad conscience—but also denied the fundamental equality of woman and man. And it did this by referring to certain New Testament passages.

2. Contrasting Tendencies

The New Testament itself already contains tendencies that do not hold to this high standard and thus remain below the norm. Paul himself once encountered a difficult situation concerning a kind of "emancipation movement" in Corinth that apparently directed itself, among other things, against the convention requiring women to cover their heads. He had a difficult theological time of it[7] and was able to write that man "is the image and glory of God," while "woman is the glory of man" (1 Cor. 11:7). In the following verse he then alluded to the second creation account in Genesis 2 by saying that "woman [was made] from man" (cf Gen. 2:18, 22). Precisely 1 Corinthians 11:7, however, is nothing less than a step backward from Genesis 1:27, according to which the human being created as woman or man is the image of God, and not just the man alone. According to 1 Corinthians 11:7, the woman is granted only a kind of derivative likeness. In verses 11 and 12, however, Paul fortunately did after all change his mind for the better and said what we actually would have expected him to say from the perspective of Galatians 3:28: "Nevertheless, in the Lord woman is not independent of man nor man of woman; for as woman was made from man, so man is now born of woman. And all things are from God" (1 Cor. 11:11f). [8] With this thesis of the equally primal nature and equal value of both sexes, Paul basically withdrew what he earlier had theologically supported so inadequately and explained so unpersuasively (cf also the contorted line of argument).

Admittedly, the New Testament does not understand equality even at the level of the creation statements as an equality in *every* respect. One could argue endlessly whether and to what extent women really are "weaker" than men, as 1 Peter 3:7 suggests. Antiquity normally spoke of woman's "weakness" in a derogatory fashion, and not always with an eye on her physical constitution, but rather also regarding her psyche and morality. When Plato, for example, fails to see "woman's nature measure up to ours [the male] as regards the ability to attain virtue" (*Laws* 781 *b*; cf later Clement of Alexandria *Paed*, II.10.107 and elsewhere), this is not what the First Letter of Peter means. Indeed, this letter challenges precisely this idea of the predominance of the male, an idea obviously often associated with thoughts of "female weakness" (cf Ep. Arist. 250f). "Weakness" is what should bring about Love and consideration—not sympathetically from above or in the fashion of a cliché, but rather with "honor."

Christology and the theology of the cross (cf 2 Cor. 13:4) were the first occasions for the common evaluation of masculinity and femininity to be radically altered. Through them, traits considered to be typically feminine—such as "weak"—became predications of Christians in general (cf 1 Cor. 2:3; 2 Cor. 12:5ff). When Paul says, "What have you that you did not receive?" (1 Cor. 4:7), "receptivity" here can no longer be stereotypically associated with femininity. Both examples show that the stereotypes and particularly the ideals of the superman and "master morality" no longer had a chance here. Nietzsche, of course, suggested the Christians were in reality a "feminine" gang, "not even men," and that Islam—with men as its fundamental presupposition—quite justifiably despised them (Antichrist 58f). His verdict would hardly have made an impression on early Christianity.

3. Areas of Danger and Misunderstanding

a. Sin[9]

According to the New Testament understanding, this order between woman and man is threatened by sin and demonization—and this is equally true for woman and man. There can be no talk here of a particular vulnerability to sin on the part of the woman. The great disturbance brought into human life by the rebellion against God also affects the sphere of human relationships, including sexual ones (cf already Gen. 3). Wherever God is no longer one's counterpart, there the companionship of the sexes can become a confrontation, and concern can become mere lust and perversion.

This appears particularly to be Paul's opinion in Romans 1:18ff, according to which all sorts of perversions result from the more fundamental perversion of the relationship between creature and Creator. Wherever the Creator no longer stands at the center, Paul says, human and sexual relationships become disordered; natural behavior becomes unnatural—something Paul sees demonstrated particularly in homosexuality, which he considers an effect of dishonoring the creator (Rom. 1:26f).

We must not overlook the fact that deeply rooted prejudices against any deviation from the norm in sexual behavior are at work here. We see this in the sharp verdicts of Judaism against the widespread, celebrated ideal of homo-eroticism during the New Testament period. In Pseudo-Phocylides 190f we read: "Do not give yourself over, against nature, to unpermitted love. Man's love to man is even detested by animals" (cf also Philo, *On the Spec. Laws* III.39; Josephus, *Ag.Ap.* 2.273). Old Testament anthropology, with its emphasis on sexual polarity, no doubt also had a part in rejection of homoerotic sexuality.

This explanation, deviating as it does from all the insights of modern medicine and psychology concerning the genesis and nature of homosexuality, does not seem very persuasive today.[10] It is, however, correct to say that sin is never an abstract or theoretical phenomenon, but that it rather pulls both denaturalization and dehumanization behind in its wake. This can, of course, also have tangible consequences for the relationship between woman and man. These destructive consequences and manifestations of sin in the sphere of corporeality and sexuality must, however, be clearly differentiated from a certain identity. A traditional attitude exists—one that to this day has not yet been overcome—concerning the so-called Christian morality and its one-sided sexualization of sin. In the face of this morality we need to emphasize strongly that the New Testament does not consider sexuality as such evil or sinful. Just as the entire human being is a creature, so also is the entire human a sinner—and not just in corporeality or sexuality. Of course, sin can indeed have something to do with sexuality. When, for example, Jesus says to the adulteress, "Go, and do not sin again" (John 8:11; cf Luke 7:47), he does not condemn her sexual relations as such as sinful, but rather only her adultery. A social outlawing or defamation of adulterers is thus just as unintentional as is some sort of defamation of homosexuals and prostitutes.

In the final analysis, the New Testament understands sin from the perspective of the Christ event. "If I had not come and spoken to them, they would not have sin" (John 15:22). Because, however, this Christ demands faith, one can also say: "For whatever does not proceed from faith is sin" (Rom. 14:23). That is true both for spiritual behavior as well as physical phenomena. When Romans 6:6 speaks about "the sinful body," it does not equate body with sin. It proceeds rather on the assumption that the power of sin (Rom. 6:12, 14) is so great that it enslaves the entire person; the person is then no longer its own master, including over body and limb.

b. Flesh/Desire

When one says "desires of the flesh" or "sins of the flesh," most people still *eo ipso* associate it with sexuality. When, however, the New Testament speaks about "flesh,"[11] it never simply equates it with sexuality. After all, the divine Word itself becomes flesh (John 1:14). Rather, the human being is flesh in contrast to God, something we must understand above all from the perspective of the Old Testament (particularly in the phrases "all flesh" and "flesh and blood"). Thus flesh refers to the human being in its corporeality, creatureliness, and mortality. Flesh is the place one experiences pain and sickness (cf 2 Cor. 12:7; Gal. 4:13; 1 Cor. 7:28) and thus also sexuality (cf the phrase "become one flesh"). That is why the Christian—to the extent life is lived within secular parameters—is still flesh without that affecting belonging to Christ (Gal. 2:20; Phil. 1:22; and elsewhere).

"Flesh" can admittedly also negatively describe the human being in contrast to God. This is the case when a person considers flesh to be the only norm and criterion, when the secular-natural sphere is the only one of concern and the only one used as a reference point. We must not believe, however, that only sensual or sexual behavior can be "fleshly" in this sense. Flesh is rather a sphere of power encompassing the person as a whole—with body, spirit, and soul. The contrast of flesh to God thus equally includes spiritual phenomena, enabling knowledge or wisdom in their own turn to become oriented toward the norm of "flesh" (cf 2 Cor. 5:16; 1 Cor. 1:26).

Not even "desire" is *eo ipso* a sexually oriented, pejorative concept. Even the spirit desires, or is after something (Gal. 5:17). Jesus desires the Passover meal (Luke 22:15); Paul desires—yearns for—his brothers (1 Thess. 2:17), or yearns to be with Christ (Phil. 1:23; cf also Heb. 6:11). Admittedly, the concept is not usually formal or positive, but is rather negatively weighted because it is given over to "the flesh" (Gal. 5:16; Rom. 13:14; and elsewhere); it is not, however, specifically coined with sexuality in mind. The commandment "you shall not covet" (Rom. 7:7; cf 13:9), for example, is a shortened formulation for the entire second table of the Decalogue, a table reducing the commandments to a common denominator, as does 4 Maccabees 2:6 (cf also James 1:15). The other objects of Exodus 20:17 and Deuteronomy 5:21 (house, field, slave, ox, and so on) alone prevent us from thinking only or particularly of sexual desire. Jesus' warning against looking at a woman "lustfully" (Matt. 5:28) is a warning against adultery, and not a prohibition against desiring one's own wife (cf IV 4 *a*). We really hear nothing about a woman's desire (as, eg, in Josephus *J. W.* 2.121 in his essay on the views of the Essenes; concerning 1 Tim. 2:14, cf III 2 *b*).

c. *Fornication/Prostitution*

The New Testament probably picked up the frequent warning against fornication from Judaism, and it often ranks first in traditional catalogues of vices (Mark 7:21; Gal. 5:19; Col. 3:5). This does not mean that it is "the mother of all evil" (as, eg, in *T. Sim.* 5:3), but it is counted among the most pivotal consequences and manifestations of the fundamental evil of sin (cf *a*). The word is occasionally to be understood metaphorically as idolatry or the worshiping of false idols (cf Rev. 17:2ff; 18:3; and elsewhere); normally, however, it means any form of illegitimate sexual intercourse that deviates from the standard norm, particularly if it occurs extramaritally.[12] If, for example, someone lives in a wild marriage with his stepmother, that counts as fornication (1 Cor. 5:1).

All forms of incest were already forbidden by the Old Testament (Lev. 18:8ff; 20:11; Deut. 27:20). In Judaism, too, sexual intercourse or concubinage with one's stepmother was considered incestuous and punished with stoning. The so-called apostolic decree (Acts 15:20, 29) possibly also intended "fornication" to mean previously forbidden marriages between relatives; the minimal requirements of this decree, however, were to make community living possible between Jewish and gentile Christians. An example of the culturally conditioned nature of such norms is the fact that leviratic marriages were excepted from the decree—obligatory marriages between a man and his brother's childless widow.

Fornication included particularly prostitution and the trafficking with prostitutes (1 Cor. 6:12ff). The Corinthians placed eating and sexual intercourse on the same level and considered them theologically indifferent; in a certain fashion this was a prefiguration of the modern "norm-free" glass-of-water theory. Paul, however, considered physical traffic with a prostitute to be a profound occurrence, and he repeatedly tried to show anew that one's very membership in Christ was at stake (cf also d). The body cannot be separated from the spiritual and real as being merely material or unreal; it is part of the whole person (cf 1). Paul argued above all that the body is the place where Christ has come to power: "The body is meant . . . for the Lord, and the Lord for the body" (v 13). Bodies are members of Christ (v 15). A person having physical intercourse with a prostitute is not doing something that is merely peripheral or inconsequential, but rather becomes "one flesh" with her (v 16). Here, too, this trafficking is certainly not rejected qua physically-sexually; community with a prostitute, however (and there is no reason to think specifically of temple prostitution) breaks one's communication with the Lord, who is not satisfied with mere inwardness but rather claims one's physical existence as well.

We cannot say for sure whether fornication also includes unnatural sexual intercourse in addition to premarital (as, eg, in *T. Benj.* 9:1). The concept of nature was, of course, still ambiguous at that time. We hear nothing, for example, about masturbation. It is thus doubtful that it was considered to be particularly unwholesome or punishable.

d. Libertinism

1 Corinthians 6:12ff cannot be understood without considering the excessive understanding of freedom and nature-oriented understanding of salvation so widespread

particularly in gnostic circles, ideas also affecting the relationship between woman and man.[13]

Despite the sheer quantity of merely moral indignation one encounters in the anti-heretical reports of the ancient church, one does see clearly enough that certain gnostics apparently held the opinion that "as free men, they can do whatever they wanted" (Hippolytus *Ref*. 19.7), for example, traffic with sexual indiscrimination (19.5). Perhaps they assume that under any circumstances a permanent divine substance is saved, so that one's manner of life is irrelevant (as maintained by Irenaeus I.6.2f). According to Clement of Alexandria (*Misc. Studies* III.34.3), a certain group committed adultery as a protest against the commandments of the creator god. In any case, it is certain that they radically despised human corporeality. If the body is the work of an anti-divine demiurge, why then should one not ruin it through libertinism?

The early church thus had to protest against all sorts of libertine tendencies because it perverted Christian freedom (cf, in addition to 1 Cor. 6:12ff, also 2 Pet. 2:1ff and Rev. 2:14, 20). We hardly need to emphasize how relevant this libertinism is during the time of a permissive and hedonistic society. Freedom and libertinage are not, however, the same for the New Testament. An unbridled "living out" of sexuality and an unbound sexual "freedom" are inhuman and ruinous both for oneself and for others. Paul completely agreed with the saying "I am allowed everything"; at the same time, however, he limited it in a twofold fashion: 1. "not all things are helpful [for the other person]" (1 Cor. 6:12*a*), and 2. "I will not be enslaved by anything" (1 Cor. 6:12*b*). Above all, however, the phrase "everything is yours" is valid only as long as its continuation holds true: "and you are Christ's" (1 Cor. 3:22f). Christ, in his own turn, extricates one from precisely this egocentricity.

e. Asceticism

Already in early Christianity, another influence was much more pervasive, one usually resulting from the same dualistic hostility and contempt toward the body, but that led to the opposite result, to asceticism.[14] It dominates not only the genuinely gnostic writings but the early Christian apocrypha as well. As we shall see, this could also lead to a rejection of marriage.

Sexual asceticism results whenever the body is equated with poverty and "corpse" (Gos. Thom. 56 and 80), whenever it is considered to be merely "animalistic" (Thom. Cont.) or a "despised thing" (Gos. Phil. 22), or whenever it is thought to be of demonic substance and is thus excluded from salvation. According to the so-called Acts of Thomas 58, the sexual impulse is dirty madness and is diabolical. The Sophia of Jesus Christ 106:5 disqualifies sexual reproduction as a "dirty practice," and in the Gospel of the Egyptians the savior says, "I have come to destroy the works of the female." One can easily add to this list of diatribes condemning corporeality and sexuality as diabolical. Non-gnostic texts also manifest this ideal of virginity or cultically determined abstinence, but this was usually limited in the cults to priests and priestesses (cf the vestal virgins) and to those visiting temples or religious celebrations. Or, for example, one wanted as a neo-Platonic or neo-Pythagorean philosopher to attain revelation and proximity to God by means of spiritual freedom from physical bonds. This association of disdain for sexuality with demonic-satanic powers, however, is typically gnostic.

In the New Testament, however, we can see that New Testament congregations and authors were not always able unambiguously to ward off the unwholesome influence of such dualistic views, though we do not encounter in the New Testament the kind of ascetic rigorism found in the gnostic texts just cited. The Corinthians already appear to have held the opinion that it is not good to touch a woman (1 Cor. 7:1), probably meaning not only the ideal of remaining single— something supported by Paul as well, though for other reasons—but also abstinence from sexual intercourse by married partners (cf further IV 2 b). Rigorous "self-abasement and severity to the body" (Col. 2:23) is a formulation of

gnostically infiltrated heresy that also advocates other prescriptions for abstinence (2:16-21). However, even the
primitive Christian writers often did not withstand such ideas,
and the effects continue to manifest themselves to the present
in rigidness and ecclesiogenic neuroses. In any case, this is
generally not limited specifically to sexual abstinence (in 1 Cor.
9:25, for example, self-restraint in general is meant), and one
does not refer to the creation faith only as regards the ascetic
prohibition of marriage (1 Tim. 4:3f); one tries rather to defend
against all kinds of outgrowths of dualistic-ecratite tendencies
(cf, eg, Col. 2:22 and further IV 2 *b*).

Even if one judges the dangers of human sexuality to a
certain extent differently today, one should not be so quick and
glib toward the New Testament warnings with the objection of
banality or prudery. Neither should one overlook the fact that
precisely here the human being really is continually threatened. Considering the fundamental significance of love (cf V 2),
the decisive question will remain whether the human capacity
to love is threatened or disturbed, and whether sexual
partnership is in danger of being pushed aside by mere
impulsive reaction or by a degrading surrogate. At the same
time—and in a fashion different than we find in the New
Testament—one will today want to speak just as strongly about
the promises as about the dangers that result from the Christian
freedom from egocentricity, promises holding true when
Christians relate as women and men.

4. Woman and Man in the Surrounding Culture

We will present here the customary evaluation of woman
and man, whereas the more specific treatment of sexual
morality, marriage, being single, and so on, will appaear in the
various later sections (cf IV 1 and 3 *a*). One can say without
exaggeration that the general attitude of New Testament times,
aside from exceptions, was a universal declassification and
discrimination against women in favor of men.

a. Judaism[15]

As much as we need to consider the Old Testament inheritance, certain alterations do become clearly noticeable. To speak of Judaism *as such* is, to be sure, still an impermissable generalization. We are more concerned here with a few basic aspects and will not be making distinctions between, for example, Palestine and the Diaspora. On the one hand, Jewish Wisdom literature held to the line of the Old Testament: "Thou madest Adam and gavest him Eve his wife as a helper and support" (Tob. 8:5f); this, of course, is a clear reference to the Old Testament creation story. One immediately recognizes the differences as well. Adam's fall is no longer the cause of the disaster; Eve is rather made to be the guilty party responsible for human misfortune: "From a woman sin had its beginning, and because of her we all die" (Sir. 25:24; cf *Apoc. Mos.* 10). Considering this, it is no wonder that "the wickedness of a man is better than a woman who does good" (Sir. 42:14 LXX; cf also 25:19); this is hardly balanced out by the praise of the virtuous (house)wife (26:1ff and elsewhere). Women in general are considered to be bad, deceitful, and more given to the spirit of fornication than men (*T. Reub.* 5), so that one must protect one's senses from them (*T. Reub.* 6:1). It is precisely Hellenistic Judaism that offers us so many statements degrading to women. The statement of Josephus is typical, namely that woman is inferior to man "in every respect" and should thus obey him (*Ag. Ap.* 2.24). Philo, too, holds the opinion that women are sensual, selfish, thoughtless, jealous, and so on; masculinity is for him the symbol of what is reasonable and eternal, femininity the symbol for what is material and transitory.[16]

Rabbinic Judaism also shares the view that the woman is an inferior being with a greater inclination to sin (as an example from Apocalyptic cf 2 Enoch 30:17). To be sure, one also hears voices pointing in another direction—namely that all are equal before God (*Exod.* 14:15 *Rab.*)—but this view carries little weight in the face of the sheer quantity of statements about woman's inferiority. Women stood on the same level with slaves and children, and the pious Jew praised God each day that he did not make him a gentile, a woman, a rabbinically uneducated person (according to *t. Ber.* 7:18 and in the Jerusalem Talmud), or a slave (as in the Babylonian Talmud).[17] Here, too, women are considered to be more inclined to sin, and according to the midrash on Genesis 2:21, the mourning women go at the front of a funeral procession because they have caused the death. The same midrash attributes curiosity, talkativeness, jealousy, and similar traits to them. To Hillel is attributed the words: "Many women, much magic; many maids, much fornication" (*Abot* 2:7). Simon ben Yohai allegedly taught that even the most virtuous among women is a sorceress (*y. Qidd.* 4:66*b*). From the oldest known learned scholar, Jose b. Johanan comes the statement: "Do not converse with a woman" (*Abot* 1.5). This is supposed to counter any neglect of one's study of the Torah, but it is simultaneously quite characteristic for the low estimation of women. It is no accident that the midrash ascertains: "Never yet has God carried on a conversation with a woman, save with that pious one (Sarah), and even then only as a result of her transgression" (*Midr.* to *Gen.* 3:16).

No wonder the woman was both legally and publicly underprivileged, and that she was not taken as a full person. Her testimony in court was not considered fully valid (cf Josephus *Ant.* 4.219). Even Hellenistic Jews, such as Philo, declare that markets, council assemblies, court proceedings, and similar things that take place in public are not suitable for women (*On the Spec. Laws* III. 169). Their place is in the house, where they admittedly play an important role. Some question still exists concerning just how far domestic seclusion and isolation went in Palestine (cf, eg, 4 Macc. 18:7).

The woman was also clearly disadvantaged in religious and liturgical life, though this naturally does not constitute any judgment concerning her piety. According to Josephus, women had access in Herod's temple only to the gentile and women's antecourt (*Ant.* 15.418f). The space in synagogues was probably originally separated by barrier and railing; women later had their own gallery that could only be entered from outside. [18] No woman is included in the enumeration of persons necessary for a synagogue service. Nevertheless, in the Diaspora we find female "synagogue superiors," though this was perhaps only an honorary title. A low evaluation of women is even unmistakably present in the Law, standing at the center of the Jewish religion. A woman is not permitted to read the Law during the worship service. Her vows can be annulled by a man. She is not responsible for studying the Torah, though no agreement existed concerning whether daughters were also to be instructed in the Torah (*Soṭa* 3.4). We do indeed find individual women versed in the Law, and even scholarly women (cf *b. Pesaḥ.* 62*b*); on the other hand, the Jerusalem Talmud could even say: "Better that the Torah be given over to the flames than that it be given to women" (*y. Soṭa* 19*a*.8). She was released from daily recitation of the Shema as well as from many other commandments (cf *Ber.* 3.1).

Nonetheless, one always remembered the creation statements, namely that "man was not created without woman / nor woman without man nor either without the glory of the *shekinah*" (*Midr. Gen.* 1:26). One also recalled the great female figures both of the Old Testament and of one's own history, such as martyrs (cf 2 Macc. 7:21 and 4 Macc. 14:11ff). Above all, however, the unbroken high estimation of the woman as a wife and mother acted as a corrective to many of the degrading prejudices.

b. Hellenistic Culture[19]

Sketching an even moderately adequate outline for the Hellenistic sphere is even more complicated. In spite of the leveling effect inaugurated by Alexander the Great, many things cannot be reduced to a common denominator. We need to differentiate between Athens and Rome just as between urban and rural populations, upper and lower classes, theory and practice, or even reactionary and emancipatory attitudes. Even individual authors display ambiguous positions. A man such as Aristotle considers both sexes to be on the same level; but then he can also say that man is to woman as something better is to something less good, or as the master is to one who obeys (*Polit.* I:1254*b*; cf 1259*b*). Even Plutarch's statements concerning the roles of woman and man sound "sometimes reactionary, sometimes enlightened."[20] Neither do we really know to what extent statements by authors and philosophers can be generalized and understood as the reflex of real conditions. In any case, one can consider statements such as those of Socrates to be not untypical, namely that the feminine nature is in no way inferior to the male; it simply lacks the insight and energy (Xenophon *Symposium* 2). Neither did the hatred of women—often called sexism today—lead merely a literary life. In all of antiquity we find testimonies of misogyny reviling women as the greatest evil created by Zeus, as the curse of the world and the source of all ruin;[21] precisely the Hellenistic sphere, however, offers such testimonies to us in quantity. To that extent, then, we cannot simply relegate Menander's bitter and hateful words to the kind of exaggeration customary in comedies and satires (eg, "Many monsters populate the land and sea, but the greatest monster is woman," *Fragment* 488). This is apparently very much a case of common opinion. Women are considered to be "an immortal necessary evil" (*Stobaeus* IV.22.30).

Hellenistic culture no doubt also brought about a certain emancipation and enlightenment to the extent that personal relationships become more valuable and a liberalization of women's living conditions takes place; we find women gaining economic and legal independence in many respects, particularly in the upper classes. Being limited to the "house" is no doubt still the norm, but we do encounter women as artists, masters, philosophers, property owners, and merchants. They are considered legal persons in the sphere of financial and marriage law, and can now acquire inheritance, draw up a will, or file for divorce; indeed, they can even hold public offices. The general low estimation, however, remains unmistakable despite any humanizing tendencies. Women are considered to be talkative and cruel, ambitious and dominating (cf, eg, Tacitus *Annals* III.33.3). Ulpianus says: *dignitas est in sexu virili* (11.1). Daily utterances also confirm this picture, such as the letter of a certain Hilarion to his wife Alis: "If thou . . . art delivered, if it was a male child, let it (live); if it was female, cast it out."[22]

Because of their philosophical principle of equality, the Stoics judged women most positively. Musonius, for example, a contemporary of Paul, emphasizes the intellectual and ethical equality of woman and man as well as their equal capacity for education (9.1ff; 8.13; concerning a more thorough view of marriage, cf IV 1 *b*). Any influence on social reality, however, was limited, and even a man such as Seneca—despite all his positive statements and his good relationship with his wife—was nonetheless caught deep in the old prejudices. Concerning the ethical inferiority of women, for example, he says the woman is "a perpetually unreasonable being and—if a great deal of knowledge and training are not added—wild and immoderate in her desires" (*De Contin. Sap.* 14.1). Boys are excused by their age, women by their sex (*De Ira.* III 24.3). Man is born to rule, woman to obey (*De Contin. Sap.* 1.1; concerning a woman's silence, cf the references in III 2 *b*).

While women were excluded from certain religious activities and cults (eg, the Mithras cult), we find on the other hand special cults for women. Women play a special role as priestesses as well in the cults of Artemis, Dionysos, Isis, and Demeter, and only women had access to the holy of holies here. Men were also strictly excluded from the festival of the *Bona Dea*. Women appear to have been particularly open for the mystery religions, since here women as well as men were initiated and took part in cultic meals and processions. A popular ploy was to emphasize the female inclination for mysticism and ecstasy, astrology and mantic elements, fertility rites and the interpretation of oracles, and to disqualify them as "authors of superstition" (Strabo *Geog.* VII.3.4).

c. Critical Reception in the New Testament

It was just not the case that the New Testament called everyone to nonconformity and separation in the face of the views just outlined above; in spite of all differences and new evaluation, the ancient standards and behavioral models often enough acted as both conscious and unconscious godparents in the New Testament. We will see this confirmed in detail in the attitudes toward participation in worship and toward marriage, family, and other spheres. To be sure, the most decisive revaluation occurs in the anthropological and religious estimation of women, as we shall see particularly in the following chapters. In spite of all the influence of patriarchal-authoritarian social conditions and concepts of hierarchy, the New Testament basically overcomes the discrimination against women. Whenever this is not upheld, one remains below one's own higher standard.

Concerning 1 Corinthians 11, for example, we already suspected the influence of a certain Jewish exegetical tradition. Even the disrespectful designation of the woman as a "receptacle" (1 Thess. 4:4; 1 Pet. 3:7) has its analogies, for example, in rabbinic language.[23] Similarly, the tracing of sin back to Eve in 1 Timothy 2:14 (cf, on the other hand, Rom. 5:12) is prefigured in Sirach 25:2f (cf I 4 *a*). This does not mean that only negative statements have analogies in the surrounding culture; positive ideas to a certain extent also have a kind of prehistory in antiquity.

We can basically proceed on the assumption that whatever corresponds to convention—"as is fitting" (Col. 3:18)—is also a quantity respected by early Christianity. "Living so that you command the respect of outsiders" (1 Thess. 4:12) presupposes that even non-Christians are familiar with ethical claims, and that one also needs to investigate critically what is considered to be God's will in the relationship between the sexes.[24] The instruction to test everything and keep what is good (1 Thess. 5:21) also holds true here (cf Phil. 4:8 and elsewhere). This kind of testing anew is always necessary, and thus renders possible the historical changeability of norms.

On the whole, however, I think the differences are usually more easily recognizable than the agreements with the surrounding culture. When today perspectives that were once almost revolutionary have long become tradition, and—also conditioned by that—when the readiness to adapt to conventional models of thought and behavior dominates, this by no means exhausts the search for new possibilities for life. Coming to rest in whatever "one" does would cause the critical potential of the New Testament to recede into the background. Christians do not live in a ghetto, but neither do they live as conformists. This is not a matter of "the Christian alternative" or of an "alternative life-style" as such. The primitive Christian authors do indeed, however, display a dialectical attitude toward the norms and behavioral models of their surroundings. On the one hand, "what is fitting" is also declared valid "in the Lord" (Col. 3:18); on the other hand, we find a clear maintaining of distance from the standards and practices of the "heathens" in this area as well (1 Thess. 4:5).

II. Woman and Man as "New Creatures in Christ"

For the most part the New Testament takes seriously what the Old Testament creation faith had already prefigured in its own way. Despite various abridgments, one generally remains true to it. Just as woman and man come from God's hand together, so also is both salvation offered and God's love promised to them without distinction; just as equally, however, are they both claimed and placed into service. Since God is not a heavenly patriarch, but rather turns his love to everyone in Jesus Christ, women and men are equal members both of the people of God and of the one body of Christ. Just as every one of them was an "old self" (Rom. 6:6), who had to be "born anew" (John 3:3; 1 Pet. 1:3), so also can each person become a "new nature" (Col. 3:9f).

1. The Gospel Prehistories

a. The Genealogy in Matthew

The so-called genealogy of Jesus in Matthew 1[25] was originally to show that Joseph—and thus Jesus as well—came from the line of David; as such it makes sense only if Joseph is the physical father. In the decisive concluding section, however, the genealogical schema is interrupted, and Joseph is shown to be the husband of Mary—of whom Jesus is born (v 16). More important here is the fact that women appear in four places, although there is no clear opinion concerning their significance. In any case, precisely these names, coming from the Old Testament into the New, show that women also play an immense role in God's plan of salvation. A comparison with Old Testament genealogies shows initially that the Old Testament only sporadically mentions mothers or daughters (Gen. 25:4; 36:10ff), and usually does so for the sake of differentiating polygamous or successive marriages. Of course, everything depends on the male line in Matthew's genealogy of Jesus as well, a genealogy designed to document the providential orientation of salvation history toward the Messiah (cf the threefold fourteen generations) and to prove the Abraham and Davidic sonship (cf Matt. 1:1). The four women's names, however, are not used here to differentiate various men. Significantly, neither do they belong to the famous matriarchs of Israel's history, such as Sarah, Rebekah, Rachel, and Leah; their names are Tamar (v 3) and Rahab (v 5), Ruth (v 5) and Bathsheba ("the wife of Uriah," v 6).

Since all except Ruth appear to be suspected of some sort of moral blemish—or even of fornication—one surmises that Matthew wanted to show that not even the sinful and despised could hinder God's sovereign work of salvation. Such moral transgression, however, would sooner be an embarrassment for the women; it is clear this moral factor is not decisive because the attribute "the harlot" has been omitted from the context of Rahab's name, in contrast, for example, to James 2:25 and Hebrews 11:31. In those passages, Rahab is even praised for her actions concerning the Israelite spies in Jericho (Josh. 2:1ff). Things stand similarly with Tamar. In Genesis 38:26, Judah acknowledges her ("She is more righteous than I") despite the fact that she slept secretly with him, her father-in-law, after she was refused the levirate marriage by Onan following the death of her husband. Concerning Bathsheba, finally, only David is held responsible for the adultery.

Thus some other viewpoint must have been behind the addition of women to the genealogy of Jesus. In the Old Testament–Jewish tradition, as a matter of fact, they are all considered to be foreigners or proselytes. True, according to Jewish exegesis Tamar is supposed to have come from a priestly family; according to others, however, she was a proselyte. Rachel, too, is considered a proselyte. The Old Testament itself calls Ruth a Moabite (Ruth 1:4, 22), and Bathsheba is the wife of a Hittite (2 Sam. 11:3). Conclusion: Even if we cannot entirely exclude other factors, this inclusion of women in the genealogy of Jesus is apparently supposed to show above all that even in the Old Testament, God alluded to Jesus' universal significance for the gentile world.

This genealogy in Matthew is then followed by several stories in which Mary recedes far into the background, as is not the case in Luke. Joseph, on the other hand, is called "just" (Matt. 1:19) because of his behavior with his betrothed, and is addressed as the carrier of the promise ("son of David," 1:20). His obedience however, is emphasized most strongly (1:24), including in the stories of the persecution (2:13ff). There he plays a special role as God's tool during the child's rescue; following the angel's instructions, he leaves his home and moves to Egypt and later Nazareth.

b. Mary and Elizabeth

In the Lukan prehistory[26] we then encounter the first extensive stories about "New Testament" women. In chapter 1 we notice particularly the picture of the two women Elizabeth and Mary, though the mother of Jesus naturally stands in the foreground.

We should look first at the intentional parallelism between the two scenes with the announcements of the birth of the Baptist and of Jesus. Both stories have Gabriel being sent (v 11 and v 26), fear (v 12 and v 29), the "fear not!" (v 13 and v 30), and an angelic messenger (vv 15-17 and vv 31-33). The difference and heightened atmosphere during the announcement of Jesus' birth consists in the fact that the woman's role is much more strongly accented. John's birth is announced to Zechariah; Jesus', however, to Mary, whereby the mother (v 31) and not the father (v 13) is called to bestow the name. It is particularly unusual that Gabriel is not sent to a priest to announce Jesus' birth, and the encounter does not takes place in a temple; he is sent rather to an undistinguished girl in Galilee. Equally unusual is the angel's greeting, since women normally received no greeting whatever (*b. Qidd.* 70*a*). Mary does not ask for any further sign as does Zechariah (v 18), but rather obediently believes (vv 38 and 45).

True, Elizabeth's praise of Mary during the encounter of the two women is not directed to her as a woman, but rather as the mother of the Messiah—only as such is she "the favored one" (v 28) and "blessed among women" (v 42). We must also take note of Jesus' corrective to this praise of Mary in Luke 11:27f ("Blessed rather are those who hear the word of God and keep it!"; cf also Mark 3:31ff). Nonetheless, precisely Mary is the unequaled model of a hearing, believing Christian who does indeed keep the word (1:38, 45; 2:19, 51). Her figure is made even more

sympathetic and significant by the fact that the most beautiful
New Testament psalm is attributed to her as a prophetic psalmist,
the so-called Magnificat (Luke 1:46ff), in which she first praises
the God who "has regarded the low estate of his handmaiden";
she then praises God's great deeds, who "has exalted those of low
degree and filled the hungry with good things."

This admittedly has little to do with the Mariolatry of later
times;[27] neither can one find here even the beginnings of a
Mariology that would be independent of Christology. There
can, however, be no doubt that Luke betrays a strong interest in
this woman who in a special way experiences God's merciful
election. She personally recedes into the background in the
face of this filling grace, but that is not specific to this prehistory
and is certainly not based on the fact that she is a woman. This
merely corresponds to the New Testament estimation of
anthropology in general. It is loquacious testimony to the fact
that everything depends on grace; God calls everyone to
service regardless of whether that person is a man or woman.

Neither Mary nor any other woman or man is an
embodiment of the divine; neither can one recognize any
particular affinity in Mary for the mysterious or religious, an
affinity allegedly peculiar to the feminine gender. Obedience to
the divine word is a specific characteristic of neither the feminine
nor the male gender, but rather is emphasized in both
prehistories once in the case of a man (Matt. 1:24; 2:14), and once
in the case of a woman (Luke 1:38, 45). We read concerning
Elizabeth and Zechariah that "both were righteous before God"
(Luke 1:6), and both Anna and Simeon are supposed to have
recognized the Messiah in the child (2:29ff and 2:38).

2. Jesus' Salvation for Woman and Man[28]

a. Concern for Both

At the center of Jesus' proclamation stands the message of
the nearness of God's rule, who with the salvation power of his

goodness is seeking precisely the have-nots and the lost ones. This God who is coming to power and who is already a liberating presence in Jesus' words and works, is not the God of the pious and the moral, nor of those activists who are religiously proud of their good works—like the "long laborers" in the parable of Matthew 20:1ff who see their image of God collapse because of the vineyard owner's generosity. This God is rather the sympathizer and advocate of the fallen and despised. Jesus' salvation proclamation thus directs itself to everyone, but particularly to those who suffer or are despised, belittled or shunned. The special recipients of his message and activity are the tired and heavy laden (Matt. 11:28), the sick and possessed (Mark 1:32), the poor and weeping (Luke 6:20f). In a very consequential fashion this consciously makes no distinction between women and men; it is virtually self-evident from the beginning that women are addressed just as much as men. It is no accident that tax collectors and harlots are the premier examples of this decisive concern precisely for the lost and outsiders: "The tax collectors and the harlots go into the kingdom of God before you" (Matt. 21:31). The male and female representatives of these religiously and socially outlawed groups thus appear together here—shockingly—as those for whom the gates of the kingdom of God stand open. Tax collectors were despised because of their collaboration with the Romans and their, in part, rabid tax-collecting practices; the harlots were the horrendous example of amorality and lawlessness. Quite aside from this openness to society's rejected female peripheral groups, however, at that time it was anything but customary for Jesus so effortlessly and without *ressentiment* to address these in many respects declassed women at all, and not to overlook them entirely. According to John 4:27, even the disciples "marveled that he was talking with a woman." This fits very well with the kind of prejudice encountered, for example, in *Abot* 1.5.

The parable material is drawn with astonishing regularity from both the male and female world of life and work, showing us how little Jesus' thoughts and words were fixed on the male

sphere. Next to the parable of the supplicating friend (Matt.
7:7ff) stands that of the supplicating widow (Luke 18:1ff); next
to the parable of the lost sheep (Luke 15:3ff) that of the lost coin
(Luke 15:8ff); next to the parable of the mustard seed (Matt.
13:31f) that of the leaven (Matt. 13:33). As an Old Testament
example of reversal and willingness to hear, the men of
Nineveh stand next to the queen of the South (Matt. 12:41f; cf
also Luke 17:27f). Just as Zacchaeus is a "son of Abraham"
(Luke 19:9), so also is the woman with the stooped back a
"daughter of Abraham" (Luke 13:16); both experience salvation
through Jesus. Both the crippled man and the sinful woman are
forgiven their sins (Mark 2:5; Luke 7:48).

Salvation, however, is not limited to the verbal bestowal of
forgiveness, and it should certainly not be mistaken for mere
spiritual salvation or pure otherworldliness—as if the wretch-
edness of this world remained untouched. Jesus' community-
oriented activities, for example, show that his salvation work
concerns itself with the whole person. His healings especially
show this, since they put an end to the shortcomings and
injuries of the human physical condition and are signs and
implications of God's rule inaugurated by Christ (cf Matt. 12:28
par). Again, however, this concerns both women and men. The
many healings of both women (Mark 1:30f; 5:21ff; 7:24ff; Luke
13:10ff; and elsewhere) and men (Mark 1:23ff, 40ff; 2:1ff; 3:1ff;
and elsewhere) illustrate this.

The striking thing here is not the healing of women as such,
but rather the circumstances—such as touching (Mark 1:31;
Luke 13:13) or letting oneself be touched by a hemorrhaging
woman (Mark 5:27; cf also Luke 7:38), which was certainly
despised. He breaks the sabbath commandment just as much
for the sake of a sick woman (Luke 13:10ff) as to heal a sick man
(Mark 3:1ff). Luke 10:38ff shows with equal impressiveness
how little Jesus was affected by traditional clichés and
conventions; there Jesus stops in at the house of Mary and
Martha and thus boldly transcends what is customary. Granting
as well as accepting the hospitality of two apparently unmarried
sisters contradicts custom. We see simultaneously that women

are also directed toward the hearing of the word—not to be mistaken for contemplation or quietism; Martha's domestic activity is by no means confirmed as typical female charisma. Just as shocking is the fact that Jesus often does not hold to the advice of Sirach 9:16 as regards his table company: "Let righteous men be your dinner companions." Jesus' actions here are, however, more than an affront to social convention and more than an act of solidarity with his fellow humans; the common meal is celebrated rather under the auspices of forgiveness and in the light of the inbreaking reign of God—as a kind of prefiguration of the eschatological meal of rejoicing: "This man receives sinners and eats with them" (Luke 15:2). Presumably this includes women as well as men, particularly because in the pericope of the "great sinner" Jesus is not only called "a glutton and a drunkard," but possibly also "a friend of tax collectors and [female] sinners" (Luke 7:34; cf v 37; the translation "male" sinners instead of "female" sinners" is also possible).[29] The unusual nature of Jesus' attitude is also reflected by the fact that he apparently had to ward off typical utterances of androcentricity even among the disciples (cf Mark 10:13ff; Matt. 15:23; concerning John 4:27, cf III 3 *b*). We do not know why Jesus celebrated his last meal alone in a circle of men, as the Gospels report. Although the reports concerning the miracle of the loaves and fish was partially determined by the eucharist practice of the early church (cf Mark 6:41; 8:6), we can still point out that women were not excluded there. Mark 8:9 mentions simply four thousand meal participants; Mark 6:44, however, mentions only five thousand men present at the miraculous feeding (Matt. 14:21 adds: "besides women and children"). Perhaps this has something to do with the presentation of miraculous increase oriented toward the Old Testament people of the covenant and its organization (cf vv 39f and also 2 Kings 4:43).

b. Faith and Following

All kinds of observations support the fact that Jesus' message elicited faith not only in men, but in women as well, who could serve just as adequately as men as models of faith. On the one hand, in Matthew 15:28 Jesus says to the Canaanite woman: "O woman, great is your faith! Be it done for you as you desire" (cf also Mark 5:34); on the other hand, the centurion of Capernaum hears from Jesus: "Not even in Israel have I found such faith" (Matt. 8:10; cf Luke 17:19). While the confession to Christ in Matthew comes from the mouth of Peter (Matt. 16:16), in the fourth Gospel it is Martha who confesses Jesus as Christ (John 11:27). In addition, the way a woman conducts her life can be just as exemplary as the way a man conducts his (cf on the one hand Mark 12:42ff, and on the other Luke 10:25ff).

Mark 14:3ff is apparently also a reflex of this fact; the post-Easter community—that in the meantime has entered upon world mission—has Jesus say the following concerning an unknown woman's act of love, an anointing: "Wherever the gospel is preached in the whole world, what she has done will be told in memory of her." Wherever Jesus is presented in the Gospel, this woman's deed will also be reported because her act is "in a way an excerpt from the Gospel,"[30] a statement seeking its own kind.

Luke 7:36ff reports another anointing of Jesus by a woman, though the traditional-historical relationship to Mark 14:3ff can here remain open. Jesus' forgiveness, as originally in the parable of verses 41f, is both the realizational and the practical reason behind the woman's act of love (Luke obscured this in v 47). That very forgiveness, however, is striking enough, since it is directed toward an apparently well-known "[female] sinner." This woman's reaction, however, is just as loquacious a testimony as the fact that Jesus allowed the act to take place. The woman was forgiven "many sins" and tries to thank Jesus by means of an excessive show of love going far beyond what is usual.

The appearance of women in Jesus' immediate proximity shows particularly well how courageous and unconcerned, but simultaneously alienating and—in the eyes of a rabbi—impossible Jesus' behavior toward women was. Whereas the Jewish groups of his time are to be viewed as elitist conventicles displaying both a particularistic and an androcentric spirit, the lay movement initiated by Jesus is characterized by extreme openness and integrational tendencies void of any hierarchical gradations; but for a few exceptions (cf *a*), it is without sexist prejudices. It is no accident, then, that Luke 8:1-3 also mentions "some women" in Jesus' company:

> And the twelve were with him, and also some women who had been healed of evil spirits and infirmities: Mary, called Magdalene, from whom seven demons had gone out, and Joanna, the wife of Chuza, Herod's steward, and Susanna, and many others, who provided for them out of their means. (Luke 8:1ff)

The Lukan stylization and generalizations are unmistakable, but it is quite possible that women could be found in Jesus' immediate circle and that they offered him continuing support (cf Mark 15:40f). Indeed, verses 1f, speaking about Jesus' proclamation in the company of the twelve and the women, might very well prompt us to ask whether these women functioned only as financial contributors and silent supporters, or whether—as the tight grammatical link with the disciples involved in Jesus' mission certainly suggests—they did not also participate in the realization of this mission.[31] Mark 15:41 also mentions women who "followed and ministered" to Jesus in Galilee; "following" implies mission and service (cf, eg, Luke 9:60). Women, however, also actively participate in this service (cf further III).

c. Necessary Separations

Admittedly, Jesus apparently did not require all his "followers" to leave their homes, vocations, and families; he probably did, however, require the willingness to endure risk and suffering (cf Mark 8:34), to be bound to his cause, and to enter permanent "service" (Mark 15:41). Following Jesus in this way also included painful separations for both woman and man equally; this fact was suppressed just as little (Mark 10:29) as was the judgment upon those for whom a secure existence was more important (Luke 17:33ff). Although we will speak later about the eschatological relativization of marriage (cf IV 4), the predictable conflict is not limited to the partnership of marriage alone. The Lukan text according to Marcion (Luke 23:2) accuses Jesus himself of "causing women and children to separate," and it is no doubt true that such alienations and conflicts occurred again and again. Recalling Micah 7:6 one can then say: "They will be divided, father against son and son against father, mother against daughter and daughter against her mother, mother-in-law against her daughter-in-law and daughter-in-law against her mother-in-law" (Luke 12:53; cf Matt. 10:35f).

Nothing suggests that Jesus actually wanted the dissolution of old ties and that only considerations for rural ownership and work conditions prevented him. It is not a matter of a fundamental rejection of marital and familial bonds, but rather of a relativization and of the consequences generated by possible conflicts.[32] This changes nothing, however, in the positive estimation of both women and marriage. In addition, a renunciation of one's fellow human beings does not stand at the center, but rather of oneself (Luke 14:26).

The fissure runs, however, right through the middle of the family and involves both male and female members. Quite the contrary of isolating a person, it rather places one into a new community (cf Mark 10:30 par); both men and women, however, risk being pulled away from traditional ties. Luke 14:26 even speaks ambiguously of "hate" within the context of following Jesus; as in the Old Testament, however, this is not meant as a passion or a feeling, but rather as neglect, as in Matthew 6:24. Matthew 10:37, however, also confirms: "He who loves father or mother . . . and he who loves son or daughter more than me is not worthy of me."

On the whole, the situation is quite clear. Jesus certainly did not preach social reform or feminism; indeed, he even paid homage to his own time (cf Matt. 18:25). However, the fact that God's grace and claim are inseparable brought about a thorough revaluation of customary values and in particular put an end to any low estimation of women. The statements concerning marriage and divorce will confirm this.

3. "One in Christ"

The primitive church basically adhered to this line of thought inaugurated by Jesus. The Gospel transmission itself indicates that one felt obligated by the Jesus tradition and wanted to remain in Jesus' footsteps. As Mark 14:3ff has already shown in an exemplary fashion, this did not prevent authors from adding their own colors to the picture, though this need not be specifically discussed here again. Wherever one believed that God gave his Son "for us *all*" (Rom. 8:32), the salvation message and the community it created could only become androcentric again at the cost of its own credibility.

a. The Beginnings

During the return of the apostles from the Mount of Olives after the ascension, we already read at the beginning of Acts[33]: "All these with one accord devoted themselves to prayer, together with the women and Mary the mother of Jesus, and with his brothers" (Acts 1:14). Whatever the significance of mentioning Jesus' family may be—not only James (1 Cor. 15:7), but Jesus' other brothers as well and their wives probably joined the Jesus movement as a result of the Easter message (cf 1 Cor. 9:5)—in any case, women were included in the community from the very beginning, and not only as spectators and ornaments. This mention of women in Acts 1:14 probably also served as a preparation for the Pentecost event, specifically for the assertion that at Pentecost women and men were equally seized by the Spirit; this is emphasized by a citation from Joel 3: "Yea, and on my menservants and my maidservants in those days I will pour out my Spirit" (Acts 2:18).

This inclusion from the very beginning of women in the fulfillment of the Old Testament promise remains the standard state of affairs later as well. This is shown with particular clarity by the fact that promises in which only men are mentioned are then altered, so that we now read in 2 Corinthians 6:18, for example: "and you shall be my sons *and daughters*" (cf on the other hand 2 Sam. 7:14). The rest of Acts also testifies to the election and calling of both women and men, and to their inclusion in the community from its earliest beginnings. "And more than ever believers were added to the Lord, multitudes both of men and women" (Acts 5:14). The house of Mary, mother of John Mark, appears to have been something like a center of primitive Christian community life (Acts 12:12). This already indicates that she participated and shared responsibility, something we will discuss more thoroughly in chapter 3.

Accordingly, both women and men together are affected by the initial persecutions (Acts 8:3; cf 9:2 and 22:4), just as we later hear repeated reports of the suffering and martyrdom of Christian women—whether they are carried off to prisons or brothels, to burnings at the stake or to the animal arena.[34] Those dispersed by these persecutions, however, only cause more women and men to believe and be baptized (cf Acts 8:12). In his own mission preaching, Paul finds acceptance by both women and men. Luke particularly mentions conversions of influential women and men (Acts 17:12) or of women alone (Acts 17:4; in Philippi they were even allegedly his only audience: Acts 16:13); Luke does not, however, suppress the fact that these noble ladies let themselves be persuaded to drive the missionaries out (Acts 13:50).

Among the women converted by the Pauline mission, Lydia is mentioned by name, the seller of purple goods. "The Lord opened her heart," and she is baptized along with her entire household and even prevails upon the missionaries to stay (Acts 16:14f). Those initially converted in a community often acquired a special reputation and were often active leaders (cf 1 Cor. 16:15). We cannot overlook the fact that the specific mention of men far outweighs that of women in Acts (only Acts 9:36, for example, mentions a "female disciple"). Neither, however, can we overlook the fact that from the very beginnings Christian communities counted both women and men among their members, and that they were never constituted as associations for women or men only. This is a serious statement to any ecclesiastical association or group, assembly or community that in principle is only open to one sex.

b. "Neither male nor female"

The Pauline letters are a particularly impressive testimony to the fact that women and men are equally "new creations in Christ" (2 Cor. 5:17) and that this comprehensive renewal also implies the equal worth of woman and man, indeed their equality "in Christ." Wherever "everything" is renewed, nothing remains as it was: "There is neither Jew nor Greek, there is neither slave nor free, there is neither male nor female; for you are all one in Christ Jesus" (Gal. 3:28). For Paul this is the consequence of baptism that includes everyone—without distinction—in Christ and in his body, into the worldwide church as the arrival of the new world (v 27). Since this body of Christ has many members with many different functions (1 Cor. 12:12ff), this "all are one" can hardly mean monotony and leveling of all differences. Sexually specific differences are not denied for the sake of some abstract ideology of equality.

The examples in Galatians 3:28 by no means all lie on the same level. One is born a Jew or Greek, but a salvation-historical dimension obtains above and beyond any national characteristics (cf Gal. 6:15). One is a slave or freeman because of a certain social order. The third example of interest here points, however, toward God's creation. The clear allusion to the creation story (actually one would have to translate "male and female"; cf Gen. 1:27) shows with incontrovertible clarity that one is "created" as woman or man.

Nonetheless, all these various differences—including those derived from creation itself—are overcome "in Christ"; one could just as well say: suspended in the double sense of the word. They are insignificant as conditions for salvation, as religious worth, and as barriers between human beings; they are, however, taken seriously as the locus of grace and commitment. Thus no formless leveling is intended here. One cannot limit the statement in Galatians 3:28—that normal categories and values lose their validity in Christ—only to the religious or spiritual sphere; and one cannot degenerate to the common assertion that woman and man are equal "before God," but otherwise nothing has changed and Galatians 3:28 only has soteriological significance. It is true that the normal classifications are not valid before God; this does, however, also affect things "in Christ," and that means in the community (cf Eph. 5:30). Being different no longer means discrimination and inferiority there. Not only are religious disadvantages eliminated—as witnessed in the common worship service—but social, societal, and sexual antagonism, fixations, and coerced roles are also broken.[35]

All this did not just remain an idea or plan. The cooperation of women in the Christian communities was a common occurrence and of great significance. On the other hand, the statements of the Jewish male cited above (I 4 a) show just how controvertible and repugnant the statement in Galatians 3:28 could be outside the community itself. All these previous distinctions and privileges could not, however, play a dominant role wherever people took seriously the assertion that God blesses woman and man equally, and that this grace manifests itself in various gifts; and wherever one not only proceeds on the assumption that all live in the salvation and ruling sphere of Christ, but also draws one's values from that sphere. Paul's statements in Galatians 3:28 are not based on the gnostic defamation of sexuality, nor on the myth of some androgynous prototype; and certainly not the stoic ideal of a homogeneous world citizen with inner independence. They issue rather from the knowledge of the beginnings of God's new world, occurring in Christ, a world already commencing in the community and totally restructuring both mutual estimation and relationships between human beings. Paul relates this "new creation" not primarily to the individual, but rather to the community; in

Galatians 3:28 he gets a "glimpse of anticipated eschatology under the conditions of the present world."[36]

c. "Joint heirs of the grace of life"

Various later authors did indeed regress behind Galatians 3:28; the Pastoral Epistles especially show an intense renewed interest in the traditional roles and conventions. This manifests itself in the resumption of typical behavioral models for housewives. The equal blessing of woman and man, however, is never again really doubted, for "God desires all men to be saved and to come to the knowledge of the truth" (1 Tim. 2:4). Men are not the only heirs to this life-giving grace, but must rather share that inheritance with women. Women, too, are "joint heirs of the grace of life" (1 Pet. 3:7). Though this is spoken specifically to husbands, it is no doubt meant as the prefiguration of life together for the sexes in general. The allusion to the "holy women" of the Old Testament admittedly intends to emphasize not only their hope, but their submissiveness as well; nonetheless, the reference to "joint heirs" is not to be understood as a kind of crumb of consolation tossed out to reconcile women in their disadvantaged social roles. It goes without saying that both women and men continue to participate collectively in the worship service and eucharist. Women are not thrown back to private piety or excluded from the congregation's community life. Furthermore, this "joint inheritance" acquires independent soteriological value and augmentation that cannot ever be limited or made retroactive by even the most irksome ecclesiastical restoration. In any case, we see nothing of this even in 1 Peter itself as regards the participation in community work (cf 1 Pet. 4:10f).

4. Sisterhood and Brotherhood

This new existence as creatures manifests itself in sisterhood and brotherhood. According to the New Testament, one is joined with others in sisterhood or brotherhood not as a result of inclination or nature, but rather as a result of being children of God. Because God has accepted humans as children and, as it were, adopted them, all are sisters and brothers as daughters and sons of the same Father. This legal conception of adoption not only serves to thwart any physical or material misunderstanding of being a child of God, but also shows that the relationship of the heavenly father to his children is one God enters in a legally binding fashion and secures with his free grace. Sisterhood and brotherhood established in this fashion is independent of family and age, origin and societal or social position, and binds all Christians one to another.

a. "Brothers and Sisters"

Jesus already understood his flock as a circle of "brothers and sisters"[37] (cf Mark 3:35) not only in the sense of being common children of God, such that both woman and man experience the same God as father and call upon him in prayer, but also in the sense of "brotherly" cooperation and a life of "brotherhood." Those who are "brothers and sisters" are precisely those who do God's will—for example, who practice love (cf besides Mark 3:35 also Matt. 5:45 and elsewhere). This at least partially extricates both woman and man from their familial roles; a different status is acquired, one oriented toward God's will and yet simultaneously related both to community and communication.

This address and designation of fellow Christians as brothers and sisters derive from the Old Testament–Jewish tradition that also understands brotherhood in a figurative sense (cf the Old Testament citations in Acts 3:22; 7:37; and elsewhere). It becomes really secured, however, in the primitive church. Jews are also addressed in this way (Acts 2:29; 3:17; and elsewhere), and in various passages "brother" can even mean simply fellow human. Such is the case when 1 Thessalonians 4:6 warns not to transgress against what belongs to one's brother, or when the parable in Matthew 25:40

originally intends "the least of my brethren" to refer to all those who suffer and need help. Usually, however, this refers to congregation members and fellow Christians and does not specifically imply men.

The figurative use of "sisters" is thus rare in the New Testament unless one is referring to specific individual women by name (cf Mark 3:35 par; 10:30 par; 1 Cor. 7:15; 9:5; James 2:15). This shows no doubt to what extent socially dominant groups can impose their value system even on language; one cannot say, however, that the community's "sisters" were excluded from the kind of sharing designated by the term brotherhood. When Matthew 23:8 says "you are all brethren," it is not defining the congregation from the perspective of the men. It rather rejects precisely any community structure oriented toward a male-centered rabbinate, and in its place it recognized a fundamental equality within the "brotherhood." What we observe in Hebrews 2:12f also holds true elsewhere: Christ himself speaks here of his "brethren" in the words of Psalm 22; within the parallelism of the Old Testament citation this is interpreted as "congregation" and then continued with "children" in verse 13.

b. Brotherly Love

The most outstanding characteristic of being a child of God and brethren is brotherly love (1 John 3:10; 5:2; and elsewhere). Here love knows no limitations, as shown by the commandment to love one's enemy. However, "brotherly affection,"[38] "love of one's brethren" (Rom. 12:10; 1 Pet. 22; 2:17), and "love for one another" (John 13:34; 15:17) are only possible among Christians. Indeed, love for one's brethren is not only characteristic, it is a commandment (1 John 3:14; 4:20; and elsewhere). One is not really interested in sharp distinctions (cf the transition in 2 Pet. 1:7), but does want to see brotherly solidarity and love actually practiced. "If a brother or sister is ill-clad and in lack of daily food, and one of you says to them, 'Go in peace, be warmed and filled,' without giving them the things needed for the body, what does it profit?" (James 2:15f). One should not dispense with brothers or sisters in need and suffering by means of kind words and wishes, but should rather give them real physical support (cf 1 John 3:17f). To be sure one normally does not speak about brothers and sisters specifically, as in Mark 3:35 or James 2:15, but rather either mentions brethren alone or makes no distinction at all. There can be no doubt, however, that in most cases where Christians are called brethren—and one does not mean physical brothers—that this does not mean the brother's maleness. Compare the passage cited from James 2:15 with 1 John 3:17: "But if any one has the world's goods and sees his brother in need, yet closes his heart against him, how does God's love abide in him?"

Matthew 5:22ff says that "every one who is angry with his brother" should "be reconciled to your brother." Matthew 7:3ff speaks about the "speck that is in your brother's eye," Matthew 18:15 about sin, and Matthew 18:21, 35 about subsequent forgiveness toward one's "brother." All these passages, however, simultaneously mean one's sister as well. This is probably also the case at least in part in other passages—for example, when Acts 11:29 speaks about the support of the brethren in Judea (cf Acts 13:39f, where in v 39 one speaks of "every one that believes"; 15:32, 36, 40; 18:18, 27; and elsewhere). When the "brethren" assemble in Lydia's house (16:40), women are no doubt present as well. This is less certain in other passages in Acts; indeed in some it is impossible (2:37; 6:3; 14:2; 23:1).

Often, however, this express designation of Christians as brothers is missing in precisely those passages that deal with the primitive Christian community from the eucharist and prayer all the way to collective ownership. We read simply that "all who believed were together and had all things in common," something that was the case all the way to the selling of property and houses (Acts 2:44). These sentences and phrases (cf also "one heart and soul," Acts 4:32) as well as the statement that to each is given according to need (4:35) are intended to include all Christians.

Paul especially makes no distinction whatever when

speaking about the solidarity of all Christians: "If one member [of the body of Christ] suffers, all suffer together; if one member is honored, all rejoice together" (1 Cor. 12:26). "Rejoice with those who rejoice, weep with those who weep" (Rom. 12:15). These and similar admonitions are directed quite naturally to both women and men together. Only in questions regarding marriage does he expressly differentiate between brother and sister—and yet then actually says corresponding things about them both (cf 1 Cor. 7:15).

The primitive Christian concern for widows[39] is a particularly impressive example of how community solidarity turns itself toward particularly disadvantaged groups of the opposite sex. Christian "brotherliness" is maintained here even though all public social concern is lacking.

Acts 6:1, a transmitted piece of tradition that Luke has admittedly severely altered, already presupposes the care of widowed women. These widows were perhaps particularly numerous among the "Hellenists," since many Diaspora Jews moved to Jerusalem when they came of age. The widows were then dependent upon congregational support, particularly if as Christians they were no longer to be supported by Jewish institutions for the poor. Neither did the congregation forget the disconsolate condition particularly of the childless widows without means, as 1 Timothy 5:3f confirms (cf also James 1:27). The conditions for their support by means of the congregation's limited resources was also determined by moral categories; the performance of ecclesiastical service was understandably a prerequisite for support by the congregation. The decisively important element here is not that someone was supported if she led a model life or if she were truly destitute, but rather that Christians were concerned at all about these women in so extensive a fashion and took steps to maintain their dignity (v 3).

c. *Other Elements*

Sisterly and brotherly concern is not just documented in helpful togetherness and *caritas*, but rather also includes a pleasant and cordial interaction in general. Because we will later speak about the "subordination" of women, we need to outline immediately the context of such admonition: "mutual subordination." "Be subject to one another" (Eph. 5:21). That is the admonition to all "classes," and is addressed equally to both women and men. "Outdo one another in showing honor" (Rom. 12:10). "Finally, all of you, have unity of spirit, sympathy, love of the brethren, a tender heart and a humble mind" (1 Pet. 3:8). These and similar admonitions are always directed to both sexes.

Another sign of the eschatological family of God is the apparently Christ-oriented custom of the "holy kiss"[40] (Rom. 16:16) or "kiss of love" as part of the primitive Christian worship service.

In the Old Testament the kiss is a gesture of greeting or reconciliation toward relatives (cf Gen. 29:11, 13; 33:4; 45:15; and elsewhere). In Greco-Roman antiquity one also kissed as a greeting or farewell, in reconciliation or play. Kisses are apparently documented only fairly late as expressions of erotic inclination. We also know of cultic kisses—of divine images or altars—as signs of religious reverence and as the medium for power transmission. The New Testament knows of these kisses as greeting and farewells and perhaps also as signs of reverence and reconciliation (cf Luke 7:38, 45; 15:20; Acts 20:37). It also, however, shows us the mutual kiss serving as the introduction to a common meal. This is probably a sign of bestowed and received forgiveness and symbolizes unity and community within the congregation joined in sisterly and brotherly concern. A Christian letter from the third century shows how strongly fear then suppressed even this sign again; according to the letter, kisses could be exchanged only between men.[41]

Some ideas, of course, would be a clear reversal of the New Testament, for example that men needed less penitence than women or were better qualified for salvation; or that women comprised only a peripheral group within the *familia dei* or were excluded from "brotherly" love. Indeed, if we recall that the New Testament writings came almost exclusively from men, this self-understood inclusion of women is even more significant. To be sure, the statements presented in chapter 2, oriented for the most part toward soteriology and ecclesiology, were not really strategies designed to overcome prejudice and disadvantage. They are rather the expression of common participation in salvation and in the community, participation including that kind of overcoming. The same is true of the equal commitment that is itself based on equal grace; this manifests itself in cooperation within the community and will be presented in the following chapter. The critical and creative forces at work for fundamental changes in the relationship between the sexes were at first more latently and indirectly effective—indeed, they were even partially dulled and suppressed in the New Testament. However, they have remained active until today.

III. Woman and Man as "Fellow Workers for God"

In part II we already saw that women stood beside men as followers of Jesus and were included in mission and service. Particularly during and after Easter, however, both women and men are equally called into service as "fellow workers of God" (1 Cor. 3:9).[42] At least in the early period there is thus no hierarchically-patriarchally structured church; we find rather a community of sisters and brothers based on free cooperation among members, with organizational forms of partnership and offices growing from the congregation itself. Cooperation with God also implies cooperation between women and men in the church ("my fellow workers in Christ Jesus," Rom. 16:3; or "these women . . . have labored side by side with me in the gospel," Phil. 4:3). Women were by no means limited to the family sphere inside the house or to their domestic activities;

they were visible rather in the public life and activity of the congregation. After all, it is not they who push to witness; rather the Spirit bestowing gifts on them draws them into service (1 Cor. 12:4ff).

1. The Testimony of the Resurrection

According to the Gospels, all the disciples without exception fled when Jesus was taken prisoner (Mark 14:50): we hear only of women beneath the cross (Mark 15:40; John 19:25ff). Both men and women, however, participate in the testimony of the resurrection. The burial scene (Mark 15:47) consciously constructs a bridge for women to Easter morning.

a. The Women and the Empty Tomb

If one compares the names of the women at the crucifixion (Mark 15:40ff) with those at the burial (Mark 15:47) and on Easter morning (Mark 16:1), discrepancies emerge. They can, however, probably be best explained in the following manner: 15:40f and 16:1 are traditions independent of each other, whereas 15:40f is a Markan combination (Mary as the mother of James and Joses).

This means that the women at the burial and at the empty tomb, particularly since their names do not coincide, already lay before Mark in his source.[43] If one draws the other Gospels into the comparison, one finds that only Mary Magdalene is mentioned in all four. Scholars have thus variously surmised that this is the original state of affairs, particularly since John 20:1 mentions only Mary Magdalene. We cannot assume with further ado, however, that a tradition only grows and adds new material, in this case new names (cf Malchus, John 18:10). We must also reckon with the possibility that at the end of a transmission process only the smallest common denominator remains, or even that names are deleted (cf the deletion of "the father of Alexander and Rufus" in Mark 15:21 from Matthew and Luke). John 20:2 ("*we* do not know") also appears to presuppose that even in the fourth Gospel, Mary Magdalene was not originally alone at the grave. In any case, John is elsewhere also inclined to emphasize individual people (cf Nicodemus or the so-called beloved disciple). We might then surmise that originally several women were mentioned in connection with the empty tomb and were called by name as witnesses.

The historical difficulties regarding the pericope of the empty tomb are well known: the senselessness of anointing the body because of its advanced putrefaction (cf John 11:39); the tension regarding the anointing in Mark 14:3ff that is not designated as provisional; or the question only occurring to the women later concerning how the stone could have moved away from the tomb.

The primitive church apparently had no difficulty with all this; indeed, this story of the empty tomb was its central kerygma (in Mark it is the only Easter story!). This is particularly the case for the angel's message, the center and zenith of the pericope (Mark 16:6). The women's variously interpreted silence is admittedly a problem (v 8). It could possibly be Mark's intention to allude to the fact that the Easter faith was based not solely on the testimony of the empty tomb, but rather also on the appearances and self-revelations of the Resurrected One; then, however, it is rather curious that Mark reports nothing of such appearances. On the other hand, the women's silence can hardly explain the late appearance of the tomb story in the primitive church. Neither can it prove that the disciples had nothing to do with the empty tomb and that we are dealing here with an independent Easter story. Mark is doubtless referring the silence primarily to verse 7, since both verse 7 as well as 8*b* come from his pen.[44]

Independent of the intention of Markan redaction, this pericope was originally to show that God said yes to the "crucified" one in the resurrection; the reference to the empty tomb was to illustrate and explain the Easter message. Verse 7 admittedly draws attention away from the empty tomb to the appearances of the resurrected Jesus; on the other hand, the empty tomb can help protect the Easter faith from spiritualizing him in a docetic-spiritualistic fashion, or from having Easter itself be a product only of the faith of the disciples.

One cannot, however, emphasize that it is women who through their testimony of the empty tomb warn of a dualism of body and soul and thus also of a lack of respect for death. On the other hand, the historical ambivalence of the empty tomb is certainly not given in the fact that women are its witnesses. What appears to the disciples to be empty and idle gossip, is in truth genuine Easter testimony; that is why Luke 24:11 specifically criticizes their "disbelief." The later tradition did indeed associate men with the empty tomb, but not in order to place dependable male figures at the side of the thoughtless women (not even Luke 24:22ff can be interpreted in this way),[45] but rather in order to concentrate the Easter events in Jerusalem and to bring the tomb and appearances closer together (cf Luke 24:12, 24; John 20:3ff).

b. Witnesses of the Appearances of the Resurrected Jesus

Whereas the original witnesses of the empty tomb were women, the original witnesses of the Easter appearances were men. Women appear just as infrequently in the long list of appearance witnesses in 1 Corinthians 15:3ff as they do in most of the Gospel accounts.[46]

First Corinthians 15 is doubtless of particular significance. Female names occur neither in the old tradition picked up by Paul (vv 3-5) nor in the additional list of witnesses who saw the resurrected Jesus (James, all the apostles, five hundred brethren, Paul). That older tradition considers the appearances to be the proof and confirmation of the awakening of the crucified Jesus, and names Peter and the twelve. One cannot, however, assume that women are not mentioned because they were, as a matter of fact, women and as such unsuitable as witnessses. There are admittedly a great many Jewish

statements concerning the inadequacy of women as witnesses,[47] but we can by no means assume the same kind of
attitude for the primitive church; Jesus himself put an end to
the declassification of women, and in Mark women even appear
as the only witnesses to the resurrection. One can thus not
interpret 1 Corinthians 15:4f as a formulation of legitimacy for
leadership claims, in which case women could not be
considered at all.

We still need to ask whether women might be meant
among the "five hundred brethren" (v 6) mentioned after
Cephas and the twelve (cf II 4 *a*). This hypothesis would gain in
probability if Paul also knew of female apostles, since for him
not all resurrection witnesses are apostles, but all apostles are
resurrection witnesses (cf v 7). We cannot exclude such female
apostles (cf *c*).

Because of the Gospel accounts in general, it is
incontestable that women were included in the appearance
stories—quite independent of any historical questions. Matthew, for example, presents an encounter between the women
and the resurrected Jesus following the discovery of the empty
tomb (Matt. 28:9f). Particularly concerning the fourth Gospel,
the question has repeatedly been raised concerning 20:1ff: is it
an old tradition of an appearance before the women or before
Mary Magdalene?

We cannot fail to recognize a certain competition between
the christophany reported here and the appearance of the angel
(cf the question in v 13 repeated in v 15). The tendency of
tradition, however, moves in the direction of a replacement of
the angel encounter with an appearance of Christ at the tomb (cf
eg Epistula Apostolorum; one important Gospel manuscript
uses first person already in Mark 16:7: "*I* am going before you").
Thus the angel scene is probably the original one. The oldest
appearances probably took place in Galilee, and not at the tomb
(cf John 21 and Luke 5). In any case, many exegetes consider
Mary Magdalene to be the oldest witness to the resurrection,
and that the protophany came to her, and not to Peter (cf also
the later conclusion in Mark 16:9).[48]

No matter how things actually stand concerning the historical solution to the question of the initial appearances, the primitive Christian tradition did not have any fundamental or sexist objections to including women among the resurrection witnesses. And why should it? If we consider the structural characteristics of the appearance accounts, we cannot really offer any plausible answer to the question of why this process of identification, mission, and so on would have to be limited to male circles. Next to the tendency of adding men to the women in the role of tomb witnesses, we also encounter the reverse inclination, namely to have women appear with men as appearance witnesses. This no doubt documents the fusion of the tomb and appearance traditions; it also, however, documents the recognition that the certainty and testimony of the Easter event binds both women and men together.

c. The Apostolate

The unsurpassable function of the apostles is tied closely to the fundamental significance of Easter. Along with 1 Corinthians 14:34f, the strongest support for excluding women from ecclesiastical offices and functions has always been the fact that apparently no women belonged to the circle of apostles. However, even the names of the circle of twelve vary (cf Mark 3:16ff par), and this group did by no means comprise the significantly larger circle of apostles, as many have thought (cf 1 Cor. 15:5 with 15:7 and elsewhere). This alone shows how loosely fixed particularly the group of apostles was. The circle of twelve doubtless comprised only men, but we do have to reckon seriously with a female element within the apostolate itself.

Even the only mention of an apostle list for the time after Easter (in Luke's Acts 1:13) includes an addendum mentioning women in addition to the family of Jesus. We can certainly not conclude from the immediate sequence of verse 14 after verse 13 that Luke wanted to bring the women into objective proximity with the apostles (according to the specific Lukan conception in Acts 1:21f, not even Paul is an apostle). Despite this reservation, however, this betrays a recognition that women belonged to the inner core of the congregation from the very beginning. Luke does not, to be sure, ascribe any leadership functions to them, and certainly not the apostolic office itself.

Recently, however, many scholars are indeed questioning much more strongly than earlier whether things did not stand differently in the rest of the New Testament. There is good reason to believe that Paul is also mentioning a female apostle in Romans 16:7.[49] In a longer list of greetings we read: "Greet Andronicus and Junia[n], my kinsmen and my fellow prisoners; they are men [ones] of note among the apostles, and they were in Christ before me" (Nestle reading). This shows first of all that the apostles were not limited to the twelve. The more important question, however, is whether the second name is that of a woman. The oldest papyrus manuscript and several old versions read Julian instead of Junian (cf also v 15) and are doubtless thinking of a woman. Even the name Junian, found in most manuscripts, is probably not a shortened form of the male name Junianus, but comes rather from Junia and is probably a female name.

The male name Junias appears nowhere in all of antiquity, whereas the feminine Junia occurs quite frequently. Ancient exegetes such as Ambrosiaster and Jerome thus considered the two apostles in Romans 16:7 to be a married couple (cf 1 Cor. 9:5). Other exegetes, such as Origen, also considered it a feminine name, and Chrysostom even says in his homily on Romans: "How great must this woman's wisdom have been that she was found worthy of the title apostle."[50] Neither the context with its male and female names, nor the more precise characterization of the two apostles in verse 7 (cf above) can be used as counter evidence.

We must then seriously reckon with the possibility that this one female exception within the circle of apostles was not

the only one in the primitive church. In any case, Romans 16:6
also mentions a certain Mary, "who has worked hard among
you." The same is said in Romans 16:12 of Tryphaena,
Tryphosa, and Persis. Paul likes to use this same Greek
word—translated as "to work hard" and referring to physical,
intellectual, and spiritual effort—in reference to apostolic
activity (1 Cor. 4:12; 15:10; Phil. 2:16; and elsewhere).

Women were also active in mission (cf Phil. 4:3), and
indeed were apparently more consistent and effective than
men. An impressive example is the married missionary couple
Prisca (or Priscilla) and Aquila, whom we encounter in Rome,
Corinth, and Ephesus. In Romans 16:3 (similarly in Acts 18:18,
26, and 2 Tim. 4:19), the woman's name is mentioned
first—something that was not customary (cf, however, Acts 18:2
and 1 Cor. 16:19), probably because she displayed the greater
initiative and effectiveness. Paul is not the only one owing a
great deal of gratitude to this couple for its cooperation; the
entire body of churches does as well ("all the churches of the
Gentiles," Rom. 16:4). Clement of Alexandria (*Misc. Studies*
III.53) shows how important women remained within the
missions; referring to 1 Corinthians 9:5, he emphasizes that
through the wives of the apostles "the teachings of the Lord
could also come into the women's chambers without the danger
of defamation."[51] If women were resurrection witnesses and
missionaries, then there is no reason not to consider them to be
apostles as well—unless one shares Luke's narrow definition of
an apostle (Acts 1:21f).

Origen calls the women who witnessed the resurrection
"[female] apostles of apostles" (*apostolae apostolorum*), and
Hippolytus declares that Christ encountered women on Easter
morning "so that women also become Christ's apostles."[52] Mary
Magdalene is still considered an *apostola apostolorum* by the
later church with reference to Augustine (cf Bernard of
Clairvaux and Rabanus Maurus).[53] In view of the quickly
generated opposite tendency, we cannot be surprised that only
a few traces of this ecclesiastically significant female activity still
remain.

2. Spirit and Prophecy

a. *The Gift of Spirit and Prophecy*

The gift of the Spirit, in the sense of spirit-induced prophetic speech, is carried on already in the story of Pentecost with its specific statement that the Holy Spirit was poured out "upon all flesh" (Acts 2:17; cf also Joel 3:1). "And your sons and your daughters shall prophesy, and your young men shall see visions, and your old men shall dream dreams" (v 17). The parallel statement in the following verse reads similarly: "Yea, and on my menservants and my maidservants in those days I will pour out my Spirit; and they shall prophesy" (v 18).

The possessive pronoun "my" added to the Joel text in verse 18 (in the original text and the Septuagint this refers to male and female slaves) probably means that sexual differences are relativized here instead of social and societal limitations. In any case, the gift of the Spirit is no longer the privilege of individual charismatics and certainly not of any one sex; all now have spiritual and prophetic competence.

The effectiveness of the Spirit is no doubt not limited merely to prophetic speech (cf, eg, Mark 13:11). Nonetheless, Spirit and prophecy belong closely together in primitive Christianity, so that prophetic speech is inseparable from the gift of the spirit not only for Acts 2:17f. Prophetic statements are introduced, for example, with the phrase "thus says the Holy Spirit" (Acts 21:11; cf 11:28). Other passages also prove that the entire congregation in the early period was considered to possess the gift of prophecy (cf, eg, Matt. 5:12). Even the late first Letter of Peter calls the *entire* congregation "a royal priesthood" (2:9) that declares "the wonderful deeds" of God. His metaphorical use of this qualification itself presupposes a "general priesthood," since the suspension of cult and sacrifice now calls all to be "spiritual sacrifices" (2:5).

We are interested above all in the fact that women also function as prophetesses; the exalted Lord is thus present in a consoling and admonishing fashion through their speaking in his name.[54] In his prehistory, Luke mentions the prophetess Anna (Luke 2:36) in addition to the prophet John (1:76), showing how naturally he attributed charismatic-prophetic speech to women as well. According to Acts 21:9, the evangelist Philip, who belongs to the circle of Hellenists, has four daughters who speak prophetically. The proximity of verses 10f should not deceive us into concluding that the primary function of this prophecy was to predict future events, or that women were particularly suitable for visionary-ecstatic occurrences. According to 1 Corinthians 14, for example, prophetic speech has a much broader scope than mere clairvoyance; it can be compared *mutatis mutandis* with what one today calls proclamation and preaching, something that is supposed to effect consolation and guidance (cf 1 Cor. 14:3). In addition to comprehensibility, its particular characteristic is its concrete, relevant nature. It also, however, fulfills a catechetical-didactic function (1 Cor. 14:31).

Within the framework of the letter to Thyatira, Revelation 2:20 also mentions a prophetess who "teaches." She must have had a large following if she is mentioned specifically as the representative of the congregation in question. To be sure, we hear that this Jezebel calls herself a prophetess and beguiles the people with her teaching. It is not, however, her prophecy as such that is contested, nor her teaching as such (cf eg also Acts 18:26), but rather its content, or more concretely, its seductions to "practice immorality and eat food sacrificed to idols." We cannot say whether it was her influence that decades later prompted Thyatira to become the center of the prophetic movement of Montanism. Most primitive Christian prophetesses are in any case just as nameless as their male colleagues. Although the Revelation of John was composed at a relatively late date, it does reflect older traditions concerning congregational structure.

In any case, we have enough clear indications showing that particularly in the early church the prophetic activity of women was more natural and less problematic than it is today, even in the case of female pastors. Even if the prophets were a relatively closed circle of charismatics (1 Cor. 12:28f), women were not excluded, as Paul clearly confirms in 1 Corinthians 11:5.

b. Mulier taceat in ecclesia

The clear and—precisely in its reserve—loquacious testimony to the prophetic activity of women in 1 Corinthians 11:5 is not contradicted by the much-cited and misused verse from 1 Corinthians 14:34f that forbids women to open their mouths in churches:

> The women should keep silence in the churches. For they are not permitted to speak, but should be subordinate, as even the law says. If there is anything they desire to know, let them ask their husbands at home. For it is shameful for a woman to speak in church.

Whereas according to 1 Corinthians 11:5 woman participates in prophecy and publicly prays in the worship service, she is categorically ordered to be silent here. These two passages cannot come from the same author, and all the previous attempts to harmonize them come across as being more or less contrived. Even maintaining that the silent women represent the hearing church begs the question of why this would only hold true for women. We have persuasive arguments suggesting that this section, symptomatic of the church's regression, is a later interpolation that does not come from Paul.[55] Several elements suggest that this reactionary passage cannot be attributed to Paul. We encounter, above all, several un-Pauline statements: "as even the law says." This is not a Pauline formula for citation, and in any case such formulations are always followed by specific citations. There is also the tension within the context itself. The dominant idea of understanding and "edification" is not even mentioned. Finally, we have the contradiction to 1 Corinthians 11:5, as well as other elements.

If 1 Corinthians 14:34f were the apostle's opinion, he

could have made things much easier for himself in 1 Corinthians 11 with his contorted argumentation. Neither can one weaken the discrepancy with 11:5 by limiting 11:5 only to house assemblies and private circles, or 14:34 only to loud "interruptions" in public assemblies. On the other hand, we encounter numerous analogies documenting the pressure of convention and thus explaining the secondary addition of this prohibition to the Pauline text. Despite parallels from the environment of Sophocles ("Silence is the grace of woman," Ajax 292; cf Aristotle *Polit*. 1260*a*, 30) to Heliodor's novel in the third century after Christ "Silence suits a woman"), the actual place of origin of 1 Corinthians 14:34f can probably be found in the vicinity of the author of the Pastoral Letters. This author himself pays tribute to his environment and declares abruptly: "Let a woman learn in silence with all submissiveness. I permit no woman to teach or to have authority over men; she is to keep silent" (1 Tim. 2:11f). Again we find a teaching prohibition linked with subordination.[56] But to what does this prohibition refer? Within the present context it no doubt refers to the worship service; this in turn shows that general rules for Christian worship were known at an early period. The spirit that according to Paul seizes both women and men equally and should be given free reign (1 Thess. 5:19) is here told to keep silent; women's public speech does not conform to custom (the same is true in the synagogue). Convention has pushed charisma aside here. The unwholesome alienation of the church by bourgeois-patriarchal models and familial-ideological structures of authority achieves its victory here, and it will dominate the life, worship, and practice of the church for centuries to come. The disaster is compounded by the fact that it indirectly even involves Paul. It is time to return to the true origins. The fatal proof used for these rules that so suppress females in 1 Timothy 2:13f makes this even more urgent: "For Adam was formed first, then Eve; and Adam was not deceived, but the woman was deceived and became a transgressor." Its normative effect has crippled congregations and lasted long enough.

A tradition similar to that in 1 Timothy 2:14 can admittedly be found in 2 Corinthians 11:3. We read that the snake deceived Eve with its cunning, but according to Paul the congregation as a whole (!) as well as Eve is in danger of falling to temptation (cf, above all, Rom. 5:12ff).

3. Other Cooperative Activity

a. Charismatic Participation

The fact that all congregation members possess the gift of the Spirit implies they all have charismatic qualification. Even the New Testament itself, however, takes a milder position later on. For Paul, however, there is no doubt that the body of Christ is an organism in which all the body members are fully integrated; his understanding thus naturally includes both women and men (1 Cor. 12:12ff; Rom. 12:3ff). The complementary relationship between woman and man is thus only one form of the cooperation between all members. In any case, woman and man can participate only collectively in the "edification" of the congregation, since despite any plurality and particularity the various functions do not stand unrelated to each other. Paul does indeed guard against leveling and uniformity within the congregation; just as strong, however, is his emphasis on the participation of *everyone*. This directs itself above all against the absolutization of individual charisma such as glossolalia. Each person brings a unique gift into the congregation. Romans 16:7 and 1 Corinthians 11:5 have already shown that even as regards the apostles, prophets, and teachers one should not think only of men. The same holds true for the other charisma, such as wisdom, healing, glossolalia, and so on. During worship assemblies, "each one has a hymn, a lesson, a revelation," or something similar (1 Cor. 14:26). Why should women have been excluded from this? The transition from a catalogue of charisma to one of "virtues" in Romans 12 also shows that even in daily interaction no limits were imposed on the effectiveness of grace.[57] One can meaningfully say that every person really does receive a charisma only if both women and men—without exception—participate in that charismatic richness and breadth. Even marriage or remaining single can become charisma. "For instance, the conditions of being male or female, of being sexually committed or virgin, or being involved in family life and social relationships" are as such admittedly not charismatic; they can become charismatic, however, if they "are overshadowed by the 'only in the Lord' of 1 Corinthians 7:39."[58]

1 Corinthians 12:22ff is also of particular interest because in it Paul specifically takes up the cause of the weaker members of the body of Christ who are not considered as respectable. He thus reverses the "natural" principles of order. Precisely those who are considered pneumatically less gifted or even unspiritual in a congregation, are extremely necessary. He reminds hyperspirituality and ascetic rigorism that the digestive system and genitals also belong to the body; without the metaphor: precisely the inconspicuous and prosaic services to a congregation are necessary and indeed indispensable. "Divisions" arise where there is no delegation of services that are taken seriously as services in the day-to-day life of the world.

Unfortunately, the author of the Pastoral Letters failed to remain true to his teacher Paul here as well. Again the official and institutional element dominates. The charismatic and dynamic element atrophies whenever everything depends on a regulated, solid official structure and ecclesiastical order, whenever the congregation itself thus becomes the mere object of bureaucratic efforts. We no longer encounter charisma within the context of baptism, but rather within the context of ordination and initiation into office (1 Tim. 4:14; 2 Tim. 1:6). We hear just as little of congregational activities as we do specifically of the co-responsibility and co-participation of women. The woman is specifically pushed back into her role as housewife and mother. A final trace of female co-participation can still be recognized in the care of widows, an activity that includes prayer and perhaps some sort of pastoral or charitable house visits as well (1 Tim. 5:5, 9 and also Titus 2:3f). In any case, women at most still retain here an ecclesiastical task involved with other women.

It is certainly to the credit of the Pastoral Letters that they remained sober in the face of gnostic speculation and asceticism (cf 1 Tim. 4:4f and elsewhere). It is another question, however, whether these threats could only be banned by means of a pragmatic stabilization of the hierarchical and institutional elements. At any rate, even Justin still knows that one can find both women and men in the Christian congregation "who have received charisma from the Spirit of God" (*Dialogue* 88).

b. Witness and Service

Witness and service are the fundamental characteristics of church activity, whereby witness can also be a deed and service a word. Women and men participate in them both, though with varying degrees of frequency (concerning the apostolic and prophetic witness, that we cannot repeat here, cf III 1 and 2). Within the context of witness and testimony[59] we normally—but not exclusively—hear about men. The "cloud of [Old Testament] witnesses" (Heb. 12:1), for example, cannot according to Hebrews 11:35 refer only to men. Neither can we except women from various other general statements. When the Johannine Jesus comes together with his followers and says, "We speak of what we know, and bear witness to what we have seen" (John 3:11), one cannot limit the subject of this witnessing to the disciples (cf also 1 John 4:14 and elsewhere). This is made all the more probable when John 4:39 says specifically that many of the Samaritans "believed in him because of the woman's testimony."

They then admittedly limit the woman's testimony to a mediating function transcended by Jesus' own testimony; that is why they say to the woman: "It is no longer because of your words that we believe, for we have heard for ourselves, and we know that this is indeed the Savior of the world" (John 4:42).

This means to say, however, that one cannot believe only on the word and authority of others; it is by no means a rejection in principle of the testimony of women. The encounter with Jesus remains tied to human testimony (cf 17:20), and women are just as capable of this as men. The example of the woman at Jacob's well shows this clearly enough. She leaves everything where it is and tries to bring people to Jesus.

Women such as Euodia and Syntyche even "labor" with the apostle "in the gospel" (Phil. 4:2f). We admittedly do not know just what kind of support the women gave to Paul's gospel proclamation, but it is already significant as such that they are called "fellow laborers." The accounts in Acts show that they were also persecuted in these "labors" (cf II 3 a). According to Revelation 12:17, those "who keep the commandments of God and bear testimony to Jesus" are pursued by the satanic power (cf also v 11). The fact that both women and men are affected here is not really suggested by the image of the heavenly women that comes from extremely old mythical sources, but rather by the fact that this woman symbolizes the entire people of God of both the Old and New Covenant.

Danger not only threatens the witnesses of Jesus in the form of the "dragon" and its earthly-secular helpers (cf Rev. 13). A non-Christian husband can also bring fear to his wife if she lives as a Christian (1 Pet. 3:6). Here, however, we hear about the chance of winning the husbands "without a word by the behavior of their wives" (1 Pet. 3:1). This kind of nonverbal witness is certainly not associated every step of the way with the intention to convert. It can, however, reflect the genuine character of the gospel, and apparently it was often the only way to fulfill one's witnessing function. According to Matthew 5:16 and other passages, however, it was by no means reserved for women only.

Our findings concerning "service" and "serving"[60] do not stand so exclusively under male auspices. This seems natural. This idea of service, however, revolutionizes all human relationships and gives them a new form. It not only reverses the customary concepts of greatness and rank, but also severely questions the typically male prejudice that serving is something specifically female. Just as Jesus himself came not to be served, but to serve (Mark 10:45; Luke 22:27), so also should his followers take up his service (Mark 10:43; Luke 22:26) and follow him as servants (John 12:26). This is also true for women (cf Mark 1:31 par; Luke 8:3; 10:40). In Matthew 25:44, service is the common denominator of all activities of love: giving food, drink, shelter, clothing, visting the sick and imprisoned. Particularly in the Pauline Letters we hear a great deal about service *(diakonia)*. There are to be sure many and various services (1 Cor. 12:5), but there is no Christian position without such service.

In the early period we thus find no well-outlined office or title of deacon (cf, however, 1 Tim. 3:8ff), and *diakonia* cannot be limited to *caritas*. The apostolate, for example, counts as service (Acts 20:24; 2 Cor. 4:1; 6:3f; and elsewhere) as well as other kinds of "ministry of the word" (Acts 6:4). Thus "service" can stand in Romans 12:7, for example, between prophecy and teaching (cf also 1 Thess. 3:2). Philippians 1:1 is probably referring to administrative service, 1 Corinthians 16:15 to co-participation in the broad sense (cf v 16), and Romans 15:25f to charitable activity (cf Philem. 13 and Acts 11:29; 12:25).

We apparently cannot determine specifically the exact nature of Phoebe's diaconal activity; in Romans 16:1 she is called the "deaconess of the church at Cenchreae." It is nonetheless significant that the Greek word *diakonos*, translated as "deaconess," stands equally for male and female "deacons." Thus passages such as Philippians 1:1 can basically mean female as well as male "deacons." The later "deaconate" as the ideal of female participation in the church is in any case not yet intended here. We also need to notice that Phoebe ranks first among the twenty-seven males and females Romans 16 mentions by name; this alone points to her special significance.

Finally, we are able to draw certain conclusions from the context here. Romans 16 is a letter of introduction (cf 1 Cor. 16:3; 2 Cor. 3:1) of the kind travelers were given and addressed to friends and acquaintances. If Paul is urging the congregation to "receive Phoebe and help her in whatever she may require from you" (v 2), we may conclude that women were apparently also traveling in the service of the Christian cause and needed shelter and aid.

The same woman is then qualified in Romans 16:2 with a word whose meaning is not quite clear. It is often rendered as "patroness" or "aid." Does this suggest she stood in a position of leadership?[61] The verbal form of the same word in 1 Thessalonians 5:12 might be rendered "lead, preside," or similarly. Yet the same word in Romans 12:8 (between "contributes" and "does acts of mercy"!) suggests more the act of giving aid than of leading a congregation. In any case, 1 Corinthians 16:16 urges one "to be subject . . . to every fellow worker and laborer," and precisely this word "labor" is attributed to women in Romans 16:12. One would thus also be subject to them. A position of leadership, however, does not fit particularly well in Romans 16:2, since Paul refers to Phoebe there as his own "helper."

The Pauline congregations especially were probably not rigidly or bureaucratically organized and lacked well-outlined, departmental divisions. In that case we can likely also expect no sharp distinction between the services of the sexes. Thus particularly in the "house congregations," to whom women gave access to their houses for assembly purposes (cf Col. 4:15, but also Rom. 16:5; Philem. 2), women rendered services other than merely taking care of the "table" (Luke 10:40; John 12:12), something that in any case was also rendered by men (Acts 6:2f). Furthermore, *all* Christians belong to those who serve in social work such as care of the sick and poor, or in other works of love (cf Heb. 6:10; 1 Pet. 4:11; Matt. 25:31ff; and elsewhere).

4. Celibacy as an Opportunity for Special Service

The New Testament does not mention remaining single or celibate[62] from the perspective of coercion or a dualistic-ascetic rejection of marriage. Remaining single in the New Testament has just as little to do with the recently fashionable fear of commitment as with the marriage fatigue of late antiquity or the fulfillment of one's individual personality, long thought to be a Christian virtue. It stands rather under the auspices of the inbreaking reign of God and is a gift of grace for the purpose of particularly intensive commitment benefiting both the Lord and others.

We cannot help noticing the difference with Judaism, where marriage was a religious-moral obligation, and failing to be married by the time one was twenty years old constituted a transgression against a divine commandment.[63] Even for stoics such as Hierocles, marriage was given by nature and was a life form commanded to humans. According to the marriage laws of Augustus, intentional celibacy was even forbidden and was supposed to be prevented by censors (cf Cicero *Laws* III.3.7). We do encounter a few isolated instances in Judaism of those who were not married, such as Simeon b. Azzai (cf his statement: "My soul clings to the Torah; let the world be maintained by others"), or (probably) John the Baptist (concerning Qumran, cf IV 1 *a*). Nonetheless, celibacy and remaining single were doubtless provocative for the average Jew. Unmarried women were also despised, since allegedly only marriage and motherhood gave a woman's life meaning and fulfillment. A profound change takes place in primitive Christianity concerning all this.

a. Jesus

The separation of the disciples from their spouses and families (cf above II 2 *c*) already suggested a certain relativization of marriage. In the case of conflict, even the most close bonds were to be relinquished (Matt. 10:37f; Luke 14:26). Whoever turns down the invitation to the eschatological banquet with the excuse, "I have married a wife, and therefore I cannot come"—as in the parable of the great banquet (Luke 14:20)—loses salvation. Mark 12:25 goes beyond even this and suggests that the marriage partnership passes away with this world, "for when they rise from the dead, they neither marry nor are given in marriage, but are like angels in heaven." The actual sense of this statement is that the resurrection is not a prolongation of earthly relationships; this, however, does make marriage (including sexual differentiation, though not communication) into something preliminary and transient. Thus under given circumstances one can do without marriage even here:

> For there are eunuchs who have been so from birth, and there are eunuchs who have been made eunuchs by men, and there are eunuchs who have made themselves eunuchs for the sake of the kingdom of heaven. He who is able to receive this, let him receive it. (Matt. 19:12)[64]

The meaning of this passage has long been a controversial issue, particularly whether "being made a eunuch" is used figuratively or not. Most exegetes believe that verse 12c is not referring to self-castration as practiced, for example, by priests in some Asia Minor cults (eg, in the Cybele or Attis Cult), and later in isolated cases even in the church (eg, by Origen). Considering the prohibition of such self-mutilation in the Old Testament-Jewish tradition, and the exclusion of castrates from the cultic community (Deut. 23:2; cf, however, Isa. 56:3ff), this is probably figurative language about remaining unmarried and about sexual asceticism. At any rate, Matthew understood it this way (cf v 10). The concluding sentence in verse 12 suggests that this was not a binding rule, something also confirmed by the fact that even Peter was and remained married (cf Mark 1:30 par; 1 Cor. 9:5). What is important here is that marriage is not renounced on the basis of ascetic-dualistic, cultic, or meritorious motives, but rather for the sake of the kingdom of God (cf Matt. 13:44f). That can only mean that the renunciation of marriage frees one for the particular gifts and tasks given with the rule of God. The most impressive example of this freedom for an unlimited existence for God and others is Jesus' own unmarried existence, though we must frankly admit that his unmarried status is nowhere documented *expressis verbis*.[65]

In Luke 20:34-36, on the other hand, marriage appears *eo ipso* to be characteristic of "the sons of this age," whereas those who are found worthy of participation in the other age and the resurrection of the dead neither marry nor give themselves in marriage. It is more probable, however, that "sons of this age" refers to all humans, and remaining unmarried—just as in Mark 12:25—is reserved for the coming age. Absolute rejection of marriage would in any case remain a singular occurrence, and even the context (the question of resurrection!) points in another direction. Revelation 14:4, where the seer characterizes the redeemed as those "who have not defiled themselves with women," is probably meant figuratively in the sense of not participating in fornication (cf the understanding of "fornication" in the sense of degenerate behavior in 14:8; 17:2; and elsewhere), and not in the sense of an ascetic ideal. This seems even more likely because, according to chapters 13 and 14:3, the entire congregation must be meant. Some old versions, by the way, contain the singular ("with the woman"), and that doubtless refers to the great whore Babylon and the Roman empire. "Virgin" are those who cling to the "bride of Christ" despite persecution, who move toward the "marriage of the Lamb" (19:7), and "who follow the Lamb wherever he goes" (14:4).

b. Paul

This becomes similarly clear in the case of Paul. For him, too, celibacy is not a strict commandment for all Christians, but is rather a gift of grace not accessible to everyone (1 Cor. 7:7). It is certainly not based on any discrimination in principle against sexuality or marriage or on any motives concerned with moral perfection—1 Thessalonians 5:23 already shows that one cannot deduce from 1 Corinthians 7:34 that celibacy bestows some sort of greater "saintliness." It is based first rather on the eschatological expectation and is a symbol of the church's expectation of the returning Lord.[66] Particularly in 1 Corinthians 7:25ff Paul recommends celibacy because of the hardships of the end time in which he believes himself to be standing, a time that according to the apocalyptic understanding brings catastrophes and misery, suffering and pain in unimaginable measure.

> I think that in view of the present (or impending) distress it is well for a person to remain as he is. Are you bound to a wife? Do not seek to be free. Are you free from a wife? Do not seek marriage. But if you marry, you do not sin. . . . Yet those who marry will have worldly troubles, and I would spare you that. (vv 26-28)[67]

Paul thus does not argue on the basis of timeless dogmatic or ethical considerations. What moves him to advise against marriage is his concern for the congregation in what he considers to be the brief period before the Parousia. The distress Paul wishes to spare the congregation is the extreme affliction of the end period that can only be compounded for married people if women and children are also drawn into the suffering. The repetition in verse 32 shows how important this motif is: "I want you to be free from anxieties." The following discussion shows that this does not challenge the ideal of self-sufficiency.

The unmarried person, according to this view, can concentrate totally on the Lord, whereas the married person must also worry about pleasing the marriage partner and becomes "anxious about worldly affairs" (1 Cor. 7:32b-33). One's "interests are divided" between the Lord and the world (v 34). On the other hand, celibacy or an unmarried life gives one the opportunity for undivided and undistracted commitment to the Lord (cf v 35). On the one hand, this defends against any absolutization of sexuality and marriage, and on the other all weight is placed on an orientation toward the Lord and toward service. Whether cultural accomplishments result from a renunciation of desires or not, the primitive Christian renunciation of marriage is in any case supposed to support one's concentration on the cause of Jesus and thus also on service. Paul apparently did not notice that this kind of concentration can also come about through marriage (cf nonetheless 1 Cor. 9:5). In celibacy he saw rather above all the possibility of an "undistracted" existence for the Lord and thus viewed marriage with a certain apprehension, or even with prejudice. One should not, to be sure, understand this in the sense of a pneumatic egoism as the acquisition of time for the sake of leisure and reflection, meditation and prayer. Commitment to the Lord is rather at the same time the possibility for service to others. "Being anxious about the affairs of the Lord" (1 Cor. 7:34) can mean nothing but "serving Christ" (Rom. 14:18), a service determined by love for one's brethren (Rom. 14:15). As charisma (v 7), celibacy is at the same time always oriented toward service (cf 1 Cor. 12:4f). The example of Paul himself is again the best illustration for this.

Today we must emphasize this freedom for service in both directions: as regards the all-too-natural marriage for church workers in Protestantism, and as regards ecclesiastically regulated celibacy in Catholicism. Remaining unmarried can be beneficial to service and render one more flexible, more concentrated, and more intensely engaged. As such, however, it can only be affirmed in free, personal decision. The New Testament in any case does not recognize any absolute difference in value or any meritorious element in celibacy. Rather, every person should live and be of service according to one's own calling—and that includes both men and women.

The New Testament does not, on the other hand, thematically treat cases in which someone must unwillingly remain unmarried because of external circumstances or fate; that is another matter altogether. This kind of celibacy, like all else, is excepted neither from the eschatological relativization nor from the possibility of accepting one's given situation as the place of calling, of preserving, and of fulfilling one's life (cf 1 Cor. 7:17). In a Christian community, those living alone should be protected from the kind of communication deficit that might sell short their humanity; indeed, considering the peripheral social position in which we often encounter them, they should receive particular attention. The mocking or sympathetic scorning of the unmarried, however, is absolutely excluded here. A sentence such as that of R. Eleazar, to the effect that anyone without a wife is not a man (*b. Yebam.* 63c) is an utter impossibility for early Christianity. We are no longer standing in the New Testament tradition when we encounter the status of being unmarried as something second-rate or unrespectable.

If we summarize the results of chapter 3, we find that women as well as men bring their gifts and activities into the community. There can be just as little talk of male superiority based on revelation as (in chapter 1) on creation. The social roles and positions dictated by the average bourgeois morality of antiquity (or of modernity) cannot be the standards for determining similar positions and co-participation of women and men in the congregation of sisters and brothers. If, as is already the case in the New Testament, they nonetheless make themselves heard again and result in an almost exclusive accumulation of functions for male office holders—as is the case in the Pastoral Letters—we must protest this from the perspective of the central statements. Neither should ecumenical considerations lead us to deny these central New Testament statements and corresponding practices and subsequently fail to recognize women as public, authorized witnesses of Jesus Christ.

IV. Woman and Man as "One Flesh"

The special treatment of marriage at the end of the last chapter should not lead one to the false conclusion that Christian marriage is not affected by the promise and task of working as "God's co-workers." Tangible impulses and activities for the sake of others can also issue from a marriage between Christians (cf 1 Cor. 9:5; Rom. 16:3f). According to the New Testament, marriage as a relationship between two people is simultaneously the reality of creation, locus of *agape*, and a correspondence to Christ. To be sure, the views concerning marital partner relationships seem to emphasize more the creation elements such as "becoming one flesh," even though that is transcended again and again. On the other hand, elements that dominated throughout later centuries hardly come into view in the New Testament: eroticism, economic interests, children, care of the elderly, and so on. Indeed, we must not draw the false conclusion that the New Testament offers us something like a complete doctrine of marriage. This is particularly important for the understanding of Paul's concept of marriage; otherwise one will come up with all sorts of brilliant misjudgments, almost all of which are based more on what Paul does not say rather than on what he actually wrote. It is correct to say that, for Paul, marriage is the only adequate and legitimate locus of sexual partnership, though this does not mean that marriage is thus adequately defined.

1. Marriage in the Surrounding Cultures

a. Judaism

Here, again, we can only sketch in a basic outline.[68] Judaism has always held fast to the opinion that marriage is a divine arrangement (cf Tob. 8:6); indeed, marriage was an obligatory commandment for rabbis (cf also the documentation in III 4). Hellenistic Judaism also emphasized the natural necessity of marriage. Anyone without a wife lives without joy, without blessing, without that which is good (*b. Yebam.* 62*b*). A man without a wife or with a childless wife has been rejected by God (*b. Pesaḥ.* 113*b*). The significance of marriage resides above all in perpetuation; hence the equating of remaining unmarried with the spilling of blood. Thus also it is unethical to enter into a marriage with an infertile woman. Sexual intercourse especially was viewed alone from this perspective: Anyone having sexual intercourse with his wife not for the sake of having children was considered a libertine (Philo *On the Spec. Laws* I.113; cf Tob. 8:7; *T. Iss.* 2). On the other hand, another reason for marriage was precisely protection against such sin; thus early marriage was recommended. R. Hisda said: "The reason I am more superior [accomplish more] than my peers is that I married when I was sixteen; and if I had married at fourteen, I would have been able to say to Satan [during the temptation to become unchaste]: 'An arrow in your eyes [you have no power over me!]'" (*b. Qidd.* 29). Other times for marriage are also mentioned (cf *T. Levi* 11 and *T. Iss.* 3).

We encounter other statements that do not just consider marriage from the perspective of having children and protecting one against fornication. Proverbs 18:22 is often cited (cf also Sir. 36:24f, 40), and R. Akiba says he owes his study of the Torah to all his wife has done for him. In isolated cases the commandment to love one's neighbor is also used in reference to one's wife: "The scriptures say the following about him who loves his wife as himself and who honors her more than himself: 'You know that your time is peaceful'" (*b. Yeban,* 62*b*). We read that Tobit loved his wife very much and that his heart yearned deeply for her (Tob. 6:17). On the other hand, in a Roman grave inscription a husband merits his Jewish wife with *amor* and *meritum coniugii* (CIJ 476).

Other factors, however, dominate: "Women are acquired through money, deeds, and cohabitation" (*Qidd,* 1:1). Certain rabbis could even say: "A man is permitted to do anything he wants with his wife. Just as with the meat that comes from the butcher: If he wants to eat it with salt, he may; fried, he may; boiled, he may; simmered, he may."[69]

One symptom of a certain low estimation of women had always been polygamy or polygyny: "From our fathers we have the custom of having several wives simultaneously" (Josephus *Ant.* 17.14). This practice, although permitted by the Mishna, was probably not very widespread because of economic and "marital-climatic" reasons; in Qumran it encountered decisive resistence (cf *CD* 4.20ff).

Marriage and the renunciation of marriage in Qumran in

general pose a special problem.[70] According to some accounts all those belonging to this order practiced celibacy (Josephus *Ant.* 18.21); according to others, they supposedly married for the sake of having offspring (J.W. II.160f). In the Damascus document we find a comprehensive marriage halakah (cf also 1QSa 1:4, 9f). Ritual prerequisites are of particular importance; because of these, sexual intercourse was forbidden in Jerusalem on the Sabbath (*CD* 12.1). We cannot say with any certainty whether this kind of temporally determined, cultic continence was expanded by other members of the sect to be in effect all the time, possibly under the influence of a hyperbolic eschatology and the ideal of a permanent priesthood.

b. Hellenistic Culture

Here, too, Hellenism is two-faced; tendencies toward both individualization as well as emancipation become noticeable.[71] On the one hand, we hear about many very good marriages, particularly because the legal framework and conditions had improved. A wife, for example, was better protected by the marriage contract than previously and maintained property rights within the marriage (Gellius *Attic Nights* XVII. 6.6-10). The view of marriage of the philosophers is also for the most part exemplary and offers a deeper view of marriage. Plato himself revised his idea of the community of women and children in which marriage no longer existed (*Republic* 449d; 457c, d; *Laws* 740; 779d, e); his traditional distribution of roles and areas of responsibility has the wife take care of the home and be subordinate to her husband (*Menon* 71e). Marriage was based both on procreation and on social duty to the state, something quite welcome to the state in its pursuit of social-political goals (cf the laws of Augustus in support of marriage and remarriage, Suetonius Augustus 34 and Cassius Dio 56:1ff); now, however, the idea of community and partnership comes more to the forefront.

This is particularly the case in the deepening of the concept of marriage among the Stoics, especially in the writings of Musonius: "Shared life and shared procreation of children is the main thing in marriage. Both spouses should stand by one another so that they live and work in full partnership, consider everything to be common property, and nothing merely as one's own—not even one's own body" (67.6ff; cf already Antipater, who compares marriage with the mixing of wine with water, so that married partners share both souls and bodies). Many grave inscriptions show that marriage indeed elicited respect, sympathy, and inclination, and not only in theory: "Onesimus, who loved you, you loved in return as no other before you [loved your husband]." At the same time we still find the traditional models of the subordination of women (cf IV 3 *b*) and the hegemony of the husband (Plutarch, *Praec. Conjug*. 11; cf 48).

In addition to these high ideals, however, we encounter the darker side as well: sexual immorality, widespread prostitution and courtesan practice, and the demoralizing effect of slavery. We cannot, of course, take the picture given us by moralists and satirists to be the naked truth; just enough truth inheres in Juvenal's exaggerations, however, so that we cannot fail to see the decadence and double morality. "With sins in abundance our age has first sullied marriage, sex, and home" (Horace, *Odes* III. 6.17f). The oft-cited statement of the pseudo-Demosthenes speech against Neaira is symptomatic: "We have courtesans for fun, concubines for daily care of the body [a euphemism], and wives in order to have proper children and a loyal keeper of domestic affairs" (59.122). Even the position of the moral philosophers was inconsistent. The Stoics Chrysippus and Zeno allegedly affirmed "that every man could have relations with every woman" (*Laertius* VII.131). Next to all this we encounter the encratite tendencies with their recommendation of sexual asceticism (cf I 3 *e*) as well as an unmarried life for reasons of abandon and lust (cf Stobaeus), on the one hand, or a cynical-stoic understanding of freedom on the other, with the intention of establishing the independence and freedom from need of the wise person (Epictetus, *Diss*. III.22.69ff). On the whole, we can say that during the

Hellenistic period "extreme immorality alternated with moral strictness."[71a]

2. Marriage as a Total Commitment

a. God's Good Creation

Knowledge of the provisional nature of marriage (Mark 12:25) had neither a destructive nor hostile effect, but rather a liberating, loosening one; wherever one is affected by the word of Jesus, there one is through with any absolute claims by *eros* and *sexus*, and God's original creation will is respected. That will, however, points toward a total, personal partnership between woman and man in marriage. In the pericope concerning divorce we read: "For this reason a man shall leave his father and mother and be joined to his wife, and the two shall become one [flesh]" (Mark 10:7f).[72] The phrase at the beginning ("for this reason"), that in Genesis 2:24 refers to the creation of woman from man's rib, refers in Mark 10 to God's creation of humans as man and woman (v 6), and thus not to an original androgynous human condition. Both ("the human being"!) yearn so much for each other that they leave their father and mother. The relationship between woman and man is thus so fundamental that it even relativizes and ends the original and most immediate relationship.

This was not everywhere understood positively. In 3 Ezra 4:20ff, for example, the Old Testament citation from Genesis 2:24 is in the given context more a sign of the man's lust, who leaves everything where it is (home is mentioned in addition to father and mother) and lets himself be dominated by his wife.

In Mark 10, however, the new integration is more important than the disintegration: "one flesh." For this reason alone one should not understand "one flesh" in opposition to "one heart and soul." "One flesh" includes all aspects of partnership and is by no means intended in a limiting or especially a negative fashion. Not something in humans, but rather they themselves—"the two"—become "one flesh," and not just partially, but rather totally. Even in Genesis 2:24 one points perhaps above and beyond sexual partnership toward the wholeness and totality of marital partnership. In Matthew (and even in some versions of the Markan text) this has been intensified by the phrase "and he shall be joined to his wife" (similarly Eph. 5:31). This does, of course, make the husband the only subject of the sentence again, but the word "join" simultaneously suggests the full personal partnership between the two spouses. The same word is also used in the Septuagint for the relationship to God (cf Deut. 10:20 and 2 Kings 18:6; in Tob. 6:17 the same word is also used to refer to the joining of the man's "soul" to the woman). Marriage is thus a personal commitment and total life partnership with the inclusion of the physical-sexual sphere. Whatever else may be the source of monogamy, for primitive Christianity at least it was neither economic reasons, the male desire for power, nor fear of sexual licentiousness. It was rather the understanding of marriage as a physical-spiritual unity joining the two marriage partners into a whole, a unity that is more than the sum of two people.

Anticipating the prohibition of divorce, the first half of verse 9 also needs to be referred here: "What therefore God has joined together." Marriage is thus not a mere social convention, private agreement, economic partnership, or product of chance; God himself has his hand in it as creator. Other elements play a part as well; parents or the law are also made responsible for this "joining" of woman and man. However, neither the parents' will nor economic interests are mentioned here, but rather quite unsentimentally God's own activity. Here, too, all strands come together in God, and heaven and earth do not fall apart.

There is no agreement concerning whether this "joining together" refers only to the institution or to the concrete individual case as well. In Jewish texts God is quite naturally made responsible for the joining together of the individual couples, and this is considered as weighty an act as the parting of the Reed Sea. In Tobit 6:17, the angel tells Tobit concerning his wife: "She was destined for you from eternity" (cf also *T. Reub*. 4.1). Jose b. Halafta offers the following answer when asked what God had been doing since creation: "He joins couples together and decides: the daughter of N. belongs to N."[73]

This divine joining together should, however, be understood as a promise; it does not alter the fact that marriage belongs to the realm of the secular and transient and can thus involve disappointments and conflicts. Similarly, one must soberly and realistically consider all the human, all-too-human factors and aspects, accidents and "pressures" involved with putting a marriage together.

Paul gives particular attention here to the "burning," and unadorned, unflattering image for the consuming power of the libido. Paul is apparently familiar with certain experiences or even vital "pressures" that one would otherwise like to negate or thwart by means of an effort of the human will. Not only does he consider it better to marry than to burn in the fire of sexual desire (1 Cor. 7:9), he also presupposes a condition of sexual urgency and distress in engaged couples that pushes one toward the consummation of physical union in marriage. Anyone living in the kind of tension that threatens to rob one of power over one's own sexual impulses, should marry (1 Cor. 7:36f).

Nevertheless, marriage is not understood simply as a completely natural state or arrangement of creation. Even in Mark 10 we cannot isolate this reference to creation. The further context stands rather under the theme of following Jesus. This implies, however, that anyone who reckons with the advent of the kingdom of God and decides to follow Jesus, will also view marriage in this light. According to Paul, both marriage and remaining single can become God's charisma (cf footnote 58), and is thus a God-given possibility of service (1 Cor. 7:7). Paul certainly does not consider marriage as such to be a work of grace; neither, however, does he exclude the possibility that grace can also encompass marriage, and that the Holy Spirit itself can bring creation reality into service (cf 3).

Indeed, in the face of the Corinthians' apparent fear of losing their consecration in mixed marriages with non-Christian partners, he even reckons with the holy power of Christ and the contagious radiant power of the Christian spouse: "For the unbelieving husband is consecrated through his [Christian] wife, and the unbelieving wife through her husband" (1 Cor. 7:14). Marriages, too, can be a force field of the Holy Spirit, for God's power cannot be confined in the world to ghettos, but rather penetrates as a consecrating power into the secular realm of marriages as well. Countering the gnostic prohibition of marriage, 1 Timothy 4:3-5 later emphasizes that God's good creation—including marriage—ought to be accepted in thanksgiving and "consecrated by the word of God and prayer."

b. Physical Partnership

Paul's answer in 1 Corinthians 7:2 to a letter from those Corinthians who apparently supported sexual asceticism (cf v 1) contains an often misunderstood sentence: "But because of the temptation to immorality, each man should have his own wife and each woman her own husband." He says that marriage is neither merely a "necessary evil" nor a "security release valve," nor is it to be equated with institutionalized satisfaction of desire, nor is sexual intercourse the only meaning and purpose of marriage.[74] Precisely in view of those people who appear to lose sight of the reality of body and sexuality in their flights of asceticism, however, he remains sober and sensible enough not to overlook the inherent dangers—despite his own high estimation of celibacy. For him marriage is thus the only appropriate way to hold human sexuality in check. One should not, of course, overplay his use of "each man" and "each woman" in verse 2; it does show, however, that Paul basically considers marriage to be the normal state of affairs. The following verses then show how things stand with this marital partnership:

> The husband should give to his wife her conjugal rights, and likewise the wife to her husband. For the wife does not rule

over her own body, but the husband does; likewise the
husband does not rule over his own body, but the wife does.
Do not refuse one another. (1 Cor. 7:3-5) ·

Nothing here suggests that Paul wishes to define marital
partnership in an exhaustive fashion. In response to the
Corinthians' inquiry, he emphasizes rather that marital
partnership *eo ipso* also includes physical partnership. The
term "body" here, above and beyond the merely physical body,
also addresses the capacity for communication and totality,
confirming that sexual union involves not just a peripheral
function, but rather the entire person (cf also 1 Cor. 6:16). In
this, woman and man are equally directed and equally
obligated one to the other. It is no accident that, as the occasion
arises, Paul mentions both man and woman, and does not
merely address one or the other; indeed, he emphatically
tailors the entire chapter to reflect the mutuality within the
marital relationship[75] rather than the obligations and possibilities for the happiness of the individual.

Verse 5 also confirms this, where Paul speaks of the
conditions for withholding physical intercourse: "Do not refuse
one another except perhaps by agreement for a season, that you
may devote yourselves to prayer; but then come together again,
lest Satan tempt you through lack of self-control. I say this by
way of concession, not of command." This presupposes first that
wish and reality—one's own needs and those of the partner—do
not *eo ipso* agree, but that a permanent refusal contradicts the
essence of marriage just as much as does a lack of
communication. It presupposes above all that at certain times
one does renounce sexual intercourse; Paul does not command
this, but rather warns of exaggeration. However, sexual
intercourse by no means renders one cultically impure. Paul
separates himself here from the Old Testament Jewish tradition
and from certain ancient cults in which the execution of
religious practices (prayer, sacrifice, visiting the temple, and
similar ones) presupposes abstinence (cf Exod. 19:15; Lev.
15:18; 1 Sam. 21:5). In contrast to the precise instructions

concerning the frequency or limitations of sexual intercourse within Judaism, we hear nothing—characteristically—of such specifics here.

According to 1 Corinthians 7:5, this "refusing one another" ought initially to be temporally limited ("for a season"). Neither should it be one-sided, but rather mutually agreed upon and arranged. Again, the actual sense of this statement is a warning against hyperascetic exaggerations. Paul's "concession" here is thus not marriage itself or the consummation of marriage—although again and again it has been interpreted as such[76]—but rather the temporally limited separation.

He thus does not think much of the so-called "Joseph marriages" or mere spiritual marriages void of physical partnership (*syneis* acts), of the kind known to us from the ancient church and also presupposed in 1 Corinthians 7:36-38 by various exegetes.[77] Of course, we cannot exclude the possibility that the Corinthians indeed preferred such Platonic marriages and that Paul simply did not quite see through that. It is, however, completely unthinkable that Paul tolerated or even favored such sexless marriages. Paul is much too realistic about the dangers of being "aflame with passion" to accept this kind of spiritually cramped situation, or even to recommend renunciation of sexual intercourse as an ethical exercise designed to strengthen one's self-discipline. A marriage without total marital partnership is a marriage of appearance only.

Significantly, there is no talk here of any necessary orientation of the marital partnership toward the procreation of children and toward the perpetuation of the family, nor of any integration of marriage into a larger family structure. The New Testament neither cites Genesis 1:28 ("Be fruitful and multiply") nor disqualifies sexual intercourse that is not governed by the will to procreate children; this is not the case with many other ancient authors. Paul does not, of course, speak of any independent significance of what is sexual and erotic; neither, however, does he offer up sexual intercourse simply as a means to an end.

Let us briefly point out that not even the virgin birth—designed to underscore Jesus' unique significance—has ever been explained by reference to ascetic motives, nor is it supposed to denigrate sexual intercourse between marital partners.[78] Matthew 1:25, taken with 13:55f (cf Mark 6:3), clearly shows that after Jesus' birth Joseph had additional sons and daughters in marital intercourse with Mary, and that there can be no talk of any perpetual virginity *(semper virgo Maria)* in primitive Christianity.

c. Consecration and Provisional Value

This unlimited affirmation of human sexuality in marriage does not mean, of course, that one ought simply to live in an unrestrained fashion within marriage. Rather, things stand such that the divine will—oriented toward "consecration," toward being claimed for God—also holds true for marriage (1 Thess. 4:3). Thus "each one of you should know how to take a wife [vessel] for himself in holiness and honor, not in the passion of lust like heathen who do not know God" (1 Thess. 4:4f).[79] The somewhat demeaning reference to women ("vessel"; cf 1 Pet. 3:7) should not obscure the fact that the relationship between woman and man is tied in here with consecration.

Some exegetes consider this to be a more specific reference to the choice of partners and then marriage (cf Ruth 4:10; Sir. 36:24 LXX); that is, one ought not to enter into marriage in the intoxication of sensual desire. The word translated as "to take" or "to win for oneself" often even refers to a process within marriage itself, and can be expanded to include the way one conducts a marriage or to be understood as a veiled expression for sexual intercourse.

In any case, whether in marriage, the way one conducts the marriage, or in sexual intercourse, the Christian cannot abstract from existence as a Christian and leave the ground of consecration. This is not a criticism of vitality and eroticism, but rather of its tendency to become independent and absolute.

The marriage partner should not be a toy or object of lust, but should rather be shown dignity and honor (cf also Heb. 13:4). Wherever women are refused this honor, prayers are hindered (1 Pet. 3:7)—not because of domestic quarrels or marital disagreements, but because of spiritual ineffectiveness. Lack of love and consideration toward the marital partner also burdens one's relationship to God. In their marriages, too, Christians do not live without the one to whom they both pray (cf 1 Cor. 7:5).

This reminds us that an ultimate freedom is given in the marriage of Christians, not in the sense of a back door, but rather as the recognition of the preliminary or provisional value of all that is earthly. "Let those who have wives live as though they [already] had none [any longer]" (1 Cor. 7:29).[80] Just as celibacy, so also is marriage something preliminary and provisional; and, just as all other life processes in this world, it stands under the auspices of a final reserve. This does not imply stoic disaffectedness and indifference, nor asceticism (cf vv 2ff). Marriage does, however, belong to the provisional things of this world age and is to that extent not something definitive. Thus Christians will also remain critical and free as regards the institution of marriage.

Nonetheless, marriage can indeed be the locus of "peace" (1 Cor. 7:15), and can be lived "in the Lord" (1 Cor. 7:39; cf also IV 4 *d* above); indeed, it can be a beneficial service to others (1 Cor. 9:5). We hear of the married couple Aquila and Prisca (cf also III 1 *c* above) that they subjected themselves to extreme mortal danger and put their lives on the line for Paul (Rom. 16:4). And where is it really written that the admonitions for accepting each other mutually, for carrying the weakness of the other person, for renunciation and caring, for forgiveness and reconciliation (cf as an example the admonitions standing directly before the domestic instructions in Col. 3:12ff)—that all these things should not also be applied to marriage, and that one's neighbor cannot *also* refer to one's partner in marriage (though certainly not exclusively, something one must emphasize now as before despite common opinion)? Jesus' commandment to do good and to save life (cf Mark 3:4), or to forgive someone seventy times seven (Matt. 18:22) is naturally also valid in marriage.

3. Love and Submissiveness

Even in 1 Corinthians 7:3 we cannot exclude the possibility that Paul understands the "debt" within a sexual relationship in the light of that "debt" he mentions in Romans 13:8 and 15:1: in the light of love. Considering the fact that in marriage a person's own body is at the disposal of another person (1 Cor. 7:4f), we can then consider this to be a specific instance of the fact that the Christian in general no longer lives merely for personal interests or seeks merely personal goals (1 Cor. 13:5). To that extent both spouses are called to love. The superscription above the so-called household instructions in Ephesians 5:21 shows that this mutuality also applies to "submissiveness": "Be subject to one another." Both, however, are now specifically assigned to the two sexes.

a. The Meaning of the Household Instructions

Paul himself had admonished his readers to prove themselves where they encounter the Lord's call: in concrete reality (1 Cor. 7:17ff). His students tried to explicate this in more detail in the so-called household or domestic instructions (Col. 3:18ff; Eph. 5:21ff; cf also 1 Pet. 2:11ff).[81] The rule of Jesus Christ should also be realized in the "home," in the larger family of antiquity. Within the arrangements and structures of this world one is dealing not so much with the Creator as with the Lord Jesus Christ, hence the numerous references to this effect within the household instructions: "in the Lord" (Col. 3:18, 20; Eph. 6:1); "serving the Lord" (Col. 3:23; Eph. 5:22); "serving the Lord Christ" (Col. 3:24); "for the Lord's sake" (1 Pet. 2:13); and elsewhere. These are not just externally displayed gestures of etiquette; rather, in sexual and social relationships as well, "in word or deed, do *everything* in the name of the Lord Jesus" (Col. 3:17). The "home" is thus not first viewed as a place for individual development and personal security, but rather as the locus of collective "service to the Lord" (Col. 3:23), and thus also of charismatic opportunities (cf 2 *a*). Its mutual relationships are balanced not by domination and struggle, but rather by the various interrelated services and functions.

Marriage and home are run not by arbitrariness, but rather by the will of the Lord; neither should this be limited merely to the religious sector, but should rather apply to familial, societal, and social questions concerning marriage and home as well. We do indeed find parallels to the hoousehold instructions in the surrounding cultures (cf *b* above), but what "is fitting" (Col. 3:18) is not simply identical with the will of the Lord. Early Christianity rather chose critically from the behavioral models of antiquity and variously modified certain details. This is also true of the relationship between woman and man within the framework of the domestic instructions (cf also I 4 *c*).

The fact that especially the "home" appears as the locus of marriage does not presuppose some sort of unblemished world. It does show, however, that there was no allergy or hostility to institutions as such, and one did not think that a life outside the existing structures was more meaningful and Christian. It is correct that this also involved suffering (cf 1 Pet. 2:18ff), and the slaves no doubt felt the pain of the authoritarian structures of this "home" of antiquity often enough—Romans 16 contains several names of female slaves. Nonetheless, one should not understand the New Testament "home" and its familial structures merely as the locus of power relationships and determination by others, but rather as the opportunity for service and orientation toward Christ. Ephesians 5 shows this well[82]: "As the church is subject to Christ, so let wives also be subject in everything to their husbands. Husbands, love your wives, as Christ loved the church and gave himself up for her" (Eph. 5:24f). It is thus decisively important that the marital life of a Christian correspond to the relationship between Christ and the congregation. At the beginning of the paranaesis in Ephesians 5:1f we already read: "Therefore be imitators of God, as beloved children. And walk in love, as Christ loved us and gave himself up for us, a fragrant offering and sacrifice to God." What we find in the household instructions is thus only a particular instance of that more comprehensive *mimesis* and cannot be extracted from this context and made independent.

One does not understand certain social structures or marriage forms to be the reflections of eternal divine arrangements; to do so would be to exaggerate and legalize them religiously. Rather, existing arrangements are limited and given a new orientation in that conformity to Christ takes the place of the cosmic structures representing God; this conformity then penetrates into personal relationships. We cannot fail to see that the relationship between Christ and the church only offers a limited field of application for this analogy, since Christ as "savior of the body" (5:23) with good reason is not used in reference to the male—in contrast to his being the "head." The basic tendency, however, is clear enough: love and service corresponding to Christ. Marriage is not taken to be an ontological metaphor for the relationship Christ-church; rather, this relationship Christ-church offers rules of behavior for the marital partners. In verses 31f this relationship of analogy is, to be sure, reversed, and marriage is considered as analogous to the relationship between Christ and the church ("this is a great mystery" refers either to the hidden meaning in the Old Testament citation, Gen. 2:24, or to the relationship itself between Christ and church[83]); verse 33, however, quickly reestablishes the decisive point of view. The marriage between Christians should be lived as a reflection of and in correspondence to that primal model. That is its real "mystery."

b. "Submissiveness"

Although the superscription of the domestic instructions in the letter to the Ephesians is an admonition to mutual submissiveness (Eph. 5:21; cf also 1 Pet. 5:5), submissiveness is then specifically required of wives at the beginning (Col. 3:18; Eph. 5:22; 1 Pet. 3:1).[84]

Whether this historically really does correspond to convention or not, the authors of the household instructions did in any case hold this opinion; a statement of Pseudo Callisthenes confirms them: "It is fitting for a woman to subordinate herself to her husband." Plutarch, too, writes in his marriage rules: "Women are to be praised if they subordinate themselves to their husbands" (*Praec. conj.* 33). Others—including Jewish authors—speak of service, servitude, and obedience (eg Philo, *Hyp.* VII.3). The First Letter of Peter presents praiseworthy examples of such submissiveness among "the holy women" of Israel, such as Sarah, who obeyed Abraham and called him "lord." Since this was the usual Oriental custom (Gen. 18:12), it actually says very little; it does, however, show that the author of the Letter believed himself to be standing in a long tradition. The First Letter of Peter also shows, however, that despite this reflex of ancient social and societal structures with their institutionalized predominance of the male, submissiveness should not be confused with docile servility and subservience; neither does it say that a wife ought to follow her husband blindly. The women addressed should not, as a matter of fact, let themselves be terrified by their husbands (3:6). Since this also addresses women living with non-Christian marital partners—partners needing to be "won" (3:1), this required submissiveness does have its limits. Whereas Plutarch, for example, explains in his own marriage rules that the woman is to worship and know only those gods in whom her husband believes (19), according to the Christian household instructions the husband by no means determines his wife's confession. There is no Griseldi-ideal[85] or anything similar here.

First Corinthians 15:28 further illuminates how little this submissiveness—despite the unmistakable patriarchal context—means degrading servility: The same word is used to refer to Christ's relationship to God (cf also 1 Cor. 14:32; 16:16). Indeed, according to the Letter to the Ephesians, this subordination of wives corresponds only to the subordination of the church to Christ (Eph. 5:24). To be sure, husbands are the "head" as is Christ, but they are not Christ's earthly representatives; "as to the Lord" refers to an analogy (cf *a* and *c*). Furthermore, the term "head" expresses both subordination as well as a mutual relationship in favor of the wife (cf Eph. 4:25).[86]

Things are admittedly different in 1 Timothy 2:13ff, where this submissiveness is based on the creation of Adam before Eve and on her particular vulnerability to temptation (cf also 2 Tim. 3:6). Submissiveness here implies feelings of inferiority, and the resentment is clearly evident. On the basis of Jewish tradition, this may possibly be referring to a sin of fornication between Eve and the snake. This would also explain the extremely problematical verse 15, where bearing children is understood as a part of the path to salvation: Atonement for the guilt and redemption must, as it were, take place in the same realm as did the sin. It is only too understandable and justified that we vehemently reject the identification with such a role today.

c. Love in Correspondence to Christ

The corresponding admonition to husbands is characteristically not a call to superiority and the exercise of power. Even the word in 1 Timothy 3:4f, 12—referring to the house and variously translated as "manage"—possibly refers more to care.

This reserve concerning repression is by no means as natural as it might seem, particularly because not even the moderate and sympathetic form—as we find it in Plutarch as an addendum to the admonition for the wife to be submissive—has a parallel in the New Testament household instructions: "The husband should rule over his wife not as a despot over a thing, but rather as the soul over the body, empathizing and permeated with affection" (*Praec. conj.* 33). This comes across much more abruptly in other places, such as in the *Praecepta Delphica:* "Rule your wife."[87] One does hear talk of love as well, but for the most part this refers to sensual-erotic love or natural inclination; in Judaism, however, we do encounter the commandment to love one's neighbor also referring to marriage (cf 1 *a*). In any case, this is not referenced as part of an admonition. Anyone arguing that this admonition to *agape* is something completely unheard of apparently does not know what the New Testament means by *agape*; this is particularly the case if it is erroneously interpreted in a sentimental fashion as a "love that merely sweetens the inequality."[88]

In any case, the Letter to the Ephesians leaves no doubt as to how *agape* is to be understood as regards content. It is that surrender, defined by Christ's deed, that pays no attention to itself (Eph. 5:25). Christ's existence as "head" is based precisely on this self-sacrifice. Husbands are accordingly not admonished to take charge of their rights and privileges, but rather to orient themselves toward Christ and let love and goodness reign. Neither does verse 28 abrogate this selflessness ("he who loves his wife loves himself"); it does, however, exquisitely underscore the deep unity of the marital partners, who are a kind of single "corporative" person. We do not, of course, know to what extent this actually overcame male property claims and methods of repression in practice. We can be certain, however, that love here is not merely a disguise for the male's privileged position of power, nor is it an anemic or even overused cliché only referring to "feeling." *Agape* does not degrade emotions, but neither does it overestimate them. The familiar distinction between heavenly and earthly love (cf Titian's famous painting that contrasts them as a prim and proper bourgeois woman on the one hand, and a naked woman on the other) is untenable as a simple contrast, and it has doubtless caused a great deal of rigidness and emotional void. Neither, however, can we change the fact that *agape* does not refer to self-realization or acquisition. *Eros* is neither denounced nor mystified, but rather is integrated. Precisely this is a part of the humanity of the New Testament.

d. Woman and Man as Parents

Woman and man in early Christianity were by no means as family-oriented or as fixed to the roles of mother and father as is often thought. The recollection of Jesus' own provocative behavior was too strong, the behavior bringing him into conflict with every average Jewish family.[89] Similarly strong were the words and experiences figuring on a separation from one's family (cf II 2 c). Not even the Christmas story, misunderstood as an idyllic family story, can serve to mystify or transfigure the institution of the family. It is not the parents who are the center of attention here (and who, according to Luke 2, are not a "normal" family), but rather the angelic message. Mary, who has only a manger for her newborn child, is emphasized neither as a symbol for all underprivileged mothers nor in her role as a mother in general. Despite verse 51, even Luke 2:41ff presents Jesus in the preliminary history as being independent from secular-familial obligations and considerations. However, he also presents the parents' pain and horror; it is no accident that Jesus' frequent disregard for convention and piety (cf Matt. 8:21f) led his parents to the conclusion that he was "beside himself" (Mark 3:21). We have other documentation as well as the rejection Jesus experienced from his own family (cf John 7:5). And his mother and brothers had to listen to such statements as: "Whoever does the will of God is my brother, and sister, and mother" (Mark 3:35; cf also Luke 11:27f). The *familia dei* is the true family.

The scene with Mary and the beloved disciple at the cross (John 19:26f) betrays the same perspective. The crucified Jesus directs them to each other, although a symbolic meaning arises that exegetes have variously interpreted: "Woman, behold, your son!" and "Behold, your mother!" In the list of greetings in Romans 16:13, Paul mentions the mother of Rufus, whom he also considers to be his own mother. This is, so to speak, the reverse side of the painful experience that Christians "are hated by all for my name's sake," and that even "children will rise

against parents and have them put to death" (Matt. 10:21f).
Even Celsus still accuses the Christian missionaries of causing
disobedience and strife within families (Origen *Contra Celsum*
III.5.50).

The fact that Jesus questions every ideology of the family
does not mean that he considers the family to be the basic
model of domination and repression, or that he expected a
liberated society to emerge when the family was eliminated.
Above all, however, this critical distance from the family did
not prevent him from holding to the Fourth Commandment
or from criticizing any "human tradition" that tried to
circumvent it, for example, by assigning to the temple the
support due one's parents and thus keeping it from them
(Mark 7:10ff).

Children are advised to follow the fourth commandment,
whereby one honors both father and mother together (Mark
7:10; 10:19; Eph. 6:2; Col. 3:20). Among parents, the father is
especially admonished, an indication of how little precisely
the wife was limited to the relationship with the child. Second
Corinthians 12:14 does say that it is not children who ought to
"lay up for their parents, but [rather] parents for their
children"; Luke 2:27 also presupposes this kind of collective
parental responsibility for the children (cf also 1 Cor. 7:14).
Other passages, however, emphasize the role of the fathers (cf
Luke 1:62f), above all the household instructions: "Father,
do not provoke your children, lest they become discouraged"
(Col. 3:21; cf Eph. 6:4). Again, we hear nothing of joy,
security, tenderness, and other advantages (neither, however, do we hear of disadvantages!) of family life, and—considering a passage such as Mark 10:13ff—the brevity of these
admonitions is indeed a problem. On the other hand, we
again find confirmation of the fact that *agape* permeates
societal and legal relationships as well, for there is no talk here
of rights and privileges, but rather of special tasks and duties
for fathers.[90] It is quite possible that these admonitions are
directed against the degeneration of *patria potestas* into
arbitrariness and brutality.[91]

4. Mutual Loyalty

One can glean from the New Testament neither a morality of prudery nor a pseudo-progressive libertinism. Whoever understands Jesus' provocative intervention on behalf of prostitutes and adulteresses—in the sense of some fashionable freedom-parlance—as a protest against any commitments or social order, not only destroys that particular partnership based on trust, but also falsifies the New Testament. An unabashed libertinism transgresses against Jesus' commandment and is carried out at the cost of others. To be sure, marriage is not, according to the New Testament, a straitjacket; neither, however, is it some sort of interlude or experiment in which back doors are kept open and one figures on an eventual change of partners from the very beginning. It is rather an irrevocable life partnership. Hence both forms of marital disloyalty are rejected equally, namely adultery and divorce, although even then this inevitably contradicted current sexual freedom.

a. Adultery and Divorce in the Surrounding Culture[92]

On the basis of the Decalogue, Judaism strongly tabooed both adultery with the body and also that with the eyes (cf *T. Benj*. 8:2 and elsewhere).[93] To be sure, the man could only violate another's marriage; the woman, on the other hand, only her own. One spoke of adultery in the case of a man only if it was committed with the wife or betrothed of another Jew, since that would violate the rights and property of another man (cf the warnings against married women in Sir. 9:9; *T. Reub*. 3:10). We must, of course, differentiate between legality and morality. We cannot fail to see the obvious legal inferiority of women here as well as a certain low moral estimation, for example, when the Essenes were convinced that no woman "remained loyal to one man alone" (Josephus, J.W. II. 121).

In Greco-Roman antiquity adultery was forbidden only for women, and then it was severely punished. A man's trysts and particularly his relationships with slaves and courtesans were considered cavalier. Cato elucidates this double morality best. He allegedly granted the husband the right to kill his wife if she were caught and convicted of adultery; she, on the other hand, did not have the right to touch him with even a single finger under reverse circumstances (Gellius, *Attic Nights* X.23.5). In the face of increasingly frequent adultery, there is no doubt also an emphasis on how badly things go with the adulterers if they lie in wait for married women, since their pleasure is then dampened with a great deal of suffering and danger (Horace, *Satires* I.2); a great many opportunities exist to satisfy one's desires of love in a less dangerous fashion (Xenophon, *Memorabilia* II.1.5). However, extramarital sexual intercourse as such on the part of men was largely considered to be quite normal and not at all immoral.[94]

Although Judaism condemned adultery, it had no qualms at all about divorce. Individual rabbis and schools offered various answers to the question of which grounds for divorce were adequate (cf *c*). According to Rabbi Akiba, it was enough simply to have become acquainted with a more beautiful woman. There was never, however, any doubt concerning the basic right to divorce. In certain instances—such as disloyalty, the refusal of honor, or childlessness—there was even an *obligation* to divorce (cf Prov. 18:22*a* LXX). We also, of course, encounter the extremely rare case of a woman being able to apply for divorce (eg, in the case of impotence, the refusal of support, hideous sickness, and similar things); such instances are, however, negligible. Here, too, rights and obligations are apportioned quite unequally. A statement from the Mishna is characteristic: "A man that divorces [his wife by means of a letter of divorce] is not like to the woman that is divorced; for woman is put away with her consent or without it, but a husband can put away his wife only with his own consent" (*Yeban.* 14:1). In any case, during the Mishna period there was no marriage "that could not quickly be dissolved by the husband in a totally legal fashion by means of a letter of divorce."[95]

Nonetheless, we do hear isolated voices of warning (cf already Sir. 7:26): "God hates the act of sending away . . . for the Eternal One was the witness between you and the wife of your youth" (b. Gitt. 89b). Actual practice likely did not reflect theory so closely, particularly in the lower classes, since not every man could afford the financial settlement this involved. Anyway, one cannot *eo ipso* conclude reality from mere possibility. Even at that time, the success or failure of a marriage did not depend solely on divorce laws. Nonetheless, divorces did one-sidedly favor the male, particularly because a certain stigma then adhered to a divorced woman (cf already Lev. 21:7).

Divorces were also on the daily agenda in the non-Jewish world, although according to Hellenistic law women could also initiate them. Indeed during the Hellenistic period the number of divorces increased. In a eulogy we read: "Rare are . . . long marriages that are ended by death and not by divorce."[96] According to Seneca, noble women counted their years not according to consuls, but rather according to the number of husbands; they divorce in order to marry, and marry in order to divorce (*De Beneficiis* III.16; cf Juvenal, *Satires* VI.229f). The reasons were often trifling and shabby, and above all egoistic. At any rate, divorce was always a legal problem of property, not a moral problem.

b. Criticism of Adultery

In the face of all this, the New Testament considers this exchanging of partners to be a clear transgression against God's commandment and a falsely liberal betrayal of one's marital partner. Freedom is not a free ticket for adultery, and promiscuity is not a prescription for a happy marriage. To be sure, one must guard against inordinately emphasizing the sixth commandment and branding it as particularly grievous and scandalous. In Mark 10:19 and Romans 13:9, for example, it stands among the other commandments of the second table of the Decalogue (cf also 1 Cor. 6:9), and James 2:11 also warns against isolating precisely this commandment: "For he who said, 'Do not commit adultery,' said also, 'Do not kill.'" God's commandments cannot be divided.

John 7:53ff is particularly illuminating here.[97] The story tells us of a woman caught in adultery; the Torah prescribes the death penalty (Lev. 20:10; Deut. 22:22), and in analogy to Deuteronomy 22:23f (concerning the betrothed) the people intend to carry it out by stoning. Jesus speaks against this and gives the woman a new beginning by his unconditional forgiveness. His actions here are not only a statement against all rigid legalism, but also and precisely against understanding adultery as being especially worthy of condemnation and death. All are sinners before God, who would have to "write them all in the earth" (Jer. 17:13), if one can interpret the puzzling "wrote with his finger on the ground" (John 8:6, 8) in this way.[98] Luke 18:11 is also an unmistakable warning against all Pharisaic degradation of adulterers (mentioned here, by the way, *after* extortioners and the unjust); certainly God can "be merciful" and "justify" the other sinners just as he does the tax collector (vv 13f).

This cannot, however, relativize the clear no spoken to all disloyalty to one's marital partner (cf also John 8:11). Waywardness and so-called free love are incompatible with marital "oneness." Above all, it transgresses against the divine commandment, and this kind of transgression is according to primitive Christian views not simply a private affair, but rather concerns the congregation as a whole (cf 1 Cor. 5:1-5, 11; 6:9f); now the commandment does not just apply only or primarily to the married woman.

Jesus did not intend to diminish the seriousness of adultery by intervening for the adulteress. The second antithesis in the Sermon on the Mount shows this with utmost clarity, since it sharpens the sixth commandment and even calls a person an adulterer who merely looks at a woman with lust (Matt. 5:27f). This does not mean one's own wife, as Tolstoy thought. Jesus did not in principle preach any sort of asceticism and certainly did not intend to elicit scrupulous anxieties and feelings of guilt. He did, however, draw clear boundaries designed to protect marriage and at the same time to free women from their role as mere objects of male desire.

Matthew is partially guilty for this fear-eliciting effect of Jesus' word. He pulled the following words about plucking out one's right eye and cutting off one's right hand (vv 29f) out of their original context (cf Mark 9:43ff par) and thus severely limited their meaning. Whereas they originally applied in a drastic fashion to any temptation (cf the omitted foot in Mark 9:45),[99] now they are limited to the sexual sphere. This conceals too easily the fact that the threats to humans are much more comprehensive, and that one ought not to stare in rigid isolation at this one small area.

There is no agreement whether these words should be understood literally or figuratively, as self-punishment or a hindrance to sin.[100] In any case, it calls for an uncompromising destruction of any bridges over which temptation comes,[101] even if actual adultery begins "in the heart" (Matt. 5:28) from which other human evils come (Mark 7:21f par).

Unbridled fantasy and lust "in one's heart" can only be followed by a ruinous cynicism that measures everything according to its own impulsive needs; and at the end there is then self-disgust, emptiness, and frustration. Whenever Christian freedom degenerates into the following thoughtless statement implying the winning of happiness, but in fact deforming both conscience and body: "Anything is allowed that I like and that gives me pleasure," there the dynamic of sexuality is misunderstood as much as the mystery of marriage and God's commandment. Marriage implies loyalty, trust, and love, and it contradicts anything that might loosen this mutual faithfulness. Free love, however, is neither free nor love.

c. The Indivisibility of Marriage

The texts themselves show clearly enough just how much this insistence on the indivisibility of marriage stood in direct contrast to what was customary during antiquity.[102] Here, too, just as was the case in section *b* as regards the inviolability of marriage, it is not a matter of claims of possession or "private property," but rather of the space protected by God in which a successful partnership can thrive freely; one does not enter into this partnership only on a temporary basis.

In Mark 10, Jesus is queried concerning the fundamental right to divorce; this question is, however, already stylized from Jesus' perspective. In Judiasm one did not discuss this fundamental right, but rather only the acceptable reasons; the fulcral passage in these discussions was Deuteronomy 24:1. Since the expression found there—"some indecency"—is rather ambiguous and could be interpreted more specifically within a sphere ranging from moral to aesthetic categories, various interpretations were circulating during the New Testament period. The more strict followers of Shammai understood the expression in the narrow sense to refer to sins of fornication, while the liberal Hillelites declared it shameful and sufficient for divorce if the wife transgressed against what was fitting, for example, if she went about with loosened hair or let food burn (Gitt. 9:10).

Jesus' words are thrown into clear and decisive relief against this background. He does not recognize the reference to Deuteronomy 24:1, because Moses "wrote you this commandment for your hardness of heart" (Mark 10:5). Jesus does not see in Deuteronomy 24:1 a concession to male weakness, since the male cannot lead the marriage according to God's creative order ("*for* your hardness of heart"). Even the Old Testament "commandment" (vv 4, 5) that Jesus uses to counter the Pharasaic question of what the law "allows" and what has been interpreted for one's own advantage (vv 2, 4; differently in Matthew), is considered rather to be a check on male impulses and as a protection of the disadvantaged woman.[103] She acquires certain legal protection through the required "letter of divorce" and the witnesses necessary for administering the document, and is guaranteed the possibility of remarrying.

Jesus' own requirement radicalizes the Old Testament commandment, whose intention was to alleviate the oppressive male hardness of heart ("your"!); this is not accomplished, however, with a reference to a certain blemish adhering to the divorced woman, making remarriage, for example, even more difficult. His reasoning emerges rather from two Old Testament citations (Gen. 1:27 and 2:24), and above all from the reference to the integral part played by trust and longevity within the totality of marital partnership; God himself has joined the couple together: "What therefore God has joined together, let not man put asunder" (Mark 10:9). This is the crux and high point of the entire pericope; the previous legitimation of the prohibition against divorce on the basis of the two Old Testament citations does not really prove the indivisibility and longevity of marriage, since the Old Testament in neither passage really establishes the insolubility of marriage.[104] God's "joining," however, implies validity and longevity; whoever reckons with his reign will also place marriage under his auspices and will avoid not only legal divorce, but anything that might separate those joined by God. Mark 10 is not blowing into the horn of romantically or ideologically obstinate apostles of freedom who celebrate divorce as liberation and then even want to give it Christian blessing. As certainly as God has joined together man and woman as unequals, virtually ensuring that marital problems and tensions will arise, it is equally certain that differences as such are not reason for separation.

There is no denial here that what *ought* not to occur in fact *can* occur, though it is not really under discussion here. Furthermore, the question of divorce is by no means considered from a legal or ecclesiastical-legal perspective. The New Testament prohibition of divorce can be legislated as little as can the prohibition of anger (Matt. 5:22). One transcends legal thinking here and contradicts all inhumanity resulting from hardness of heart. That is why an address is made to the responsibility of the partners themselves not to dissolve the marital bond arbitrarily. Even though justice or law cannot guarantee the personal relationship within marriage and its longevity, it can indeed protect and support the will to faithfulness. This is not contested here.

Even Paul emphasizes in 1 Corinthians 7:10f that the Lord himself commands a wife not to separate from her husband nor a husband from his wife. Whereas originally only the man was probably addresed, since according to Jewish law the wife normally had the right neither to write a "letter of divorce" nor to remarry without his permission,[105] here the wife, too, is addressed in this matter of prohibition of divorce.[106] This expansion corresponds to Roman-Hellenistic legal conditions and is a necessary actualization of the will of Jesus to oppose "hardness of heart" and to hold both marital partners together in loyalty and solidarity. Marriage is considered here unmistakably not just from the perspective of the male alone, but rather from that of the mutual orientation and co-responsibility of woman and man.

Paul also expands this in another direction. Christians living in mixed marriages also should not obtain divorces as long as the non-Christian partner is willing to continue in the marital relationship (1 Cor. 7:12ff; cf on the other hand the religiously based divorce commandments in Ezra 9–10; Neh. 13:23ff). Paul is not, however, proposing any fundamental or even metaphysical insolubility of marriage. If the non-Christian partner wants a divorce, one is obligated neither by some order of creation nor by the Lord's word prohibiting divorce to maintain that marriage under all circumstances. To push one's own understanding of marriage onto the non-Christian or to bring about a lazy *modus vivendi* at the cost of faith (v 15) can only rob marriage of its "peace" (v 15) as well as its harmony (v 5). Thus one is "not bound" here, but rather is free.

Particularly considering that Paul has concrete problems in view here, one can ask whether it is permissable to stylize this so-called *privilegium Paulinum* into the only exception, or whether it might function as a model for other instances; in the latter case, failing marriages would then require responsible dissolutions taking applicable circumstances into consideration (cf below). The most interesting element here is the parenthetical remark in 1 Corinthians 7:11: "But if she does [get divorced], let her remain single or else be reconciled to her husband."

We cannot be certain that Paul is referring here to a divorce that has already taken place, one that took place perhaps before the conversion; however, in view of the strict words in verse 10 this is more probable than that he is figuring on future divorce cases.[107] In any case Paul again expands the circle of those addressed. On the one hand he suggests that the Lord's word is not to be understood slavishly and literally as a rigid quantity (cf also the initial admonition to the wife in v 10), and on the other that one should take seriously the validity of Jesus' prohibition of divorce. We recognize this same polarity of validity and flexibility elsewhere.

We see that rigid prohibition of divorce in the sense of a practical rule cannot be followed very long when, in a secondary statement, Matthew recognizes adultery or fornication (echoing the Shammaite divorce practice) as an exception (Matt. 19:9; 5:32).[108] One could not and did not want to presume that anyone would live with a woman who would not give up an adulterous relationship or had become a prostitute (cf 1 Cor. 5:11). Thus Matthew must again pragmatically reconsider the "hardness of heart" instead of insisting on some strict ideal requirement. The alleviation of the divorce prohibition into a prohibition of a second marriage (cf *d*) also shows that one cannot maintain the divorce prohibition itself under all circumstances. The justification of such rules of exception and individual cases is that they really do take seriously Jesus' word for one's practical life and try to mediate it with concrete reality; the danger is that they themselves become legally rigid in the course of time and hinder other means of mediation. That would be the case, for example, if one were to accept only the adultery of the wife as a reason for divorce, as is the case in Matthew.

Today, too, there will be cases in which divorce is acceptable without having to give up one's recognition of God's commandment or having to propagate a *laissez faire* attitude. It was Jesus' intention to grant a certain protection to the disadvantaged, such as, for example, to the to a large extent unprivileged and unprotected woman; this intention should be the common standard and the criterion of all concrete, individual rules. The correct path is neither self-righteous condemnation nor a reduction of divorce into a mere mechanical accident or a cavalier offense. Particularly in view of the fact that those suffering most from divorce are usually the weaker partners and the children, today, too, we need to recall that marriage is a partnership arranged for life according to God's will. Since the failure of marriages also always involves human guilt (not only, by the way, that of the marriage partners), a church making more strictly legal and rigorous judgments here than elsewhere among the Lord's word will only lose credibility. The Catholic Church especially needs to ask itself whether it can refuse to divorced and remarried persons precisely what it does not refuse to murderers and exploiters, whose deeds it also does not approve, but who certainly can be reintegrated into the ecclesiastical community.[109] If the church is the locus of forgiveness, then divorced persons should also find in it both a new beginning without continuing guilt feelings as well as a reintegration into service and responsibility without discrimination.

d. Remarriage After Divorce or Death

A much more complicated matter, one we cannot discuss here at great length, involves the original meaning of the other tradition concerning divorce, the one found in Mark 10:11f and in the so-called sayings-source (Matt. 5:32; Luke 16:18).[110] Divorce is initially equated with adultery—a provocation for every Jew, since, as we saw, the wife belongs to the husband as a piece of property acquired by the bridal payment, and the husband cannot possibly violate his own marriage, but rather only that of another man: "As a husband, a man can violate his own marriage just as little as he can his personal property, which stands at his complete disposal."[111] Above all, however, one could not possibly consider the divorce approved by the Torah to be a transgression of the Decalogue. The institution of divorce was to prevent people from committing precisely that transgression. The version in Luke 16:18 is probably the older to the extent that it considers the prohibition of divorce, remarriage, and marriage of a divorced woman only from the perspective of the male, something directing itself to Jewish legal conditions and meaningful only within the Palestinian sphere. We cannot determine with any certainty whether remarriage was also prohibited from the very beginning. Luke possibly expanded his source under the influence of Mark 10:11 ("and marries another"; cf on the other hand Matt. 5:32). In Mark we read: "Whoever divorces his wife and marries another, commits adultery against her; and if she divorces her husband and marries another, she commits adultery" (Mark 10:11f).

What we immediately see quite clearly is that in a manner similar to 1 Corinthians 7, the woman is also affected by the divorce prohibition. The question, however, is whether the accent lies on the divorce prohibition at all, or whether in the meantime the interest has not shifted rather to the prohibition of a second marriage. Not the divorce from the first, but rather the marriage to the second wife would then be equated with adultery.[112] Why? Because the divorce prohibition could not be maintained for any length of time in an absolute fashion and was thus alleviated into a prohibition of the second marriage (cf *c*). This possibly also emphasizes more strongly that only the new marriage made the separation definitive, a marriage that normally followed the divorce quite automatically, particularly in the case of the husband (marriage as such is not given up, as is often the case today, but rather only one with a certain woman).

It is also uncertain whether this reference to the second

marriage after a divorce (or after remarriage) as adultery presupposes that the first marriage was still considered to be in effect.[113] Adultery "against her" doubtlessly fits together better with the relationship to the first than to the second wife; particularly if remarriage was originally not even mentioned, this "against her" could then only refer to the first wife, against whom one committed adultery in the case of divorce. The equating of the remarriage of a divorced woman with adultery (Luke 16:18b) also appears to presuppose the continued existence of the initial marriage. However, it is also possible that the designation adultery was simply chosen from the perspective of the Decalogue, in which case "against her" merely points out that—differently from in Judaism—adultery can also be committed against the wife, and that she is the one who suffers during divorce. Divorce not only transgresses against a divine commandment, but is also—like adultery—a form of the continued existence of the first marriage, this holds true only before God, and not legally as if one were offering a definition here in the fashion of an undocumented legal form.

In 1 Corinthians 7:11, Paul sees only two possibilities for divorced persons: either remaining unmarried, or reconciliation. His advice to remain single in case the separation has already taken place, however, is based not on a knowledge of the prohibition of a second marriage, but rather on his familiar preference for "remaining" in the same basic circumstances in which one encounters the call (v 20). This alone makes his advice comprehensible, namely to remain unmarried in the case of divorce. He is not thinking here of a mere "separation from table and bed" as opposed to an actual divorce.

Today we would want to ask, of course, why one could not advise or make possible a second marriage for the abandoned partner in the case of an unwanted separation, when no "reconciliation" is possible because the other partner has already remarried. If one takes 1 Corinthians 7:9 or 7:36 seriously, one cannot limit the advice to widows and betrothed.

Possibly in contrast to the later Pastoral Letters, Paul in

any case sees no hindrance in principle to a second marriage following the death of a spouse. Marriage lasts only till the death of the partner (1 Cor. 7:39; cf also Rom. 7:2). Paul would no doubt personally prefer an unmarried life here as well; nonetheless, a widow "is free to be married to whom she wishes, [but] only in the Lord." In my opinion this should not be understood such that in that second marriage one should only choose a Christian. Paul would probably consider this the most sensible and useful thing to do simply in order to exclude differences in questions of faith as far as possible. A constant reference to the Lord, however, is above and beyond that the basis and standard of *all* Christian behavior; the New Testament contains no strict prohibition of mixed marriages as we find in the Old Testament (Deut. 7:3) and in Judaism (Jub. 30:7 and elsewhere).

Finally, in the Pastoral Letters we frequently encounter the admonition that a bishop and deacon should "be the husband of one wife" (1 Tim. 3:12; Tit. 1:6).[114] It is highly unlikely that this is specifically prohibiting polygamy or bigamy. It either refers to the renunciation of a second marriage following a divorce, or is an admonition to remain unmarried after the death of a spouse. The former seems to fit better, since something similar is required of the widow as of the bishop, namely that she be "the wife of one husband" (1 Tim. 5:9), whereas younger widows are advised to remarry (1 Tim. 5:14). If this meant, however, that following the death of a spouse one should not remarry—something possibly supported by epitaphs praising women (but only women) as *univira*—then the ideal of the single marriage would even have gone past the limits for marriage set by God.

"Loyalty beyond death": Despite all high estimation of the exclusive nature of marital partnership, this is not a biblical statement. The New Testament was much more sober. As with the Sabbath, marriage was created for the sake of humans, not humans for the sake of marriage—not, it is true, to live at the cost of the marital partner, but rather until death to share joy and suffering and to maintain faith, love, and hope together.

V. "Encounter"

The purpose of this "encounter" cannot be simply to justify the New Testament apologetically. What the New Testament says, however, should indeed be brought into dialogue with our own time. The previous chapters have already opened this dialogue repeatedly in specific instances, but now we will discuss the problem a bit more thoroughly. In itself, such discussion would require a thorough and comprehensive analysis of today's world and the inclusion of the insights acquired by modern humanistic sciences; this, of course, cannot be carried out here. It must suffice to outline a few points—without excessive oversimplification—one needs to keep in mind for a meaningful dialogue.

1. Analogies

We live in an age of ethical disorientation and behavioral insecurity, an age in which the relationship between the sexes is a particularly controversial issue. Diagnoses and therapeutic recommendations contradict one another, and even theologians emphasize different areas according to whether one is thinking more of the dangers inherent in the so-called sexual revolution,[115] or is able to glean something positive from it as well.[116] Our age is probably fluctuating—just as did the New Testament period—both between an under- and overestimation of sexuality, as well as between patriarchal and emancipated slogans and behavior.[117] Some see the very foundations of morality and order shaken; others see now as before nothing but a moldy and prudish morality of repression. Not even the words of the church are characterized by a clear evaluation of the state of affairs with an instructional perspective.[118] Accordingly, any reference to the biblical tradition awakens different hopes. Some promise a dam against ethical relativism; others fear a renewal of rigorous Puritanism.

We find no consensus whatever; our age is full of both confusion and insecurity as well as insuperable conflicts and false hopes. On the one hand, this lack of consensus is not surprising, since we live in a pluralistic society and our knowledge increases in so many areas so rapidly that the individual loses even the possibility of an adequate overview. On the other hand, psychology and sociology, medicine and biology, anthropology and the historical sciences—with their ever new informaton and empirical data, and despite the ambivalence and variability of that data—all justifiably claim to offer support in solving these problems. We today know a great deal more than the New Testament authors—about early childhood influences concerning sexual behavior; about complementary sexual images in the unconscious (with feminine components in the male and masculine in the female); about sociocultural and psychosocial factors behind marital crises; about group-dynamic processes within the family, and so on. Everyone can see the incisive changes wrought by contraception and abortion. The legal and cultural framework of the cohabitation of the sexes has also been fundamentally altered. One need think only of the separation of working and living spheres in the "industrial life-style," of the relatively late age at which people marry—despite any acceleration in other areas (in New Testament times Jewish girls normally became betrothed at twelve!), of tax laws and divorce rights, of permanent relationships which resemble marriage, and so on. All this has had an unavoidably strong influence on the relationship between woman and man.

Can our New Testament findings relate at all to this? In view of the phenomena just mentioned, a mere biblicist transferal is immediately excluded. However, anyone who, for example, is no longer convinced that the woman was created from the man—in my opinion that person should also consider the consequent position of the man as the "head" of woman and

the subordination of the housewife to be completely antiquated; otherwise that person is being inconsistent. And
anyone refusing women the right to the office of pastor on the
simple basis of 1 Corinthians 14:34, is on the wrong track not
only because this does not follow the central New Testament
line of thought, but also because this presumes a direct
transferal of the New Testament without any consideration of
today's situation.[119] Indeed, the New Testament, situation-
oriented as it is, virtually prohibits this kind of direct
transposition. An unhistorical acquisition of New Testament
views for the present is excluded by the historically conditioned
and transient nature of New Testament conceptions as well as
by the clear agreement between it and certain conventions of
antiquity at large—not only with unconsciously active conventions, but consciously acquired ones as well. The sense of such
reception, after all, is to maintain a reference to one's own
present.

The New Testament doubtless does not simply sanction
the ideas of morality and cultural models predominant at that
time, nor does it simply stabilize certain structures such as the
"home" without further ado. The New Testament is more than
merely a reflection of cultural factors or an archive of ancient
behavioral standards. Neither however, does it pursue a
general strategy of conflict or seek out Christian alternatives for
their own sake. Rather, an "encounter" took place even then in
a critical dialogue with that particular present. It is quite
natural that Jesus' divorce prohibition—within the Jewish-
Palestinian sphere originally directed only to men—was
expanded in the Hellenistic sphere to include women as well so
that its real intention could be understood and actualized.

Today, too, Christians can neither simply orient themselves according to the models of thought and behavior of their
age and surroundings, nor adapt effortlessly to fashionable
trends and the spirit of the time; neither can they in a cliquish
fashion preach a basic nonconformity or question conventions
as such. In every case, however, a discussion with the present is

indispensable, and for that reason alone a mere repetition of New Testament statements is a senseless undertaking.

We certainly cannot conceal the fact that in the course of church history Christians have usually swum *with* and not *against* the current as regards woman and man. Today we have particular reason to recall nonconformity and not to conceal some highly out-of-season truths and alternative forms of life found in the New Testament. Even if the rest of the world considers adultery to be quite normal or even a healthy act of liberation, Christians will not want to participate here. And even if divorce becomes more and more an everyday occurrence, divorce can never be equated for Christians with the obligation of loyalty; at most it may represent an "emergency solution," but "not a solution for the emergency."[120] Precisely here one must withstand the normative power of the factual; Kinsey reports with their sexual statistics should not be elevated in Christian communities to the level of legitimizing documentation for certain behavioral models.[121] At most they can draw attention to the fact that one can fall prey in various ways both to unreal fantasies and to a constriction of perspective; one ought not, however, to declare such empirical-demoscopic findings to be natural, normal or even scientific, behavior-regulating norms.

All the temporally conditioned, changeable factors within historical relationships and communal forms cannot, of course, conceal the fact that humans now as ever live as woman and man, and that many former basic models for their mutual relationship are still valid and practiced.[122] Anyone turning to the New Testament will not, in any case, expect to find answers to all questions as if it were a recipe or reference book. The New Testament is first a testimony to God's historical salvation activity in Jesus Christ, and not a compendium for the correct relationship between the sexes. However, wherever the liberating power of this salvation becomes active and this witness of Jesus Christ finds faith, certain consequences issue concerning a way of life that also affect the association and relationship of woman and man, consequences that can even lead to incisive changes. The New Testament offers a person quite definite ways and signposts in order to help one realize both one's freedom and one's obedience. These cannot, to be sure, be systematized into detailed ethical-casuistic rules, but they do point in certain directions. Here, too, New Testament ethics is thus conceived in the fashion of a guide or model, and not deduced from principles. Within this model, however, certain fundamental decisions are made, and certain criteria emerge that still should be considered today (cf *b*).

Certain questions have no doubt taken care of themselves in the course of time. No woman goes to church in a veil anymore, even though 1 Corinthians 11 specifically requires it. The Puritanical polemic against women's makeup in 1 Peter 3 also finds very little understanding today, or is understood at most as a warning against excess. It would be a premature conclusion, however, to think that for this reason the New Testament has nothing more to say to us, if for no other reason than that both of these problems are peripheral ones; one cannot put all New Testament statements on one level (cf the introduction). Even here—and particularly in the other examples—certain fundamental attitudes emerge that are worthy of reflection.

Within the disparate individual statements, however, we find a great many fundamental insights that can only be counted as our own loss if we overlook them. All the change of the past centuries has changed nothing here. One can in the meantime be sure that differentiation between the sexes is not a result of class-oriented society; not even significant political and social changes such as the alteration of the means of production or the conditions determining society can *eo ipso* improve the delicate mechanism and subjective realities of relationships between the sexes ("Pashas are also comrades"). In view of Jesus' liberal behavior, one cannot really consider the differences between the overwhelmingly agrarian Galilean sphere on the one hand, and the Hellenistic cities with their upward-striving classes on the other, to be responsible alone for "emancipatory" or "reactionary" tendencies and attitudes. The same holds true today. Whether one considers woman and man only from the perspective of their biological functions and thus of their traditional roles; whether one associates in the manner of a partnership and does not limit women's participation to emergency situations in divorce cases and church business; whether one separates whenever a marital crisis arises, or holds to the other; whether one becomes infected by the marketability and commercialization of sexuality; whether one allows oneself to be led and traumatized by the worship of a hedonistic standard of desire—these and many others are still unsolved problems today.[123]

Certainly many questions remain unanswered in the New Testament—we must often say, fortunately. We hear equally little about "ordination" and the administering of sacraments by women, or about premarital sexual intercourse and "marriages without certificates," the kind becoming increasingly popular today, for example, because of financial considerations. From the perspective of the New Testament we cannot even say exactly when and how a marriage begins, what the external circumstances and signs of its declaration of commitment are, and what should be considered to constitute a marriage. This, by the way, already opens to us today a certain preliminary sphere of marriage with measured, cautious steps; in view of the finality of the decisions to be made on the part of both partners, this cannot be dismissed simply as noncommittal infatuation. On the other hand, in relatively inconspicuous statements we can find many indirect guides and instructional hints capable of furthering the discussion today despite any allegations of obsolescence.

Paul, for example, says in 1 Corinthians 1:16f that Christ did not send him to baptize, but rather to proclaim the gospel; if women are also called to the proclamation, then there can be no question of withholding the administration of the sacraments from them as something "higher" from this perspective. If greatness in the church means actual service (Mark 9:35; 10:43f; and elsewhere), then any male leadership claims and any purely masculine positions are fundamentally called into question. There is all the more need for change if, despite the readiness to work and sacrifice and participate on the part of women, they are still not adequately represented within the responsibility and leadership of the church—indeed are hardly represented at all. Yet even this example (despite the "among you" in Mark 10:43f) extends beyond the ecclesiastical sphere and refers service to interpersonal and social relationships as well, thus warning us against limiting the New Testament statement in an introverted, overly private fashion to the interior ecclesiastical sphere.[124] Today, for example, this might mean that it will not suffice merely to prevent the "male illusion" of accomplishment, success, and competition from finding its way into marriage, family, and church; one must rather make the Christian marriage and church attractive as a paradigm of true humanity beyond these more narrowly limited spheres. Only those who think unhistorically could object that during New Testament times the equality of woman and man did not yet imply equality of educational and vocational opportunities. One impulse for us that can acquire exemplary significance today is the fact that the woman's activity went above and beyond what was expected and accepted of the average woman at that time—indeed, it even went beyond what the later New Testament scriptures themselves tolerated.

2. Criteria

We can avoid the Socratic misunderstanding that knowledge and enlightenment of themselves produce the correct attitude and practical application, and we can recognize that we do not simply find timeless and absolutely relevant principles from which we can deduce certain concrete decisions. Nonetheless, criteria do emerge, as a kind of aid in decision-making, with which we can find our way through the labyrinth of modern values and behavior as well. Anyone who listens to the voice of the New Testament will again and again find certain guiding principles capable both of protecting one against threatening distortion within a mass society "directed from outside" with its behavioral laxity, as well as of disclosing new practical vistas of Christian love. It helps very little if one knows that the New Testament took a position for or against something, and yet remains unreflective concerning which reasons caused that very position to be taken. If Christians, in their relationship with the opposite sex, are mature and responsible as well as in need of help and capable of receiving it, then precisely these kinds of criteria can be a tremendous aid in making one's own decisions.

First of all, the *idea of creation* has emerged as one point of view that has protected the New Testament against the various forms of dualistic devaluation of the physical and sexual. This idea of creation alone would have prevented anyone from considering woman to be "God's second mistake" (Nietzsche, *Antichrist* 48) or from viewing marriage as a curse and burden as did gnosticism.

The Old Testament creation tradition, it is true, is cited directly only in isolated instances, and is used, for example, to refute any prohibition of marriage (1 Tim. 4:4) or to determine divorce questions (Mark 10:6). In an unspoken fashion, however, this also criticizes ascetic exaggerations or the degradation of women, and the adoption of "natural" morality is doubtless a result of this kind of thinking. The New Testament understands "nature" (cf Rom. 1:26 and I 3 *a*) only in the sense of "creation," and treats it as relevant only as such. One cannot despise the body, sexuality, or marriage if the world and humanity are not the work of an anti-divine demiurge, but rather of the Creator, and if the new creation in Christ is the fulfillment and realization of the Creator's original intention. It is no accident that the struggle against even Christian discrimination against sex and *eros* is taking place today for the most part by referring again to the creation faith.[125]

The biggest danger is that one understands empirical data as an unchangeable arrangement of creation and nature, and then fails to recognize the temporally conditioned nature and variability of these quantities. This was shown already by Romans 1:26 (cf also 1 Cor. 11:14) as well as by the most recent theological discussion, particularly the Catholic discussion concerning the "pill." Quite aside from the fact that there is such a thing as "denaturation" of sexuality, the old question remains concerning just what "by nature" means specifically. Is woman really passive, receptive, emotional, sensitive, monogamous, and so on "by nature," and man the opposite of all these? Despite this ambiguity and despite the relativity of any scientific or cultural data, recourse to creation faith is unavoidable and is probably most prudent, particularly because enough experiential material is treated to address people today as well (eg, the need for giving and communication in sexuality).

According to the New Testament, creation faith necessarily includes *eschatology* as a corrective. This is the element that has held the New Testament within a field of tension and dynamic and prevented any fixation of a status quo or absolutization of creation norms and naturally privileged orders of existence.

The call to extraordinary behavior, such as the renunciation of marriage, cannot be reconciled with any purely "natural" or bourgeois morality, nor can the demand that one sacrifice marriage and family if a conflict arises concerning one's "following." Naturally enough, this eschatological motif is interwoven with other motifs. The radicalization of the prohibition of adultery, for example, no doubt also guarantees a certain protection of marriage, and thus should not be understood merely as an eschatological insistence on total obedience. Above all, the unmistakable rigorism (cf the unconditional exclusion of "the immoral" and "adulterers" from the kingdom of God in 1 Cor. 6:9f) can only be understood from the perspective of eschatology. One should not pass off this kind of rigorism merely as cheap, noncommittal moralizing. Regardless of how things stand with the historicity of the events leading to the death of John the Baptist, Mark 6 in any case proceeds on the assumption that John's criticism of marriage, or of the adultery of Herod Antipas with his sister-in-law Herodias, cost him his head. Above all, however, the eschatological proclamation involves participation and self-discipline (cf 1 Cor. 9:25), and this doubtless includes the freedom from impulsive sexual satisfaction.

In the New Testament, eschatology means not only expectation, but the inbreaking of the eschaton as well. Galatians 3:28 proved to be a piece of anticipated eschatology, and the reversal of status (Mark 10:43ff and elsewhere) is an attempt "to turn the expected reversal of inner-worldly arrangements and relationships into present behavior." On the other hand, Mark 10:31 and other passages hold fast to the future-oriented expectation.[126] We would like to ask how this eschatological perspective might be brought into the discussion today; this would, of course, involve a larger investigation to be done persuasively.[127] We can say in a preliminary fashion, however, that even in the New Testament, eschatology cannot be identified with an expectation of a near end—something our own contemporaries can in any case no longer share as mode of eschatological faith.

This near expectation is, to be sure, a particularly intensive form of future expectation, but neither Jesus nor Paul nor any other New Testament author represented any sort of "interim-ethical" position. According to such a position, the present would be understood only as a brief interim. One would wait in rapturous impatience only for the end, and in this apocalyptic fever of escapism would no longer need, for example, to take body and marriage seriously. And it is simply not true—despite Simone de Beauvoir[128]—that the New Testament, by offering the promise of a better future with pseudo-equality, is really only offering women passive resignation here.

Now, things do not stand such that statements concerning the correct relationship between woman and man only became possible after the experience of the non-arrival of the *parousia*, when a sobering period followed the alleged eschatological enthusiasm of the earlier period and one once again settled down with the world itself (cf, eg, 1 Cor. 7). To be sure, in the later New Testament texts we find a marked decrease in eschatological expectation; yet precisely there is where the genuinely New Testament beginnings of the correct view of that relationship between woman and man gave way to a reconciliation with the average bougeois morality.

Today, too, we need to ask of all conceptions and behavioral forms whether they share the New Testament eschatological sobriety and expectation, or obscure the dimension of hope and make something final out of what is in fact only preliminary; that would then result in a kind of *carpe diem* (1 Cor. 15:32) and excess, would prompt utopian programs,[129] and overlook the temporal as well as the substantial limitation of all that is earthly. Protestantism has seldom known any creation-theological forgetfulness as regards marriage and remaining unmarried; it has, however, often known a repression of the eschatological reservation. It is true that the ideal of virginity has caused a great deal of trouble, but calling it an "antichristian inheritance"[130] does a bit too much violence to the "arrangements" and pays too little attention to eschatology.

The real criterion of all individual New Testament statements is—here, too—*the salvation message of Jesus Christ* as promise and claim of God's love, resulting in the unlimited equality and equal worth of woman and man. God's salvation deed in Jesus Christ determines the life of *all* Christians. Since God's love seeks us *all,* any devaluation of individuals is excluded *a limine*. Since it lays claim to everyone, no one can be excused from service. All love is thus a gift and the reflection of previously received love; but it is also a commandment and obligation. It is grounded in being loved and to that extent is not simply a calculable human possibility or universal principle.[131] The person loved by God, however, is now also endowed and called to love; the relationship between the sexes in the church and in marriage should correspond to that love as an unconditional self-giving, void of any selfish claims, as Ephesians 5 shows especially well. In any case, the New

Testament is one protest against G. Benn's well-known statement that love today has "no content" and no longer brings about any change. We admittedly need to remove the aftertaste of "mere feeling" from this severely misued word (though without devaluing emotions!) and emphasize, in the sense of the New Testament, that love does cost something.

The basis of love's decisive significance in the New Testament clearly lies in its correspondence to the salvation activity of Jesus Christ. The "new commandment" is just that: to love one another "even as I have loved you" (John 13:34; cf 15:12 and elsewhere). Thus the household instructions themselves show conformity to Christ to be a decisive criterion.

This simultaneously draws the limits of ethical evidence and the capacity for consensus, something the argumentative style of the Pauline Letters cannot conceal. So-called healthy human understanding can also offer unreasonable advice, such as the kind of culture recommended by Herbert Marcuse, characterized by "the self-sublimation of sensuousness . . . and the de-sublimation of reason."[132] Reason can also be eclipsed; it can be of promise then only if it orients itself toward love. Thus humane sexuality and mutual sexual relationships were not a necessary consequence even as early as the stoics, and even today reason can be an instrument and justification for inhumanity and hedonism.[133] "Hardness of heart," however, such as discrimination against women, is still "hardness of heart" even if it is alleged to be reasonable, and love—with Jesus—will oppose it.

This double commandment of love is not just one commandment among others, but is rather the first and greatest (Mark 12:28ff par). and is the quintessence of all other, more specific commandments. Thus even the commandment "you shall not commit adultery" is summed up in this sentence, "You shall love your neighbor as yourself" (Rom. 13:9). If "everything" should be done out of love (1 Cor. 16:14), then the relationship between woman and man is included as well. One can then no longer excuse one's selfishness and intransigency by referring to laws (eg, to the divorce possibility set up by the

Mosaic law). The priority of love also supercedes that of the law, though love's significance cannot be reduced to a formal impulse or a specific, spontaneous act. Despite a great deal of flexibility, love is still marked by permanence and consistency as well as by a certain content and certain contours.[134] It is a goal-oriented motif, and as such it is indispensable both as a guiding criterion and as a dynamic force helping to overcome difficulties and to order ever new situations with imagination for the benefit of others. In sexual ethics it makes considerable difference whether one proceeds on the basis "of the negative criterion of the *neminem laedere* or the positive one of the radical demands of the commandment of love."[135] This kind of love—always thinking from the perspective of the other person—is all the more necessary precisely because the New Testament presents so many problems in which at least two behavioral possibilities are under discussion and both decisions demand Christian responsibility, for example, being unmarried or married. Who, besides one who loves, will do the right thing when it is a question of making a marital decision "in accord" (1 Cor. 9:5) or of letting the other charismatic speak in the congregation (1 Cor. 14:30)? Indeed, even when one's own interests require consideration, love supplies the deciding impulse, for example, if one stands before the question of whether to marry one's betrothed or not (1 Cor. 7:36-38).

Today, too, if we wish to think further along New Testament lines, we must grant the last word to nothing else but selfless love. First Corinthians 13 is no doubt not just reserved for weddings, but it is obvious this chapter is critically important as a guide in the question concerning the correct relationship between woman and man, and not just in marriage. The problems of such relationships can in the final analysis be adequately and successfully solved not with considerations of consumption and privilege, nor according to subjective needs, but rather with the kind of commitment and sacrifice that is not egocentric. The fact that such solutions differ from case to case does not mean that one has to make do with commonplace slogans. Whenever Paul offers the kind of detailed advice in his letters such as that found in 1 Corinthians 7, his pastoral care no doubt also implies considerations regarding "counseling for families, marriages, and singles." Today, too, if this kind of counseling takes place under the light of love and with tactfulness and flexibility—rather than "laying a constraint" around the neck of the person seeking counseling (1 Cor. 7:35) and thus without any pressure on conscience or law—it can open up new spaces and possibilities for communication, awaken the willingness for change and understanding, and guide one into a shared perception of responsibility.

All these criteria must admittedly be viewed against the background of the perpetual threat to humans. Just as certainly as "the cultural ordering of sexual impulses" belongs to the cultural accomplishments of humanity, so also must we take note of its reverse side, the "inclination to deterioration" and the "tendency toward degeneration."[136] Considering the excessive pressure of distorting conventions and overdue traditions with all their disastrous consequences, the need for encouraging humanizing love is all the greater; such love could put a stop to the erosion of norms as well as to the various psychological strictures. Above all, however, it will discover ever new spaces for resonance and ever new arenas for Christian humanity.

3. Perspectives

Regarding the topic woman and man, here, too, the New Testament is better than the reputation it has acquired as a result of a somewhat inadequate history of exegesis and effect. Although it lacks the pathos of emancipation and does not offer any contribution to the general struggle against taboos, this does not at all mean that one can—as has often been the case—pigeonhole it under patriarchalism and the propagation of taboos.

The first thing one notices is a beneficial sobriety. We find none of the exaggerated, illusory, stifling, excited, excessive, and aggressive elements so often associated with this topic, the kind that again and again have resulted in blind slogans and experiments (cf already the ascetics and libertines in Corinth).

The relationship between woman and man is specifically treated only in a relatively small number of New Testament texts; despite the fragmentary nature of our sources, it does not appear to have been a particularly important topic in primitive Christianity. That, however, means that there were no special problems here. This was not the case because in a conservative fashion the male-oriented thinking and acting was simply accepted as natural, and then the domination of the male simply supported anew or even increased. It was rather because certain consequences naturally issued from the center of the New Testament message that these conditions were altered.

Quite justifiably, however, this topic was never absolutized or isolated. The relationship between woman and man is not more urgent than that between Jews and Greeks or between slaves and free men. Adultery and divorce, for example, are not a greater wrong or a more serious problem than anger or hatred of one's enemy (cf Matt. 5). Primitive Christianity on the whole did not make the mistake of later centuries by letting one's concern for justice and peace, for example, recede behind one's support of the indivisibility of marriage. Even in certain writings in which ethical problems stand in the foreground, such as the Letter of James, the topic in question here is not addressed at all, while others certainly are—such as the question of social exploitation or the causes of strife and war.

The New Testament thus disappoints anyone hoping to attain a world free of alienation and pain by correcting the relationship between the sexes. Indeed, such hopes can only suffer shipwreck according to the New Testament. Even modern authors have long seen that sexual "liberation" does not automatically spur one on to oppose social repression.[137] A person also errs, however, by believing that at least the family is something like an absolute, inviolable value according to which everything else should be ordered. The family is neither *the* guiding model nor *the* hostile model in the New Testament.

This does not imply that a general hostility toward institutions as such is the case, nor that only an abstract personalism or an anthropology oriented toward personal relations predominates. The New Testament is quite clear about the fact that humans do not exist as isolated individual beings, but rather only in community with other women and men. However, this relational aspect cannot do without institutional elements and an ordering into certain social forms; this is already shown by the structure of marriage or even the congregation itself, that does manifest certain ordered services even though it lacks rigidly outlined offices and organizational structures.

We cannot, of course, overlook the fact that marriage is understood primarily as the coexistence of two people. Institutions are just as little final ends as are personality or personal duality. We must also admit that the New Testament fails to reflect adequately just how this total life renewal and the accompanying human capacity for love involves institutions themselves; nor does it adequately reflect on how in a reverse fashion evil and secular factors can structurally and institutionally take over so completely that they repress the people concerned and condemn marriages, for example, to almost certain failure. The New Testament does not, however, simply abstract from these structural and institutional aspects and orient everything toward interpersonal relations.

Love does not wantonly break up the institutional framework, but rather both fills it out and changes it. There is no emigration into interiority or into the private sphere in which those concerned simply deal with everything by themselves; there is, however, a kind of subterranean movement by love beneath those structures.

More recent social ethics thus also justifiably opposes spiritualistic-protestant prejudices presuming that a person can be played out against an institution or interiority against external order.[138] Individual and institutional determinants, it is true, are difficult to balance; it is decisive, however, that the "structures" in which Christians live do not simply remain the same as before. The necessary structures are thus indeed "not only a barrier against evil, but also possibilities for the coming kingdom of God as well as forms for the new life already beginning here."[139] The New Testament certainly does not outline any plans or strategies for a comprehensive alteration of culture and society for the sake of improving relationships between the sexes, but it does prepare the way for such improvements.

Certain factors need more emphasis today than previously. The church's language, for example, needs to withdraw more decisively than did the New Testament from the excessive use of the male element; it needs to pick up on the kind of beginnings suggested, for example, by the synonymy of "sons of God" and "children of God" (cf Rom. 8:14 with 8:17), or by the natural completion of the Old Testament citation 2 Samuel 7:14 in 2 Corinthians 6:18 by the addition of "daughters."[140] The problem of God the "Father" and Jesus Christ the "Son" would need to be discussed separately. In any case, we need to consider that certain consequences for our image of God emerge from the fact that Christ is the reflection and representative of God (2 Cor. 4:4; Col. 1:15), and, on the other hand, that man and woman are one in Christ (Gal. 3:28), or are at least inseparable (1 Cor. 11:11). And this does not even take into consideration the "feminine" characteristics in Jesus' own conception of God.[141]

Considering the conditions and factors determining life at that time, we cannot be surprised that compared to our own situation a great many deficiencies and negative reports arise regarding the role of women outside the church and marriage in the public, social, and political sphere. Admittedly, however, precisely the conspicuously important role and participation of women in those early Christian congregations can today be considered a pioneering effort as regards the role of women in society as well. Christian faith is commensurate neither with "male religion" nor with "male society," but rather liberates one for responsible maturity and participation in *all* spheres of life.

The expansion of all this should be carried out much more decisively today than in the New Testament, where it only takes place in a preliminary fashion. The church is neither an island for the blessed nor an enclave with rigid borders, but rather stands in a reciprocal relationship with society. Despite the conservative legitimation of convention in 1 Corinthians 11:3ff, I do not believe one can recognize a "sharp division" between the "religious breakthrough" and the "breakthrough on the level of social justice."[142] The traditional lines of demarcation are not drawn again until the later New Testament period.

Not even in the case of marriage does the New Testament incline toward a shielding from community or a concentration on the intimacy of duality. It guarantees neither love nor partnership, but rather might also support an individualism between two people that actually has no promise. The reduction of marriage to the personal relationship, without the earlier customary shared work and living space of the generations, and without neighbor relationships and social obligations, has in reality only increased the fragility of marriage. Neither marriage nor remaining single can do without the dimension of society at large, without a social reference point, or without service. The success of human relationships and communication certainly is not limited to marriage alone, if for no other reason than that love in the New Testament sense transcends marriage, and Jesus' commandment to love one's enemy puts into question any identification of one's neighbor with one's marital partner.

The basic model of female-male relationships in the New Testament is everywhere that of partnership, whether in marriage or the church.[143] Partnership, however, means competent mutual activity with reciprocal respect, and it is something different than external determination of one by another, dependence, or stricturing of one's developmental possibilities. We thus recognize this mutuality and reciprocity again and again, whether in marriage (that, too, is no doubt one reason for the exclusively accepted heterosexuality) or in the church (cf "fellow workers," "fellow female laborers"). Among Christians, this partnership and community is determined by a "third member," to whom everyone belongs both in life and in death (Rom. 14:8) such that "fellowship in Christ" (John 13:8; 1 Cor. 1:9) *eo ipso* places one into the reference field of "fellowship with one another" (1 John 1:7; Acts 4:32). Whenever polarity in the church—as has often enough been the case—becomes polarization, it is usually primarily because these common relational reference points and this common context have been lost from view.

The primary concern of this community of partnership is thus not that the—so to speak—classical roles are either accepted or altered, but rather that they emerge as the locus of reconciliation and liberation, of service and commitment. Self-realization at the cost of others is allowed neither in nor outside marriage, neither in the home nor in the church; indeed, not even the so-called "patriarchal" texts show us anything resembling an egoistic "master-of-the-house" behavior.

Partnership certainly does not imply a lifeless leveling or uniformity that obscures the variations of gifts and tasks. In the decisive points, however, woman and man really are equal: equally blessed and equally obligated. Grace, however, like duty, is neither an undifferentiated nor a generalized quantity, but is rather always given in concrete, specific apportions (cf 1 Cor. 12) that as such are consciously accepted and lived. This legitimizes neither prejudicing, discriminating role models, nor diminished life opportunities. Fixed hierarchical structures only gradually acquire influence again, and even then are not intended as a degradation and repression of women. The relationship between woman and man is not, to be sure, simply *the* model of fellowship and partnership, since love of one's neighbor and commitment do not depend on whether the neighbor encountered is male or female, and since partnership is not limited to marriage.

Nonetheless, or rather: precisely for that reason, partnership is the decisive, key word for the relationship between the sexes, since it first of all suggests that all creaturely existence is limited and in need of a complement, and is rich both in risk and in potential. Above all, however, it crystallizes the solidarity and cooperation—made possible by God's liberation salvation activity—of the various members of the body of Christ. Woman and man are partners precisely to the extent that they live together in freedom, openness, and community; to the extent that they act in love both for each other and for others; and to the extent that they remain together until "the perfect" (1 Cor. 13:10) comes, when woman and man—who are already "children of God"—will be "what has not yet appeared" (1 John 3:2). Until then, however, "in the Lord woman is not independent of man nor man of woman" (1 Cor. 11:11).

Notes

Translator's note: The reader should refer to the *International Glossary of Abbreviations for Theology and Related Subjects* by Siegfried Schwertner (Berlin: de Gruyter, 1974) for an explanation of the periodical and series abbreviations used below.

1. Cf. E. Schlüssler Fiorenza, "Die Rolle der Frau in der urchristlichen Bewegung," Conc(D) 12 (1976), pp 3-9, particularly in reference to E. C. Stanton.
2. K. H. Deschner, *Das Kreuz mit der Kirche* (1974), p 64. J. Kahl, *The Misery of Christianity* (Harmondsworth, England: Penguin, 1971), pp 73ff, accuses the entire New Testament of defamation both of women and of sexuality. S. de Beauvoir, in *The Second Sex* (New York: Bantam, 1970), p 90, finds that "through St. Paul the Jewish tradition, savagely antifeminist, was affirmed."
3. Cf W. H. Leslie, *The Concept of Woman in the Pauline Corpus in the Light of the Social and Religious Environment of the First Century* (Evanston, 1976), p 6.
4. A different view is taken by K. Niederwimmer, *Askese und Mysterium Über Ehe, Ehescheidung und Eheverzicht in den Anfängen des christlichen Glaubens,* FRLANT 113 (1975), p 53. Concerning Mark 12:25 cf also III 4 *a*. In the Gospel of Philip, on the other hand, we read: "When Eve was still in Adam death did not exist. When she was separated from him death came into being. If he again becomes complete and attains his former self, death will be no more" (68).
5. Cf K. Barth, *Church Dogmatics* III, 4, pp 116ff. On the other hand, according to G. Friedrich, *Sexualität und Ehe, Rückfragen an das Neue Testament* (1977), p 9, J. P. Sartre has made us aware (in *Being and Nothingness*) "that existential philosophy has not at all been concerned

with human sexuality, and that Heidegger's concept of 'existence' is to a certain extent sexless."

6. Cf S. Sapp, *Sexuality, the Bible, and Science* (1977). H. H. Schrey, in his status-of-scholarship report concerning "Sexuelle Revolution und 'neue Moral'," ThR 35 (1970), pp 33-64, 327-65, emphasizes that contemporary theological sexual ethics on the whole "takes its point of departure not in marriage, but rather in the creaturely differentiation within sexuality" (p 57).

7. Concerning 1 Corinthians 11 cf Wm. O. Walker, "1 Corinthians 11:2-16 and Paul's Views Regarding Women," JBL 94 (1975), pp 94-110; J. Murphy-O'Connor, "The Non-Pauline Character of 1 Corinthians 11:2-16?" JBL 95 (1976), pp 615-21; L. Cope, "1 Corinthians 11:2-16: One Step Further," JBL 97 (1978), pp 435 ff. A. Funk, in "Mann und Frau in den Briefen des heiligen Paulus," US 32 (1977), pp 280-85), explains the contradictory evaluations in Paul from the perspective of social psychology. According to that view, Paul's "primary socialization" as a Jew led him to value the male sexual status more highly. His "secondary socialization" as a Christian, with its new affirmation of equality, was not able to eradicate, but only to cover over the values "internalized during the initial socialization process during childhood, values that were thus particularly stable" (p 283). It is indeed striking that inequality is supported by Jewish tradition (1 Cor. 11:3ff), while equality is supported by Christian arguments (Gal. 3:28).

8. Cf J. Kürzinger, "Frau und Mann nach 1 Kor 11,11 f.," BZ 22 (1978), pp 270-75; he, however, translates as follows: "For the rest, neither woman is different than man, nor man different than woman in the Lord."

9. Cf R. Bultmann, *Theology of the New Testament*, I (New York: Scribner, 1951), pp 239ff; E. H. Maly, *Sin: Biblical Perspectives* (1973); H. Harsch, *Das Schuldproblem in Theologie und Tiefenpsychologie* (1965), pp 44ff.

10. Cf, eg, S. Bailey RGG III, pp 441-44; Friedrich (note 5), pp 46 ff; Schrey (note 6), pp 353ff.

11. Cf E. Schweizer, *Theological Dictionary of the New Testament* VII, pp 98ff; Bultmann, *Theology of the New Testament*, note 9, pp 232ff.

12. Cf F. Hauck/S. Schulz, *Theological Dictionary of the New Testament* VI, pp 579ff; J. Jensen, "Does porneia mean Fornication?" NT 20 (1978), pp 161-84 (contains a criticism of B. Malina, NT 14 [1972], pp 10-17, who suggests that it refers only to cultic or commercial prostitution).

13. Cf Niederwimmer (note 4), pp 74ff, 200ff.

14. Cf H. Strathmann, RAC I, pp 749 ff; H. Chadwick, RAC V, pp 343ff; W. Schrage, "Zur Frontstellung der paulinischen Ehebewertung in 1 Kor 7, 1-7," ZNW 67 (1976), pp 214-34; Niederwimmer (note 4), pp 80ff and 169ff, overestimates—in my opinion—the ascetic enthusiasm and presupposes even in Jesus a link with Jewish "sexual rigorism" that is a bit too direct.

15. Cf L. Swidler, *Women in Judaism* (1976); A. Oepke, *Theological Dictionary of the New Testament* I, pp 781ff; (H. L. Strack and) P. Billerbeck, *Kommentar zum NT aus Talmud und Midrasch* I-IV (1922–1928), particularly III, pp 468, 558f, 611f. Most of the citations for Rabbinic Judaism are taken from Billerbeck.

16. Cf R. A. Baer, *Philo's Use of the Categories Male and Female*, ALGHL 3 (1970); further I. Heinemann, *Philons griechische und jüdische Bildung* (1932; reprint 1962), pp 231ff.

17. K. H. Rengstorf, *Mann und Frau in Urchristentum*, Arbeitsgemeinschaft für Forschung des Landes Nordrhein-westfalen 12 (1954), pp 11f (cf p 14 concerning Greek predecessors); Swidler, (note 15, pp 80ff, 199f; W. A. Meeks, "The Image of the Androgyne: Some Uses of a Symbol in Earliest Christianity," HR 13 (1974), pp 165-208, particularly pp 167f.

18. Cf W. Schrage, *Theological Dictionary of the New Testament* VII, pp 817ff.

19. Cf J. Leipoldt, *Die Frau in der antiken Welt und im Urchristentum* (1954), pp 10ff; C. Schneider, *Kulturgeschichte des Hellenismus* I (1967), pp 78ff; K. Thraede, RAC VIII, 197ff; by the same author, "Freunde in Christus werden . . ." Kennzeichen 1 (1977), pp 35ff.

20. Thraede (note 19), p 59.

21. Cf E. Borneman, *Das Patriarchat* (1975), pp 197ff.

22. A. Deissmann, *Light From the Ancient East* (New York: Doran, 1927), p 168.

23. Cf Ch. Maurer, *Theological Dictionary of the New Testament* VII, pp 358ff.

24. Cf W. Schrage, *Die konkreten Einzelgebote in der paulinischen Paränese* (1961), pp 187ff, 210ff.

25. Cf G. Kittel, *Theological Dictionary of the New Testament* III, pp 1ff; A. Vögtle, "Die Genealogie Mt 1, 2-16 und die matthäische Kindheitsgeschichte," BZ (1964), pp 45-58, 239-62 and BZ (1965), pp 32-49; F. Schnider/W. Stenger, "Die Frauen im Stammbaum Jesu nach Mattäus," BZ 23 (1979), pp. 187-96.

26. Cf Paul S. Minear, "Luke's Use of the Birth Stories," in *Studies in Luke-Acts. Essays Presented in Honour of Paul Schubert*, ed. Leander E. Keck and J. Louis Martyn (Nashville: Abingdon, 1966), pp 111-30; M. Dibelius, "Jungfrauensohn und Krippenkind," in *Botschaft und Geschichte* I (1953), pp 1-78.

27. Cf G. Stählin RGG IV, pp 747f; W. Michaelis, *Theological Dictionary of the New Testament* IV, p 643; *Mary in the New Testament*, ed. R. E. Brown, K. P. Donfried, and others (1978).

28. Cf J. Leipoldt, *Jesus und die Frauen* (1921); by the same author (note 19), pp 115ff; A. Craig Faxon, *Women and Jesus* (Philadelphia: United Church Press, 1973); L. Swidler, "Jesu Begegnung mit Frauen. Jesus als Feminist," in *Menschenrechte für die Frau*, ed. E. Moltmann-Wendel (1974), pp 130-46. In *Jesus der Mann. Die*

Gestalt Jesu in tiefenpsychologischer Sicht (1975), pp 80ff, H. Wolff calls Jesus the "first man who broke through the androcentricity of the ancient world. The despotism of exclusively male values has been toppled. Jesus is the first to break the solidarity of men, ie of non-integrated men, and their anti-feminine or antagonistic attitude. Jesus stands before us as the first non-hostile or non-animus man."

29. F. Heilder, *Die Frau in den Religionen der Menschheit* (1977), p 90. Concerning Luke 7:36ff, cf U. Wilckens, "Vergebung für die Sunderin," in *Orientierung an Jesus* (Festschrift für J. Schmid) (1973), pp 394-424.

30. W. Marxsen, *Der Evangelist Markus*, FRLANT 67 (²1959), p 86.

31. Cf Leipoldt (note 19), pp 125f; Heiler (note 29), p 88.

32. Cf H. Greeven, *Das Hauptproblem der Sozialethik in der neueren Stoa und im Urchristentum* (1935), p 126; a different view is taken by H. Preisker, *Christentm und Ehe in den ersten drei Jahrhunderten* (1927).

33. Concerning the historical and theological question of this passage in Acts, compare the commentaries by G. Haen-chen, *The Acts of the Apostles: A Commentary* (Philadelphia: Westminster, 1971), and H. Conzelmann, *Handbuch zum Neuen Testament* 7 (1972).

34. Cf L. Zscharnack, *Der Dienst der Frau in den ersten Jahrhunderten der christlichen Kirche* (1902), pp 27ff.

35. J. Dewey, "Images of Women," in *The Liberating Word: A Guide to Nonsexist Interpretation of the Bible*, ed. Letty M. Russell (Philadelphia: Westminster, 1976), pp 62ff, speaks of "the absurdity of this division in realms of application" (p 77). Cf also K. Stendahl, *The Bible and the Role of Women* (1966); by the same author, "Die biblische Auffassung von Mann und Frau," in *Frauenbefreiung. Biblische und theologische Argumente*, ed. E. Moltmann-Wendel (1978), pp 118ff, particularly p 126. A different view is taken, for example, by Rengstorf (note 17), pp 10ff. J. J. Davis, "Some Reflections on Gal. 3:28;

Sexual Roles and Biblical Hermeneutics," JETS 19 (1976), pp 201-8, also denies any social implications for Galatians 3:28; he considers hierarchical structures of authority natural and constitutive for man and woman, though not for slaves and freemen.

36. D. Lührmann, "Wo man nicht mehr Sklave oder Freier ist," WuD (1975), pp 53-83, citation on p 70. Cf also H. Thyen, "'. . . nicht mehr männlich und weiblich . . .' Eine Studie zu Gal 3,28," in F. Crüsemann/H. Thyen, *Als Mann und Frau geschaffen,* Kennzeichen 3 (1978), pp 107ff. For Thyen, too, the Christian church is "the bridgehead of God's new creation in the middle of the continuing history of the world" (p 135; concerning the history of reception of Gal. 3:28, cf pp 188ff).

37. Cf H. v. Soden, *Theological Dictionary of the New Testament* I, pp 144ff; K. H. Schelkle, RAC II, pp 631-40; J. Friedrich, "Gott im Bruder?" CThM 7 (1977), pp 220ff; H. R. Schlette, "'Und voll Sanftheit jeder Schritt': Über die Brüderlichkeit Jesu," in *Brüderlichkeit,* ed. H. J. Schultz, Gütersloher Taschenbücher/Siebenstern 310 (1979), pp 39-47.

38. Cf R. Schnackenburg, *The Moral Teaching of the New Testament* (London, 1965), pp 381ff.

39. Cf G. Stählin, *Theological Dictionary of the New Testament* IX, pp 440ff; Leipoldt (note 19), pp 205ff.

40. Cf G. Stählin, *Theological Dictionary of the New Testament* IX, pp 119ff and 138ff.

41. Heiler (note 29), p 139.

42. Cf Zscharnack (note 34); J. M. Ford, "Biblical Material to the Ordination of Women," JES 10 (1973), pp 669-94.

43. Cf L. Schenke, *Auferstehungsverkündigung und leeres Grab,* SBS 33 (²1969), pp 20ff.

44. Cf U. Wilckens, *Resurrection: Biblical Testimony to the Resurrection* (Atlanta: John Knox Press, 1978), pp 34ff. A different view is taken, for example, by H. v. Campenhausen, "Der Ablauf der Osterereignisse und das leere

Grab," SHAB (1952), 4. Abh., pp 22ff; H. Grass, *Ostergeschichten und Osterberichte* (²1962), pp 21ff.

45. E. Schüssler Fiorenza, "Interpreting Patriarchal Traditions," in *The Liberating Word: A Guide to Nonsexist Interpretation of the Bible* (cf note 35), p 53, sees androcentric tendencies in Mark 16:8 as well as in Luke 24:11 and John 20:1ff; cf also Wolff (note 28), p 85f, who also sees anti-feminine tendencies in 1 Cor. 15:5ff. One cannot deny that in these passages such tendencies did play at least a *part*.

46. Cf K. Lehmann, *Auferweckt am dritten Tag nach der Schrift*, QD 38 (1968); J. Kremer, *Das älteste Zeugnis von der Auferstehung*, SBS 17 (1966); J. E. Alsup, *The Post-Resurrection Appearance Stories of the Gospel Tradition*, CThM 5 (1975).

47. Billerbeck (note 15), III, pp 217, 251.

48. Heiler (note 29), pp 97f; cf also M. Hengel, "Maria Magdalena und die Frauen als Zeugen," in *Abraham unser Vater* (Festschrift für O. Michel), AGSU 5 (1963), pp 243-56, particularly 251; R. E. Brown, "Die Rolle der Frauen im vierten Evangelium," in *Frauenbefreiung* (note 35), pp 133ff, particularly 139; Thyen (note 36), pp 143f.

49. B. Brooten, "Junia . . . hervorragend unter den Aposteln," in *Frauenbefreiung* (cf note 35), pp 148-51, refers an extensive study concerning the name as regards the findings in inscriptions.

50. Cited in Brooten (note 49), p 148.

51. Cf Zscharnack (note 34), pp 52f. On the other hand, the reservation becomes noticeable in the Syrian *Didascalia*: "If the heathen hear the word of God proclaimed by a woman, they laugh and mock" (III. 6.2).

52. Hippolytus, *Cant.* XV (GCS I.1), 354ff; Origenes *PG*. 14.474; P. Jordan, *Die Töchter Gottes* (1973), p 71.

53. References in Heiler (note 29), p 99; Jordan (note 52), p 71; Hengel (note 48), p 251.

54. Concerning primitive Christian prophecy, cf G. Friedrich, *Theological Dictionary of the New Testament* VI, pp 828ff.

55. Cf G. Fitzer, *Das Weib schweige in der Gemeinde. Über den unpaulinischen Charakter der mulier-taceat-Verse in 1 Kor 14*, TEH 110 (1963); Heiler (note 29), pp 116ff.

56. Many suspect as a background emancipatory tendencies among the heretics. Cf, eg, R. R. Ruether, "Frau und kirchliches Amt in historischer und gesellschaftlicher Sicht," Conc(D) 12 (1976), pp 17ff, particularly 19; H. v. Lips, *Glaube-Gemeinde-Amt*, FRLANT 122 (1979), p 153.

57. E. Käsemann, "Gottesdienst im Alltag der Welt," in *Exegetische Versuche und Besinnungen*, II (1964), pp 198-204 (translation not contained in *Essays in New Testament Themes*; see note 58); U. Brockhaus, *Charisma und Amt* (1972); H. Conzelmann, *Theological Dictionary of the New Testament* IX, pp 402ff.

58. E. Käsemann, "Ministry and Community in the New Testament," in *Essays on New Testament Themes* (London, 1968), citation on p 71; cf Schrage (note 14), pp 233f.

59. Cf H. Strathmann, *Theological Dictionary of the New Testament* IV, pp 489ff; A. A. Trites, *The New Testament Concept of Witness*, MSSNTS 31 (1977).

60. Cf H. W. Beyer, *Theological Dictionary of the New Testament* II, pp 84; W. Brandt, *Dienst und Dienen im Neuen Testament*, NTF Reihe 2, 5 (1931).

61. Heiler (note 29), p 110; also Ford (note 42), pp 676f, with a reference to the masculine form of the word that is used, for example, for royal administrative officials (1 Chron. 27:31) and envoys (2 Chron. 8:10 and 14:11), or of the head of temple administration (2 Macc. 3:4).

62. Friedrich (note 5), pp 58ff; E. Gössmann, *Ehe und Ehelosigkeit. Eine Literaturübersicht*, BiLe 9 (1968), pp 230-36; cf T. Matura, "Le célibat dans le NT d'après l'

exégèse récente," NRTh 97 (1975), pp 481-500 and 593-604.

63. Billerbeck (note 15), I, pp 807; II, pp 372f; III, pp 367f.

64. Concerning Matt. 19:10-12, cf J. Schneider, *Theological Dictionary of the New Testament* II, pp 763ff; H. Greeven, "Ehe nach dem Neuen Testament," in *Theologie der Ehe* (1969), pp 37-79, particularly pp 43ff; Niederwimmer (note 4), pp 54ff; Matura (note 62, pp 487ff.

65. Some exegetes consider "eunuch" in Matthew 19:12 to be a word of derision used to refer to Jesus and his followers' nonconformist habit of remaining unmarried, a word Jesus then uses apologetically; cf J. Blinzler, "Eisin eunouchi. Zur Auslegung von Mt 19.12," ZNW 48 (1957), pp 254-70.

66. Cf K. H. Schelkle, "Ehe und Ehelosigkeit im Neuen Testament," in *Wort und Schrift* (1966), p 192; H. Rusche, *Ehelosigkeit als eschatologisches Zeichen*, BiLe 5 (1964), pp 12-18.

67. Cf G. Delling, *Paulus' Stellung zu Frau und Ehe*, BWANT 56 (1931), pp 84ff; E. Kähler, *Die Frau in den paulinischen Briefen* (1960), pp 31ff; H. Baltensweiler, *Die Ehe im Neuen Testamant* (1967), pp 167ff.

68. Cf Swidler (note 15), pp 139ff; Billerbeck (note 15), index of word "Ehe"; Heinemann (note 16), pp 261ff; Preisker (note 32), pp 66ff.

69. Billerbeck (note 15), III, p 68; cf the wife's letter of complaint against her husband who has treated her wrongly in various ways (CPJ 128).

70. Cf H. Hübner, "Zölibat in Qumran?" NTS 17 (1970/71), pp 153-67; A. Steiner, "Warum lebten die Essener asketisch?" BZ 15 (1971), pp 1-28; Swidler (note 15), pp 62ff.

71. Cf A. Oepke, RAC IV, pp 650ff; C. Vatin, *Recherches sur le mariage et la condition de la femme mariée à l'époque hellénistique* (1970); K. Gaiser, *Für und wider die Ehe. Antike Stimmen zu einer offenen Frage* (1974); H. Cancik-Lindemaier, "Ehe und Liebe," in *Zum Thema*

Frau in Kirche und Gesselschaft (1972), pp 47ff; Preisker (note 32), pp 13ff.

71.*a*. Gaiser (note 71), p 94.

72. Cf Baltensweiler (note 67), pp 54ff.

73. Preisker (note 32), p 72.

74. Concerning this and similar judgments cf Schrage (note 24), p 218; Preisker (note 32), p 126f; Delling (note 67), p 45; a different view is taken—and with some justification—by Greeven (note 32), p 136.

75. Cf E. Kähler (note 67), pp 14ff.

76. Cf the discussion in Schrage (note 14), p 232.

77. Cf R. H. A. Seboldt, "Spiritual Marriage in the Early Church: A Suggested Interpretation of 1 Cor. 7:36-38," CTM 30 (1959), pp 103-19 and 176-80; Baltensweiler (note 67), pp 175ff; Thyen (note 36), pp 178ff.

78. Cf G. Delling, *Theological Dictionary of the New Testament* V, pp 834ff.

79. Cf Ch. Maurer, *Theological Dictionary of the New Testament* VII, pp 365ff; Niederwimmer (note 4), pp 72f.

80. Cf W. Schrage, "Die Stellung zur Welt bei Paulus, Epiktet und in der Apokalyptik. Ein Beitrag zu 1 Kor 7,29-31," ZThK 61 (1964), pp 125-54.

81. Cf J. E. Crouch, *The Origin and Intention of the Colossian Haustafel*, FRLANT 109 (1972); W. Schrage, "Zur Ethik der neutestamentlichen Haustafeln," NTS 21 (1974/75), pp 1-22.

82. Concerning Eph. 5:22ff, cf Baltensweiler (note 67), pp 221ff; J. P. Sampley, *"And the Two Shall Become One Flesh." A Study of Traditions in Eph. 5:21-23*, MSSNTS 16 (1971); Friedrich, (note 5), pp 85ff; Greeven (note 64), pp 77ff; R. Schnackenburg, "Die Ehe nach dem Neuen Testament," in *Theologie der Ehe* (1969), pp 9-36, particularly pp 28ff.

83. Cf G. Bornkamm, *Theological Dictionary of the New Testament* IV, pp 822ff.

84. Cf E. Kähler, "Zur 'Unterordnung' der Frau im Neuen Testament," ZEE 3 (1959), pp 1-13, and note 67, pp 88ff; G. Delling, *Theological Dictionary of the New Testament* VIII, pp 39ff.

85. Heiler (note 29), p 50, refers a Brahman citation from *Manusmrti* 5.154 as an example for this heroine (from one of Petrarch's narratives) who is severely tested regarding her humility and submissiveness: "Even if a husband is void of all virtue, is a slave to desire, and has absolutely no good qualities, a virtuous wife must always honor him as a god."

86. Cf Friedrich (note 5), pp 92f.

87. Cf also *sura* 4.38 of the Koran, where this goes as far as sanctioning the striking of a wife.

88. Thraede (note 19), p 61; a correct evaluation is made by H. Greeven, "Zu den Aussagen des Neuen Testaments über die Ehe," ZEE 1 (1957), p 122; by the same author, RGG II, p 319; Gaiser (note 71), p 99: "The object here is not the self-realization of the individual, but rather a partnership of mutual service arising from the experience of divine love."

89. Cf R. A. Harrisville, "Jesus and the Family," Int 23 (1969), pp 425-38; H.-H. Schoeder, "Eltern und Kinder in der Verkündigung Jesu," ThF 53 (1972), pp 110ff.

90. Cf Rengstorf (note 17), p 35.

91. G. Schrenk, *Theological Dictionary of the New Testament* V, pp 982ff and 1004ff.

92. Cf the article "Ehebruch und Ehescheidung" by G. Delling, RAC IV, pp 666-77 and 707-19.

93. Billerbeck (note 15) I, pp 299ff; Niederwimmer (note 4), pp 27f.

94. Cf Friedrich (note 5), pp 22ff; Gaiser (note 71), p 98.

95. Billerbeck (note 15) I, pp 319ff; cf also K. Schubert, "Ehescheidung im Judentum zur Zeit Jesu," ThQ 151 (1971), pp 23-27. Concerning Josephus *Ant.* 4.253 and Philo *On the Spec. Laws* III.30, cf Delling (note 92), p 709. Cf also note 105.

96. Delling (note 67), p 15, and (note 92), p 713; cf Preisker (note 32), p 20, and Borneman (note 21), pp 407f.

97. Cf U. Becker, "Jesus und die Ehebrecherin," BZNW 28 (1963); Niederwimmer (note 4), pp 35ff.

98. Cf Baltensweiler (note 67), pp 125ff; R. Schnackenburg, "Das Johannesevangelium," HThK IV, 2 (1971), pp 288 f.

99. Niederwimmer (note 4), p 31, sees "the experience of self-alienation" coming to expression in the concretely named members.

100. Cf G. Stählin, *Theological Dictionary of the New Testament* III, p 859.

101. G. Eichholz, *Auslegung der Bergpredigt*, BSt 46 (²1970), p 80.

102. Cf R. Pesch, *Freie Treue. Die Christen und die Ehescheidung* (1971); D. W. Shaner, *A Christian View of Divorce According to the Teachings of the New Testament* (1969); G. Schneider, "Jesu Wort über die Ehescheidung in der Überlieferung des Neuen Testaments," TThZ 80 (1971), pp 65-87; P. Hoffman, "Ehescheidung," in P. Hoffman/ V. Eid, *Jesus von Nazareth und eine christliche Moral*, QD 66 (1965), pp 109ff.

103. Cf R. Pesch, *"Die neutestamentliche Weisung für die Ehe,"* BiLe 9 (1968), pp 208-21, particularly pp 213f; a different view is taken by Greeven (note 88), p 114, who also rejects the common interpretation concerning a concession to human weakness, but then explains it such that Moses, in the fashion of Jesus, "drew guilty behavior out of secrecy and anonymity and held it before God and world." Cf also by the same author, note 64, p 58; Schnackenburg (note 82), p 15.

104. *CD* 4.21 uses Genesis 1:27 not to support divorce, but rather polygamy. Cf however K. Haacker, "Ehescheidung und Wiederverheiratung im Neuen Testament," ThQ 151 (1971), pp 28-38.

105. Cf Josephus *Ant.* 15.259. The Aramaic documents of the Jewish military colony in Elephantine also, however,

mention the wife's right to divorce her husband; cf Schubert (note 95), pp 24f.

106. Cf Schrage (note 24), pp 241ff.

107. Cf R. Pesch (note 102), pp 60ff.

108. The subsequent effect of these two passages has prompted an incalculable number of secondary works. Hardly anyone represents the inclusive understanding any longer ("even in the case of fornication"). It is debatable, however, whether one ought to think of adultery regarding the exceptions. Cf F. Hauck/S. Schulz, *Theological Dictionary of the New Testament* VI, 591; Hoffmann/Eid (note 102), pp 124ff; Niederwimmer (note 4), pp 51f. Others refer to incestuous relationships, eg, Baltensweiler (note 67), pp 92ff, though hardly with any justification.

109. Cf F. J. Schierse, "Das Scheidungsverbot Jesu. Zur schriftgemässen Unauflöslichkeit der Ehe," in *Die öffentlichen Sünder oder: Soll die Kirche Ehen scheiden?* ed. N. Wetzel (1970), pp 13-41, particularly pp 35 and 38.

110. Cf B. Schaller, "Die Sprüche über Ehescheidung und Wiederheirat in der synoptischen Überlieferung," in *Der Ruf Jesu und die Antwort der Gemeinde* (Festschrift für Joachim Jeremias) (1970), pp 226-46; G. Bornkamm, "Ehescheidung und Wiederverheiratung im Neuen Testament," in *Geschichte und Glaube* I (1968), pp 56-59.

111. H. Greeven (note 64), p 66. The provocation consists in the fact that the woman ceases to be a "legal object" and becomes a "legal subject," and the loyalty claim of the man becomes that of the woman; Hoffman (note 102), p 119.

112. Schaller (note 110); cf also Baltensweiler (note 67), p 62. A different view is taken by R. Pesch (note 102), p 33.

113. Baltensweiler (note 67), pp 63 and 66.

114. Cf W. A. Schulze, "Ein Bischof sei eines Weibes Mann . . ." KuD 4 (1958), pp 287-300; A. Oepke, *Theological Dictionary of the New Testament* I, pp 362ff, p 789; Baltensweiler (note 67), p 240.

115. Friedrich, for example (note 5), pp. 7ff particularly emphasizes the "sexualism" and considers it to be a reaction to the "totally rationalistically oriented existentialism"; however, he also considers it to be a consequence of the existentialist understanding of freedom, of psychoanalysis (W. Reich), and of the loss of the meaning of life.

116. W. Rohrback, *Humane Sexualität* (1976), pp 59ff and 84ff, for example, also refers to the humane progress made and warns quite justifiably against an overexaggeration because of negative symptoms. That happens often enough in the generalizing Cassandra-cries and moral indignation on the part of the church as well, particularly if it distorts one's perception of one's own guilt in ecclesiogenic fears and neuroses and only offers legalism as a means of combating it. Rohrback also sees, however, that the "new standard of a more free, mature, and human sexual behavior . . . is accompanied by a deeper abyss, and that the danger of falling . . . has become greater" (p 121).

117. Davis, for example (note 35), p 201, traces the confusion in the role identities of man and woman back to the industralization and urbanization processes that have alienated people from the traditional roles.

118. Cf the various positions taken by the state churches (*Landeskirchen* in Germany) regarding the question of divorce in the marriages of the clergy. A persuasive and insightful study has been done by a committee of the Protestant Church of Germany (EKD) and co-published by the church administration; the study treats the common life of woman and man and appeared in 1979 under the title *Die Frau in Familie, Kirche und Gesellschaft*. Cf also, *Ehe: Institution im Wandel. Zum evangelischen Eheverständnis heute*, Heft 18 of the series *Zur Sache: Kirchliche Aspekte heute* 18 (1979).

119. Concerning the other legal scriptual views and their leveling, cf already E. Hahn *Partnerschaft* (1953), pp 34ff.

120. R. Pesch (note 102), p 21.
121. Cf Friedrich (note 5), pp 14 f; Schrey (note 6), pp 43ff; Rohrback (note 116), pp 33ff.
122. Concerning one of these "fundamental models of sexual relationships," namely the "mutual permeation of *eros* and *agape*" in marriage even after the hiatus of Romanticism, cf, eg, H. Thielicke, *Theological Ethics* III (Grand Rapids: Eerdmans, 1979), pp 295ff.
123. Among the vast number of secondary works on the modern problems, cf D. S. Bailey, *The Man-Woman Relation in Christian Thought* (London: Longmans, 1959); S. Keil, *Sexualität* (1966); K. H. Wrage, *Mann und Frau. Grundfragen der Geschlechterbeziehung* (1966); St. H. Pfürtner, *Kirche und Sexualität* (1972); H. Ringeling, *Die Frau zwischen gestern und morgen* (1962); by the same author, *Theologie und Sexualität* (1968); K. Lüthi, *Gottes neue Eva. Eine theologische Untersuchung über die Wandlungen des Weiblichen* (1978).
124. Cf Hoffmann/ Eid (note 102), pp 194ff.
125. Cf Rohrbach (note 116), p 164.
126. Hoffman/Eid (note 102), p 202. Concerning the relationship between eschatology and ethics in the New Testament, cf Schrage (note 80).
127. Concerning the relationship between eschatology and ethics today, cf W. Kreck, *Grundfragen christlicher Ethik* (1975), pp 139ff.
128. Cf note 2, p 631.
129. Concerning secularized eschatologies, cf the chapter "Der utopische Optimismus in der neueren Sexualtheorie" in Rohrbach (note 116), pp 13ff.
130. E. Brunner, *The Divine Imperative* (London: Lutterworth, 1953), where this is, however, spoken in the context of discrediting of sexuality. Cf p 365: "It is of course a false and exaggerated statement to say that only in marriage or at least through sex experience can anyone become fully human; time after time experience has disproved this statement."

131. Cf G. Friedrich, *"Was heisst das: Liebe?"* CwH 121 (1972); *Prinzip Liebe, Perspektiven der Theologie,* with essays by E. Biser and others (1975).

132. H. Marcuse, *Eros and Civilization* (Boston: Beacon, 1956).

133. Concerning nature and *ratio* as normative factors in B. Russel, A. Comfort, and others, cf Rohrback (note 116), pp 18ff.

134. Concerning the problems of inadequate radical situation ethics that, with their pithy commandment of love, do as little justice to the New Testament findings as to the complex situations and conflicts of modernity, cf Schrage (note 24), pp 249ff; Rohrbach (note 116), pp 107f; Kreck (note 127), pp 36ff, 153ff, 213ff.

135. Ringeling (note 123), p 143.

136. Cf the citations of A. Gehlen and H. Schelsky in Rohrbach (note 116), pp 46f.

137. Cf R. Reiche, *Sexualität und Klassenkampf* (1968); cf Schrey (note 6), pp 52ff.

138. Cf Schrey (note 6), p 331; Rohrbach (note 116), pp 46f, 123f; cf p 20ff in the study mentioned in note 117.

139. Cf p 21 in the study mentioned in note 117.

140. Some impulses for "inclusive" language can be found in L. M. Russel, "Changing Language and the Church," in *The Liberating Word: A Guide To Nonsexist Interpretation of the Bible* (1979), pp 82ff; cf also pp 13ff.

141. Cf also II 2 *a* as well as E. Moltmann-Wendel, *Freiheit—Gleichheit—Schwesterlichkeit,* KT 25 (1977), pp 16 ff, and Wolff (note 28), p 121.

142. A different view is taken by E. Schüssler Fiorenza, "Frau und kirchliches Amt in historischer und gesellschaftlicher Sicht," Conc (1976), pp 17ff, citation p 18. Cf W. Schrage, "Barmen II und das Neue Testament," in *Zum politischen Auftrag der christlichen Gemeinde,* ed. A. Burgsmüller (1974), pp 127ff.

143. Cf Hahn (note 119) and pp 17ff of the study mentioned in note 118.

Bibliography

General

Bebel, August. *Woman and Socialism*. New York: Socialist Literatur, 1910.

Daly, Mary. *Beyond God the Father*. Boston, 1973.

De Beauvoir, Simone. *The Second Sex*. New York: Bantam, 1970.

Faber, Heije. *Gott in vaterloser Gesellschaft*. Munich, 1972.

Friedan, Betty. *The Feminine Mystique*. New York: Dell, 1977.

Goldberg, Herb. *The New Male*. New York: Morrow, 1979.

Hite, Shere. *The Hite Report*. New York: Dell, 1977.

Keil, Siegfried. *Sexualität, Erkenntnisse und Massstäbe*. Stuttgart/Berlin, 1966.

Kentler, Helmut (ed.). *Texte zur Sozio-Sexualität*. Opladen, 1973.

Marcuse, Herbert. "Aggressiveness in Advanced Industrial Society," *Negations: Essays in Critical Theory*. Boston: Beacon, 1968.

Mead, Margaret. *Male and Female*. New York: Morrow, 1945.

Moltmann-Wendel, Elisabeth (ed.). *Frauenbefreiung*. Munich, 1978.

Pross, Helge. *Die Wirklichkeit der Hausfrau*. Hamburg, 1975.

———. *Die Männer*. Hamburg, 1978.

Richter, Horst E. *Lernziel Solidarität*. Hamburg, 1974.

———. *Der Gotteskomplex*. Hamburg, 1979.

Rosenbaum, Heidi. *Familie als Gegenstruktur der Gesellschaft*. Stuttgart, 1973.

Ruether, Rosemary R. *Religion and Sexism*. New York: Simon & Schuster, 1974.

Scharffenorth, Gerta and Thraede, Klaus. *Freunde in Christus werden*. Gelnhausen, 1977.

Vinnai, Gerhard. *Das Elend der Männlichkeit*. Hamburg, 1977.

Willi, Jürg. *Die Zweierbeziehung*. Hamburg, 1975.

Concerning the Old Testament

Beer, Georg. *Die soziale und religiöse Stellung der Frau im israelitischen Altertum*. Tübingen, 1919.

Crüsemann, Frank. *Als Mann und Frau geschaffen*. Gelnhausen, 1978.

De Vaux, Roland. *Ancient Israel: Its Life and Institutions*. New York: McGraw-Hill, 1961.

Gollwitzer, Helmut. *Song of Love: A Biblical Understanding of Sex*. Philadelphia: Fortress, 1979.

Grelot, Pierre. *Le couple humain dans l'écriture*. Paris: Cerf, 1964.

Köhler, Ludwig. *Hebrew Man*. Nashville: Abingdon, 1956.

Otwell, John H. *And Sarah Laughed*. Philadelphia: 1977.

Patai, Raphael. *Sex and Family in the Bible and the Middle East*. New York: Doubleday, 1959.

Plautz, W. "Zur Frage des Mutterrechts im Alten Testament," ZAW 74 (1962), pp 9-30.

———. "Monogamie und Polygamie im Alten Testament," ZAW 75 (1963), pp 3-26.

Römer, Willem H. Ph. *Frauenbrief über Religion, Politik und Privatleben in Mari*. Neukirchen-Vluyn, 1971.

Stendahl, Krister. *The Bible and the Role of Women*. Philadelphia: Fortress, 1966.

Trible, Phyllis. *God and the Rhetoric of Sexuality*. Philadelphia: Fortress, 1978.

Wolff, Hans-Walter. *Anthropology of the Old Testament*. Philadelphia: Fortress, 1974.

For New Testament bibliography, see notes.